THE ARCHITECTURE OF AFFORDABLE HOUSING

The publisher gratefully acknowledges the contribution
provided by the General Endowment Fund of the
Associates of the University of California Press.

THE ARCHITECTURE OF AFFORDABLE HOUSING

SAM DAVIS

UNIVERSITY OF CALIFORNIA PRESS   BERKELEY   LOS ANGELES   LONDON

University of California Press
Berkeley and Los Angeles, California

University of California Press, Ltd.
London, England

Library of Congress Cataloging-in-Publication Data

Davis, Sam.
    The architecture of affordable housing / Sam Davis.
      p.   cm.
    Includes bibliographical references and index.
    ISBN 0-520-08758-5 (alk. paper)
    1. Architecture, Domestic—United States. 2. Public
housing—United States. 3. Architecture, Domestic—
California. 4. Public housing—California. I. Title.
  NA7540.D38 1995
  728′.1′0973—dc20   94-7469
                               CIP

Printed in the United States of America
9 8 7 6 5 4 3 2 1

CONTENTS

When I would tell people I was writing a book on affordable housing, I usually deflected their disbelieving glances by joking that it was to be one of the shortest books ever written, or that my first chapter would be one sentence long: "Move out of California." If pressed, I would further confound people by adding that the book focused on the architecture of affordable housing. Certainly this is an oxymoron of classic proportions!

I am no Pollyanna, nor do I have that special treasure map that will lead us to a new promised land with a home for every person and a garage for every car. This is not a guide or reference book that will disclose new standards, dimensions, or technologies. But I am optimistic that if we understand the constraints, pressures, and problems that surround affordable housing, we can see ways to do it better. This book is about issues in the design of housing for those whom the private marketplace has failed to serve, and the architectural responses to these issues. Its focus is housing for people who have historically and chronically been without housing options, who need some manner of assistance or subsidy in order to live in decent and dignified conditions (most likely by renting). This segment of the population is growing and will continue to do so. I do not mean to diminish the problem confronting increasing numbers of families, many with two incomes, that find themselves shut out of home ownership. They, however, still have some housing choices.

Designing and building affordable housing in the United States poses unique problems in part because of our national obsession with the single-family house and in part because of our historical ambivalence about subsidized housing. People all over the world live in detached houses, but nowhere else has this housing type been deified as the socially and morally acceptable form. Moreover, in other industrialized countries the provision of housing to populations in need, with the concomitant governmental intervention, has usually been viewed as integral to a humane social policy. In the United States, however, social policy vacillates between helping the needy and stigmatizing them, between allocating funds and decrying the impulse to throw dollars at problems, between believing in activist government and trusting the mechanisms of the free market.

My emphasis on California is part chauvinism, part practicality, and part necessity. I live and work in California, and it seems that for many things, if it happens at all, it happens here. Design trends, government policy, and social activism are part of the affordable housing context in California, both for good and for bad. The practical side of my emphasis is my knowledge of the state's regulations and my access to the officials, architects, builders, and community activists I interviewed. I did conduct interviews in other parts of the country, and I include examples in the book from all over the United States, but the focus is California. It is a necessary focus, because this state has the worst housing affordability crisis by all measures. Seventeen of the country's twenty least affordable housing markets are in California. And its problems are not limited to urban areas; rural and suburban communities are struggling as well. Fifty percent of Californians rent, compared to a national average of 43 percent.[1] Nearly one-third of the state's renters are paying a disproportionate share of their income for housing, and 20 percent live in overcrowded circumstances.[2] If there are solutions or answers for the country as a whole, they must work in California.

Several people assisted in the preparation of this book in countless ways, from sitting for interviews to providing materials, information, and data. I am indebted to them all.

Throughout the preparation of this manuscript, I asked people knowledgeable in the field to read and comment on the work. Keith Bloom, Mary Comerio, Robert Herman, Lisa Joyce, John Landis, Roger Montgomery, Barton Phelps, Rob Wellington Quigley, and Ben Weese all graciously provided their insights and criticisms.

When undertaking to write a book, one hardly considers the vastness of the entire enterprise, including the research, referencing, acquisition of artwork, and general administrative details. Carolyn Greis was instrumental in all these. Elizabeth Byrne and Kathryn Wayne of the Environmental Design Library at the University of California at Berkeley were also untiring in their reference and research assistance.

This book underwent several iterations, each the result of thoughtful and astute editing. Amy Einsohn and Carolyn Greis provided initial editing and reality checks, and Rose Vekony the final, and very thorough, edit.

I am grateful to my colleagues at Davis & Joyce Architects for their understanding and patience while I was writing and not designing. James Clark, director of the University of California Press, deserves special thanks for motivating me to write what had been building up inside and then giving me moral support to complete it. And I owe a very special thanks to Barbara Gross Davis, who had just finished her book when I began mine, and so served as the model of a dedicated author while providing ongoing support and advice.

During the year of research and writing I was fortunate to have support from the following at the University of California: the Committee on Research of the Academic Senate; the Department of Architecture; the College of Letters and Sciences, for a Humanities Research Fellowship; and the Center for Real Estate and Urban Economics, for a Faculty Associate Grant.

"Affordable housing" is the latest in a long list of synonyms to denote housing for those who cannot afford the free-market price. Earlier in this century it was called "poor housing" or "subsidized housing." The rubric for all of these, and the term used by most Europeans, is "social housing," which expresses both the intention and the need. "Social housing" implies that a responsible and humane society has an obligation to assist those of its members who could not otherwise have decent housing.

For our purposes, affordable housing is housing that receives direct or indirect financial assistance, housing that is developed outside the purely market-rate private system. Few projects today are wholly public financed, and some market-rate projects subject to inclusionary zoning may be considered partly subsidized. If in order to obtain financing or approvals a private developer is compelled to make some of the units affordable, the project falls within my definition. In these cases the project may have been built no differently from a purely market-rate development, but the

rent for some of the dwellings is lower than for others, or if they are sold, some prices may be higher to subsidize the affordable units. The projects discussed in this book benefited from some sort of subsidy, grant, tax credit, or land donation.

That the United States is suffering an acute shortage of affordable housing is indisputable. In 1989, the shortage of housing for those most in need stood at over five million dwellings[1]—more if one includes units whose size or location made them unsuitable for those prospective residents. And this figure is growing at an alarming rate.

The increasing number of homeless families on our nation's streets is the most dramatic manifestation of this housing crisis. These families are living out the most desperate and tragic results of a decade of national neglect and a stagnant housing policy. In 1980, $26.6 billion of the federal budget went to housing, but by 1989 that figure was $7.4 billion, a drop of 72 percent.[2] Perhaps as many as 250,000 children in the United States were homeless in 1991, and according to some estimates, seven million Americans are so poor that they may soon become homeless.[3] While these statistics and predictions are hotly debated, if this dire scenario comes to pass, Homelessness would be the second largest city in the nation, behind only New York.[4]

Other symptoms of the housing crisis are less readily visible. Many working-class and middle-class people sense that they too may be only one illness, accident, or layoff away from homelessness. Their insecurity reflects the fact that housing costs have continued to vastly outpace incomes. During the 1980s, for example, family income rose by 6 percent while rents increased by 19 percent.[5] By 1987 over 10 million households were paying half their income for housing. For the poorest families—those with incomes below the federal poverty line—rent may consume as much as 70 percent of their income.[6] With the federal poverty line at $10,000 a year for a family of four, that family would then spend $7,700 a year (or $642 a month) for rent and then have $2,300 remaining ($192 a month) for all its other needs. Even families who receive other assistance, such as food stamps and medicaid, are hard pressed to decently feed and clothe themselves, pay for transportation and utilities, and cover all other necessities on what is left after the rent is paid.

Paradoxically, although 75 percent of the households below the poverty line receive no housing subsidy, one large category of Americans who are not among the neediest—homeowners—receives the lion's share of government housing assistance in the form of tax deductions for mortgage interest and real estate taxes. As a result $50 billion of government housing assistance goes to middle- and upper-class homeowners each year, rather than to low-income renters.[7]

It seems fitting, nonetheless, that our tax code reinforces one aspect of the American Dream: we aspire to be a nation of homeowners. Our identities and values are tied to the location and charac-ter of our dwellings. That so many Americans cannot afford to rent, much less purchase, a decent dwelling in the community of their choice has become a political bombshell that is finding its way onto the national agenda.

Who needs affordable housing? Not just the homeless, and not just those living at or below the poverty line. All sorts of people with incomes above the poverty line still cannot afford market-rate housing: single parents, seniors, twenty-year-olds fresh on the job market, and the new unemployed are probably the largest groups. In Los Angeles the waiting list for public housing reached twenty thousand, and the city stopped taking names. And consider the plight of those who live in the San Francisco Bay Area, one of the country's most expensive housing markets. Federal guidelines recommend that low-income families pay no more than 30 percent of their income for housing. By these standards, a household earning $18,000 should spend no more than $450 a month for housing, but the median rent in the Bay Area is nearly $700 a month.[8] No wonder a new 100-unit affordable project in San Francisco attracted two thousand applicants.

THE VALUE OF DESIGN

With a problem so urgent and widespread, why even discuss architecture? Why not concentrate on stimulating production to increase supply? What is the value of design in so basic a need as housing? A common view is that good design costs more, and that while architects add value and quality to buildings, they rarely add economy. It seems no one ever goes to an architect to save money. Architects can blame both themselves and the media for this perception. The rise of a few architects to celebrity status and the lavish magazines devoted to high-style homes perpetuate the stereotype that architecture, like couture, is only for the lucky, moneyed few. Not so. The all-too-obvious mistakes in public housing of the last fifty years overshadow the long and occasionally honored history of architects' participation in affordable housing.

Seventy percent of the cost of a new dwelling is affected by planning and design.[9] Careful planning and sensitive design that save even 10 percent of those costs can reduce the monthly payments by $100 in perpetuity. Although any single design decision is unlikely to yield dramatic savings and improved quality, thoughtful unit planning will. For example, a plan that uses space inefficiently may call for long hallways, which add little to the livability of a dwelling and cost money to construct. Moreover, they need to be lighted and heated—an ongoing expense for the occupants. For all that one might save by using poor-quality materials and scrimping on space, such short-sighted penny-wise attitudes are ultimately costly—both economically and socially.

Housing is not merely shelter, or basic protection from the elements. It also must bestow on its inhabitants a sense of dignity ("one's home is one's castle"). Do you take pride in your dwelling? Does it make you feel secure, safe, and satisfied when you are there? To ignore this aspect of housing, or to consider it a perquisite only for those who can afford market-rate housing, is to invite both social and financial disaster. Moreover, housing is a key ingredient in community building. Islands of low-income projects that are socially, economically, and architecturally cut off from the surrounding communities compel their inhabitants to be detached and alienated.

An approach to affordable housing that relies primarily on stimulating production is the result of two long-standing attitudes. The first is that housing is a commodity, like refrigerators. It is not. Housing cannot be produced in a single location and distributed throughout the nation. Local needs, codes, customs, and climates vary. Dwellings are big, costly, and generally immovable. They are set on a specific site and stay in their basic form for decades. Decisions made at the outset about size, form, materials, layout, and aesthetics affect all the generations who reside in that house. If the rooms are too small, the plan poorly conceived, or the construction too costly to maintain or operate, residents can't easily exchange it, move it, or ignore it. If a family of six wants to live in a particular neighborhood and only a small apartment or a one-bedroom house is available, neither will suffice. If that family has special needs or requirements, the dwelling must accommodate them.

The second misconception is that affordable housing should not exceed a minimum standard. It should be basic, safe, and clean—but no more. That it should meet the cultural and psychological needs of its residents or have the quality and amenities of market-rate housing is often seen as a misguided use of money, particularly if the housing is subsidized. This patronizing attitude has led to the construction of housing that stigmatizes and penalizes its residents, that denies their dignity and their humanity. It has doomed publicly assisted housing.

MYTHS AND HALF-TRUTHS

These two erroneous ideas—that housing is a commodity and that the barest minimum is sufficient for subsidized housing—have engendered a complex set of half-truths, myths, and misunderstandings about the design of affordable housing. I list them briefly here; they are discussed further in the chapters that follow.

Housing is a technical or production problem. If we could find more efficient ways of building, we could make more houses for more people. This myth has guided much of our low-income housing. It has an element of truth, and it appeals to the mind-set of a nation intent on technology and manufacturing solutions. But the dispersed nature of the nation's building industry and the diverse needs of vastly different communities make it impossible to rely on centralized production models as a keystone to our housing policy.

We need housing for families with children, since such families make up the majority of needy households. There are many families with children who need good housing, but in only 26 percent of the nation's households do mother, father, and children live together, as in television's Ozzie and Harriet or the Cleavers. The fastest-growing segments of the population are actually unmarried people—now 30 percent of all households—many with children; and an increasing number of seniors.[10] Affordable housing must include solutions for diverse populations—seniors, homeless, families, and singles.

Affordable housing is an urban problem. We need projects of high density in cities to accommodate the urban poor. Clearly there is a need for affordable housing in urban areas. In the 1950s and 1960s some 425,000 mostly low-cost dwellings were destroyed in the name of "renewal," a misguided effort to rid our cities of blight. But only 125,000 new dwellings replaced them, and half were market-rate, not affordable.[11] We have yet to catch up. Moreover, high-density elevator housing in urban areas has proved an ill-advised strategy. Far more successful are moderate-density, low-rise, and infill projects. Nevertheless, this is not the only area with housing needs; suburban and rural communities also must add affordable housing and must likewise rely on moderate-density, low-rise buildings.

Regulations and codes protect low-income occupants from poor construction. Building codes do offer protection. But housing is probably the most regulated of all building types, and many rules serve only to increase costs or to protect an inter-est group or industry. Zoning ordinances that exclude higher-density housing from some communities, for example, are one of the primary factors in increasing housing costs.

Standardization and replication of buildings is the best way to lower housing costs. It is true that standardization can produce efficiencies, but the cookie-cutter approach to housing is what has doomed so many public housing projects. The key is to find means of including architectural variety and diversity within recurring building systems.

Building large projects that gain economies of scale is the best way to lower costs and increase production. Large projects may be more efficient to construct, but the increasing costs of aggregating land and the approval process often offset the savings. Because the surrounding communities, particularly stable existing neighborhoods, do not want a large project in their midst, the ultimate social cost is greater than the front-end savings achieved by making large projects. Rather than create isolated enclaves, we need to integrate affordable housing into communities.

The single-family house is the best form of housing, and we ought to do everything we can to make it affordable. Despite the many virtues of the single-family house, it is an environmentally unsustainable form. We cannot continue to convert agricultural land into tracts of single-family housing and the roadways that connect those houses to job centers. The cost of transportation, utilities, and service networks, as well as the resulting air pollution and environmental degradation, preclude construction of a single-family home for every household in America. The strategy for the architect is to incorporate as many of the features of the single-family house as possible at increasing densities.

Affordable housing is a temporary solution for those in need. Although any one household's neediness may be temporary, our nation will always have a need for affordable housing units. To think otherwise is pure, utopian fantasy. It is preferable to view affordable housing as a permanent solution, so that it becomes a stabilizing aspect of the community.

Affordable housing costs less to build than comparable market-rate housing. This logical statement was once true. But because affordable housing was cheaper, it wasn't as good, and because it wasn't as good, the inhabitants, who had no other housing choice, were seen as unworthy. This cycle needs to be broken by making affordable housing that is indistinguishable from market-rate housing.

Architects have a limited role in affordable housing. Housing, in the end, is building; it is what we see after all the regulation, process, and politics have run their course and the money is spent. The buildings stay much longer than the remembrances of how they came to be. The lives of the people who live in them, and of those who live near them, are forever affected by their design. This realization is what motivated me to write this book.

Fifteen years ago I wrote this passage in the preface to *The Form of Housing*. I believe it still:

Architecture is public domain. Even the private house makes use of our diminishing natural resources and is affected by many individuals, laws, and institutions. As material resources dwindle further and more people become involved in various aspects of building, the problems grow in complexity and in their interdependence. Nowhere in the field of building and architecture is this more true than in housing. For those interested in architecture and its relationship to society, the place for fruitful investigation is housing.[12]

In the intervening time many projects have been built, some of them my own, and while I believe that we are improving what we build and how, the issues and problems discussed in that book persist. The continuing housing crisis in the United States has been exacerbated by poor economies and policies. Housing is still very much a fruitful place to look for how architecture can serve society.

THE ARCHITECT AND AFFORDABLE HOUSING

Architecture has become a recognized, highly visible part of popular culture. Architects grace the covers of national news magazines, their trials and tribulations are front-page stories in the *Wall Street Journal*, and architect-designed dinnerware, housewares, and furniture are sold in department stores. Some architects are household names. But one would be hard-pressed to name the architect of an affordable housing project, and some might even claim that such works are not really architecture. For much of our housing history, they would be right. While public housing was first seen by reformers as a means of engineering social change, the public's ambivalence about subsidizing it and the pervasive penurious attitude of government agencies empowered to sponsor it shifted the focus to highly regulated public utility that militated against good design. During this time the architect's involvement was continuous, albeit tenuous. But architects have also been leaders in social housing, particularly when it was envisioned either as a manufactured commodity or as an instrument of community activism.

THE REFORMERS:
HOUSING DESIGN AS SOCIAL POLICY

The earliest social housing in the United States was motivated by concerns about the growing maladies of urban life, the diseases and social pathologies that tenements were thought to generate. The mission was not so much to improve the quality of life and environment for the residents living in squalid conditions as to protect the rest of society from them.

In the mid to late 1800s, with increasing industrialization, foreign immigration, and migration into urban areas, high-density living, primarily in multistory tenements, dominated sectors of American cities, particularly New York. From today's architecture and urban design perspective, the continuous walls of housing built over shops were not altogether bad, for they formed a consistent backdrop for lively social interaction. But these facades masked desperate circumstances. Poor ventilation, inadequate plumbing, and infestation of rodents and roaches fostered smallpox and tuberculosis, creating such mean conditions that civil unrest erupted. Responding to the public's anxiety, New York City passed the Tenement

House Act of 1867, which included codes, regulations, and policies that made for cleaner, safer, and sturdier housing. In 1901 the efforts of housing reformers in New York led to an even stricter tenement law that prescribed many features for new housing, including even the size of courtyards.[1]

Housing reformers who pushed for legislation, some of whom were architects, fell into two camps: those who looked to European examples of high-quality, dignified urban housing as the model for both building types and public policy, and those who saw housing as a device to promulgate and legitimate social values. This distinction translated into two views of architecture. The first camp was more amenable to a variety of building types, as long as they were safe and affordable, while the latter was interested only in the one type that was seen to represent wholesome American values, namely, the single-family house. The opponents of public-housing legislation also fell into two camps, one financial and the other philosophical. There were those within the building industry who feared they would have less business and would lose control of their operations, and there were those outside the industry who saw the intended inhabitants as unworthy. This latter group may have begrudgingly accepted that the need for decent shelter was real but would concede no more than a minimal definition of "decent."

Throughout the late nineteenth century and into the early twentieth, housing reform and design focused on safety and health. Fire protection, sanitation, and ventilation were the major concerns that affected building form and construction. Architects worked out the logistics by positing "model tenements" plans that ensured there would be ample light, air, and means of escape from fire.[2] Rather than advancing distinctive or creative designs, they strove to master a puzzle of tightly organized spaces. Many architects who participated in these efforts did so in response to competitions sponsored by magazines or organizations that had a financial interest in building.

Plumber and Sanitation Engineer magazine initiated one such event in New York in 1879, and the winning design, by James E. Ware Jr., promised both safety and economic returns.[3] It soon became the basis for codified standards for the configurations and sizes of air shafts. But Ware's "dumbbell" scheme, so named because the air shafts, carved into the long plan, made the configuration look like a barbell, was not universally praised. Residents used the ample ventilation shafts as garbage chutes, thereby reinforcing the perception of socially inept tenants who, without appropriate housing forms to provide clues, did not know how to live.

Some architects' efforts resulted in sizable structures, such as William Field's Riverside Tenement Yard in Brooklyn (fig. 1). While representing an early move by philanthropists toward large-scale housing for those with low incomes, this project, created in 1890 for the Improved Dwelling Association (a development organization that limited dividends to 5 percent), included a courtyard that not only provided ventilation and light to units but also served as an area for children's play and shared social activities. The series of projecting bays reduced the overall scale of the building by delineating sets of apartments within it.

Whatever improvements the new regulations motivated, apartments were still seen as less desirable than individual houses. Early professional housing reformers like Lawrence Veiller and Henry Wright, who wielded significant influence based on their professional credentials, made public pronouncements against apartments, both luxury buildings and tenements, tying their disdain for the type to a likely degradation of social values.[4] Their views played on the ingrained mean image of the tenement and its occupants and reflected the cultural values of independence, self-

FIG. I. The courtyard of William Field's Riverside Tenement Yard in Brooklyn (1890).

determination, and self-sufficiency, all of which were embodied in the detached single house. In order to behave like an American you had to live like one, and that meant living in, and preferably owning, a house.

Architects seemed ambivalent about this issue. They were used to designing houses, albeit for the well-off; they clearly understood the form and were comfortable working in it. But they were aware that their talents could be useful in higher-density housing. Some early reformist architects created inexpensive houses that emulated middle-class homes but were built on new tracts. Others saw apartments as necessary for cost efficiency but felt that higher-density buildings should include some physical elements of houses, or at least maintain a residential scale. For example, Frank Lloyd Wright's Francisco Terrace, built in 1895 in Chi-

FIG. 2. Frank Lloyd Wright's Francisco Terrace (1895).

cago, comprised two stories of apartments, nearly all of which were entered through a shared court-yard (fig. 2). The second-level apartments, though accessed from a balcony, each had private entries with awnings that emphasized the individual dwelling within the collective form.[5] Still other architects were convinced that apartments had benefits unavailable in single houses, the most important being a sense of community. Enclosed courtyards were particularly favored, both for their community functions and for the protection they afforded from the ills of the city beyond. The courtyard apartment is still popular today for the same reasons.

Government housing subsidies were not yet prevalent, and social housing was sponsored by interest groups or by industrialists, who were increasingly criticized for creating the demographic shifts that gave rise to the tenements. In some cases the owners of major industries saw housing as yet another way of controlling workers and making a profit. Railroad car magnate George Pullman created a whole town with 1,400 dwellings in 1884, all company-owned and rented to employees. His town, designed by both an architect and a landscape architect, physically reinforced the notion that worker status and housing type were interrelated. Workers with families and responsibilities had rowhouses, which were outfitted and sited according to employment rank. Newcomers and laborers lived in boardinghouses.[6]

The Depression provoked serious government financial intervention into housing, in part to meet the increased need for housing affordability but primarily to stimulate the economy. The Wagner-Steagall Housing Act of 1937 legitimized direct federal subsidies to housing. For reformers like Catherine Bauer, who helped draft the law, the new policy rightly affirmed that government had a role to play in housing. The opponents cited business or political arguments, fearing socialism, a shackling of capitalism, or even an end to segregation.[7] Many early programs continued the focus on single-family houses by subsidizing their purchase through guaranteed mortgages, thereby encouraging the proliferation of a tacitly approved housing form while appeasing those who favored demand-side intervention.

The supply side of subsidized housing, that which stimulated new construction through government financing, became more prevalent in the New Deal, with three focuses: programs to build whole new model communities, rural assistance programs, and urban slum clearance. The poor economy and the spirit of the New Deal attracted social-minded architects to all these causes. The Public Works Administration built several projects in the 1930s that represented much of the reformers' agenda: sound housing supported by communal amenities. Many of these projects were modest

in scale, rarely more than four floors, and were architecturally suited, at least in terms of style, to their area. They were only partly subsidized and were developed by nonprofit organizations like trade unions.

The Carl Mackley Houses (fig. 3), built in 1931 for the Hosiery Workers' Union in Philadelphia, is a noteworthy example, one made possible by the political efforts of Catherine Bauer and the architect, Oskar Stonorov, which resulted in funding for low-cost housing within the National Recovery Act. Although a survey of prospective tenants indicated that the Depression-scared union members expected only minimal housing, Stonorov had greater ambitions: "Housing . . . is no longer so much a question of naked shelter only. It is the demand for the reorganization of rotten communities into stable, sane and healthy societies."[8] The result, designed by Stonorov and Alfred Kastner, was a humane modern housing complex built around two courtyards, with terraces shared by sets of apartments. It included several recreational and social facilities, such as tennis courts, a swimming pool, and a rooftop laundry. Most significant, the complex had meeting rooms intended to encourage seminars on current political and social issues, a nursery school, a library, and a cooperative market. Its sturdy construction of reinforced concrete, an unusual material for residential designs at the time, was seen as providing the best available technology to low-income housing.

The first fully subsidized project, called First Houses and built in 1936 in New York (fig. 4), was created by reworking a block of existing tenements, removing some and reconfiguring others. The complex knitted itself into the block, and the entries were moved from the street to the interior courtyard, which was replete with artwork. Also included were several social services.[9] Because such projects were undertaken by the government to improve the economy, budgets were irrelevant—

FIG. 3.   The Carl Mackley Houses in Philadelphia (1931) featured social and recreational areas, modern architecture, and concrete construction.

indeed, the more spent, the better. Their high-quality design, in stark contrast to tenements, attested to the goal of improving the cities.

HOUSING AS PUBLIC UTILITY

By the 1940s and into the 1950s two changes had occurred in the public's and government's attitudes about public housing that affected its archi-tecture for two decades. The first change was that the high quality and level of amenities of the earlier projects were now viewed as extravagances. In her *Modern Housing* of 1934, Catherine Bauer had already suggested that housing had become a public utility—that while we might have accepted the need for decent housing, it was viewed as one of the "national minima," like water and sanitation.[10] Cost-containment measures for federally funded

FIG. 4.   First Houses in New York (1936),
the first fully subsidized housing project,
had a courtyard and social spaces.

projects became the cornerstone of public housing. Architects had not only to manage the increasing regulations for health and safety but also
to meet cost restrictions. The programs became
mean-spirited, the dwellings spartan.

Second, the "towers-in-the-park" philosophy,
which espoused the construction of isolated high-
rises in bucolic settings, gave impetus to the notion held by some of the reformers that large projects, through their dramatic image and scale,
would better distinguish the new housing from
the disdainful slums it was replacing. The smaller,
more integrated public-housing projects were seen
as too close, conceptually and geographically, to
tenements. Large projects of repeating high-rise
buildings would be strong visual reminders that
the poor were being attended to in a dynamic
fashion. It was also believed, but never confirmed,
that such projects were less expensive to build.

Typical of the era is San Francisco's Yerba Buena
Plaza, where delicate Victorians were replaced by a
large, high-rise slab with continuous rows of access
balconies. Every major city had its "Pink Palace,"
as the project was sarcastically named. This con-
spiracy of ideas by those who had the power to
employ them would be discredited in less than
twenty years, but its legacy remains.

THE ARCHITECT AS BYSTANDER

With the return of veterans in the late 1940s,
households that had placed their aspirations on
hold began to search for housing. Government-
sponsored home-ownership programs encouraged
the continued preference for the single-family
house, while the availability of inexpensive land,
the pervasiveness of the automobile in American
life, and the proliferation of highways spurred the

exodus to the suburbs. Cities were dirty, noisy, and ugly; suburbs, only a short drive away in an elegant car on an uncongested superhighway, were clean, quiet, and bucolic. Developers like William Levitt, the creator of Levittown, New York (1949), had little need for architects. Strong demand from young families, available financing, encouragement from the government, and a product with an unassailable image combined to create a market boom in which design had little impact on homebuyers' acceptance of the new communities.

The 1949 Housing Act was the first in a series of government pronouncements on the need for a decent home for everybody. It seemed to anticipate the growing disparity between haves and have-nots, between suburb and city, between homes and housing, and between mainly white, middle-class Americans and the poor. One group had choices and control, the other had few options and little say in their housing circumstance. But while these issues were becoming clearer, the ultimately deleterious effect of single-family houses at low density, both on affordability (even for the middle class) and on the environment, was either not yet understood or not yet acute enough to be worrisome.

In both forms, the single-family house and urban social housing, the role of the architect was increasingly superfluous. For both the production home builder and the land speculator, the front-end cost of design seemed to have little effect on the salability of their product. Before this huge potential market architects only saw their status diminish, a situation all the more lamentable because the builder houses were of uninspired design. The Federal Housing Administration, which insured the mortgages, further undermined the position of architects by discouraging design innovation, particularly modernism, as a potential financial risk. Houses were generally designed by a builder's in-house staff, only some of whom were architects; other designs came from plan services,

which simply sold them, or "lumberyard architects" who offered minimal design services when building materials were purchased, much like interior design services at present-day furniture stores.[11] A few enlightened developers did understand that architectural design was a means of communicating a lifestyle and thereby increasing sales. Joseph Eichler in California was one such developer. His courtyard houses, many designed by Anshen and Allen and Jones & Emmons, were distinctly Californian; with large expanses of glass, patios, and open courtyards for outdoor living, they embodied an unencumbered and unadorned aesthetic, a relaxed modernism for an increasingly informal and active lifestyle.

In public housing architects were needed, but they were kept on a short leash. As the expansive and humane attitude of the early reformers was replaced by the myopia of bureaucrats, the rules, regulations, and standards multiplied. By the inception of the "alphabet soup" programs of the 1960s, like 221(d)3, the guidelines for design filled a prodigious manual of several hundred pages.[12] These programs recognized the political imperative for clearing the slums and dealing with increasingly intransigent poverty, but they could not reconcile that imperative with qualitative issues like design.

Standards intended to protect the disenfranchised poor had the opposite effect, as the prescribed minimums were interpreted as maximums and low cost became the primary goal. Architects working in this context became only more frustrated and beleaguered as the logistics of building planning and rule conformance led to a stalemate: if a project was innovative, it would be criticized by the funding agencies; if it was uninspired, it would be criticized by the public.

Several architects succeeded in spite of the federal government, often in collusion with local authorities or communities. One example is Marin City, built north of San Francisco in 1962 (fig. 5).

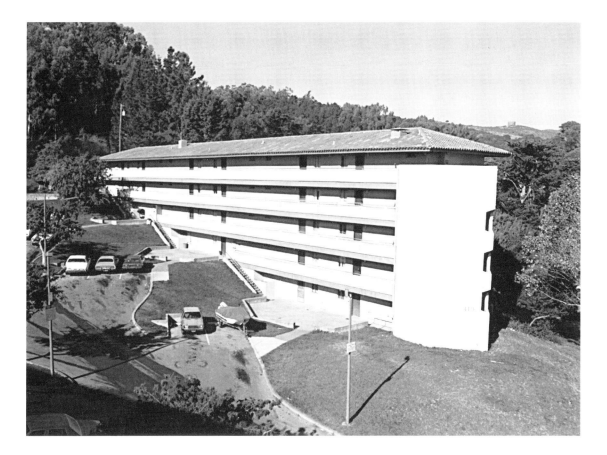

FIG. 5.   Marin City (1962), north of San Francisco, circumvented cost-containment rules to make a sturdier and more dignified housing complex.

Its architect, Aaron Green, a protégé of Frank Lloyd Wright, bent all the rules for design and material specification. The complex was set on a slope with wonderful views, and its design included clay tile roofs, concrete balconies with solid molded handrails, and lavish landscaping. In 1964 it won the first award for design excellence given by the Department of Housing and Urban Development (HUD), but the Government Accounting Office lambasted the excesses of the completed project, which stands today, over thirty years later, in relatively sound condition.

These small successes notwithstanding, by the early 1960s social housing was a mess, both administratively and architecturally. The reformers' agenda had been perverted and demeaned. The projects of the previous decades were in decay, and the remedies of increasing regulations and government control seemed to exacerbate their condition. The social turbulence of the 1960s emphasized the divisions between urban and suburban living, and the rapid successes in the space program only reinforced the misconception that the solution to social problems lay in technology. Pathologies set in, this time in the form of crime, drugs, and degradation rather than the viral epidemics of the 1860s, but the results were similar: violence. The Kerner, Douglas, and Kaiser Commissions appointed by President Johnson each cited the availability, affordability, and condition of housing as national problems. Under the banner of Johnson's Great Society, the Housing Act of 1968 encouraged much new subsidized housing, but various and seemingly unfocused attempts at remedies were short-lived. In 1973 President Nixon suspended the programs.

Pruitt-Igoe, a large public-housing project in St. Louis that was demolished by 1976, only nineteen years after its construction, is emblematic of the failure of the concept of social housing as a public utility, demonstrating the fallacy of the nation's attitudes about architecture, public policy, and urban renewal. As many have pointed out, the architecture of Pruitt-Igoe, a series of identical, repetitive high-rise buildings set on an undifferentiated flat site, was merely the most visible aspect of its flaws.[13] This is not to diminish the impact of the design errors, not the least of which was the absence of viewable, controllable, and accessible play areas for children. The project was the culmination of a grim public policy to warehouse the poor, to move thousands of very low income people into a single enclave that ignored the needs and aspirations of the tenants and denied them all but the most utilitarian features—even insulation on steam pipes.

There are several ways to look at the architect's position in Pruitt-Igoe and in similar failures. One can condemn the architect for having bought into both the policy and the anonymous high-rise building form it implied. One can view the archi-

tect as relatively powerless, able only to make the best of a misguided public policy. As a "hired gun," the architect merely facilitates the ideas of others, translating policy into physical form.[14] Or one can conclude that the architect simply did not know better. The idea of asking prospective residents what they preferred, of having them participate in the decisions that would affect their homes and their lives, was just not part of the impersonal, patronizing public-housing process.

HOUSING AS AN INSTRUMENT OF COMMUNITY ACTIVISM

In the 1960s and early 1970s a dynamic paradigm shift took place in the reform movement in social housing, one that paralleled much of the change in consciousness in other social and political arenas. The new wave of reformers focused not so much on legislation or regulation but on information in the form of literature, research on occupants, and criticism. Among several important books on the topic of livable cities and housing, the most influential was Jane Jacobs's *Death and Life of Great American Cities* (1961). Jacobs's key insight was that cities work when a sense of community is reinforced, when housing looks out on its territory, so that its residents may guard it and care for it. "The buildings on a street equipped to handle strangers and to insure the safety of both residents and strangers, must be oriented to the street. They cannot turn their backs or blank sides on it and have it blind."[15] The requirement of "eyes on the street" became the determinant factor in housing design; high-rises and balkanized projects that turned away from the city's streets were seen as antisocial and antiurban, and therefore inappropriate.

A decade later Oscar Newman took this approach further. In *Defensible Space: Crime Prevention through Urban Design* (1972), he outlined the causal relation between building form and the growing pathologies around housing projects. His emphatic criticism of high-rise housing as inappropriate for poor families, supported by his research on the dire conditions of many such projects, signaled the end of that building type for public housing. From the early 1970s until now, the favored form for affordable projects has been the low-rise development of medium to high density. Courtyard housing, townhouses, and garden apartments with as many as fifty units an acre are now the dominant type.

The new wave of housing reform was also supported by a growing movement of behavioral research in architecture. Based on field research in which people were asked about their preferences and needs, much of this work generated guidelines, similar to the earlier standards but more tailored to individual occupant profiles and community needs and allowing greater interpretative freedom to architects. These guidelines generally focused on performance rather than rigid prescriptions. Instead of requiring a set amount of space for play, for example, they would discuss different types of play and the design conditions that facilitate them.

Armed with critical literature, field research, and a heightened social consciousness, the new generation of architects and government administrators were less interested in regulation than in quality. Perhaps the boldest example was set by the Urban Development Corporation (UDC) in New York. This "super agency" had the power to cut through local jurisdictions and regulations in order to smooth the way for affordable housing. The UDC retained high-profile architectural firms and provided them with the latest research and guidelines on user groups and their preferred amenities. It even compelled its own project managers to live in their developments for a period upon completion, both to lessen the psychological dis-

tance between housing supplier and occupant and to learn firsthand what really worked architecturally.

Some large and celebrated urban projects, most notably Yerba Buena in San Francisco and Cedar Riverside in Minneapolis, stimulated a broader wave of social activism in the public sector, much of it focused on community preservation and advocacy for those with housing needs.[16] Rather than push for a particular building type or program, these reformers became advocates for the occupants whose housing and communities were at risk. Their efforts to stop or dramatically alter the plans of the projects were successful, with strategies that often included alternative architectural designs.

While this social activism was directed on behalf of those without political might and lacking access to design professionals, the system also worked for people who had both. Protectionism of property and lifestyle, which became known as "NIMBYism" (Not In My Back Yard), began in earnest. Cities created design review boards with non-architect members to arbitrate on design issues. Environmental impact legislation, initiated by the federal government in 1969 to protect the community from the environmental abuses associated with manufacturing, added new layers of regulation to housing.[17] Under the National Environmental Policy Act of 1969 (NEPA), projects receiving federal funding had to submit lengthy environmental impact statements (EIS; also called environmental impact report, EIR). The EIS approval process was adroitly manipulated by people determined to stop projects or protect their investments: "The courts usually found that a plaintiff's eyes were fixed, not on the beauties of nature nor the public good, but on the dollar sign."[18] But another consequence was that builders, developers, and housing authorities, all under increasing pressure to present projects good enough to overwhelm the opposition, began to pay more attention to design issues. Architects were necessary not just to solve design problems, as they had done before, but also to bestow some vitality on the work and help convince the evaluators of the merits of the design. Thus, architects and architecture were finally deemed crucial to the social housing endeavor.

The 1960s and 1970s presented the first drift away from the single-family house and toward higher-density housing. In 1960 only 22 percent of all new housing was multifamily, but this figure doubled by 1970.[19] Several factors influenced this trend, including increased construction costs and a greater difficulty in gaining entitlements to develop open land. Architects who had already been proponents of higher-density low-rise designs, strategies that fit into communities more comfortably, were encouraged by this movement and enjoyed new employment opportunities.[20] Many gained national recognition for work done primarily with for-profit developers.

In 1973, just as high-density low-rise housing was gaining a foothold and architects were having an impact on both design and affordability, the Nixon administration suspended housing subsidies. Instead of intervening on the supply side by funding new construction, the federal government moved toward the demand side and instituted a housing voucher program, comparable to food stamps. Under the voucher system low-income renters received direct cash payments that allowed them to live in market-rate housing and pay no more than 30 percent of their income for rent.

It might seem that architects should fall on the demand side of the supply-demand debate. For when rent rather than construction is subsidized, architects can focus on design issues without obsessive bureaucratic oversight and budgetary constraints. From a social standpoint, vouchers also make sense. The housing is not identified as exclusively for the poor, since those who receive assistance live alongside those who do not; only management knows who is who. Moreover, the housing often has amenities that would be considered "too good" for a purely affordable or subsidized project but are necessary if the developer is to attract residents who do not receive assistance.

In reality, however, vouchers may not stimulate the construction of much new affordable housing. In a weak economy, for-profit developers simply lie low. In better financial climates they have ample market-rate tenants, often in suburban areas, where those with dire housing needs are fewer. And when they do build, the for-profit developers have their own set of rules, criteria, design obsessions, and cost-containment measures that are often as draconian as those of government agencies.

THE COMMUNITY DEVELOPMENT CORPORATIONS

The abdication of active supply-side intervention by the federal government was greeted with shock and dismay by those who understood the breadth and depth of the nation's housing shortage. But now released from the golden shackles of federal subsidies, the states began to establish agencies and programs that mirrored previous federal efforts. Most of these new programs were less onerous and more responsive to local conditions, culture, and control. The design review components were more focused on quality and less on cost containment or rote compliance to rules.

States also began to enact laws that compelled jurisdictions to formulate plans to create affordable housing or else face punitive cutbacks in state funding. For some cities that resisted affordable housing, the monetary threat proved insufficient. In California the state responded by threatening these cities with lawsuits if their obligations were not fulfilled. But the cities replied that planning was wasteful as long as there was little available funding for construction. For other cities, however, the promise of state money is indeed an enticement and there is ample competition for it.

These local efforts are undertaken through local housing authorities, community development corporations (CDCs), or private developers. More often than not, local housing authorities are tainted by their association with previous generations of failed federal programs and by the general perception that they did not maintain or manage the subsidized projects well. Tenants of buildings managed by the Oakland Housing Authority (OHA), for example, often wait months for minor repairs, and they label the OHA the city's largest slumlord.[21] In a few cases, however, local housing authorities have been rejuvenated by younger, more entrepreneurial directors and compete admirably in the housing arena.

The role of private developers has been strongest in rural communities, where affordable housing is not controversial and where the majority of residents are laborers. Private development has been successful in creating affordable housing in these areas in part because land costs are low and the nonconfrontational process does not drain financial resources.

But perhaps the most positive result of the demise of federal programs has been the rise of the nonprofit, community-based CDCs, which act very much like private developers but do not have the same motive of profit. The CDCs cannot be oblivious to finances, but they are more interested in serving their affordable-housing constituency and providing a high-quality product; whatever profit they generate must be reinvested in the system. Neither a government agency nor a private company, this third-sector developer evolved from the social activism of the 1960s. Many CDCs focus their efforts on economic development rather than housing production. But when they choose to develop housing, they are armed with a missionary zeal, spirited leadership, community involvement through a citizen board of directors,

and most important, the support of the local politicians. These groups stand the best chance of providing affordable housing in the decades to come.

Unlike a private developer, the CDC need not worry about how to entice renters or buyers to quickly fill a new project, since there are always long waiting lists of needy tenants. Instead, the CDC is more concerned about the long-term image and vitality of the project. Thus, while for-profit developers are more likely to create islands or enclaves, detached from their surroundings to promote feelings of safety, seclusion, and eliteness, nonprofits strive to integrate their projects into existing neighborhoods, so that their tenants can be part of the community. And while for-profit developers might undertake an innovative design to provide leverage in the marketplace, nonprofits are generally conservative, not willing to risk disfavor among the politicians and local residents in the communities in which they operate.

The nonprofit housing developer is fast becoming a major provider of affordable housing. The first such group was formed in the 1960s in New York's Bedford Stuyvesant; by the early 1990s five thousand organizations had created over three hundred thousand affordable units, primarily in urban and rural areas.[22] Perhaps the country's most famous nonprofit affordable housing developer is Habitat for Humanity, an ecumenical organization that relies heavily on volunteers to help build and renovate housing; its most visible laborer is former President Jimmy Carter. By 1992, Habitat for Humanity had created seventeen thousand homes throughout the world; it will be the nation's largest builder by 1994.[23] To date, Habitat for Humanity has focused most of its efforts on detached, low-density single-family houses, largely because of the organization's home-ownership orientation, but also because it is easier for volunteers and temporary labor forces to work at this scale.

A nonprofit community-based developer, sensitive both to neighborhood concerns and to the needs of a huge market of low-income people, seems like a wise, responsible evolution of the reformist housing movement of the 1800s. The projects are architecturally sound, if not innovative; they are financed through a combination of public and private funds; and they are managed carefully by an organization that will own them in perpetuity and maintain their affordable status. But this ingenious combination of entrepreneurial, mercurial, and ecumenical spirit still faces the stubborn problem of attracting sufficient funding.

The CDCs do receive some direct subsidies, but much of the funding comes through federal or state tax-credit programs that grant businesses and individuals tax breaks for investing in affordable housing. Budget-balancing maneuvers, however, may prompt Congress or state legislatures to reduce or suspend future tax credits. Meanwhile, there are limitations on the tax-credit pools, for which nonprofits must compete. This competition has several negative side-effects, particularly for the architecture and for costs.

The CDC must have control of the land on which it intends to build before it can apply for the tax credits. Finding developable property and ensuring its suitability, both technically and politically, takes time, pushing the organization against the application deadlines. It is usually at the last minute that the architect is given instructions as to the site and program, and thus the design—the element that will have the greatest effect on the costs and the most lasting effect on the project— is a hasty set of decisions. Although the design can be refined if the application is approved, changes in unit size or mix and in overall costs are not allowed. And since so little of the public review process can be undertaken before the land is optioned and the application submitted, there is an inevitable disjunction between what is contractually required for funding and what may be most desirable for the community. Finally, the deadline for spending the funds once they have been granted is also much shorter than is feasible under the best of circumstances. Since any hitches may jeopardize the financing, the CDC and the architect must get it right from the outset, without much opportunity to work with the community.

The application process has two other costly side-effects. The tax-credit application is evaluated on a point system that is convoluted enough to have spawned a growing consultant industry. It may cost a CDC $15,000 just to submit an application that may not be successful, and this sum does not include the CDC's in-house staff costs or the cost of the schematic architectural design. It would not be unusual for a CDC to have invested $25,000 or more for each project submitted in a highly competitive process. In the 1992 round, for example, there was $100 million in requests for $61.5 million in federal tax credits. In California that year, there were $96.7 million in requests for tax credits of $46.4 million.[24] The point system rewards projects that have a high level of amenities, such as security systems or exercise parcourses. While these make for good projects, they also drive up the costs. It is a catch-22: in order to gain access to affordable housing funds, you must make your project less affordable. The competition also turns CDCs into suspicious rivals rather than cooperative collaborators in their shared goal to create affordable housing.

The successes of the nonprofits have spawned new CDCs, some of which are energetic, enthusiastic, and adept at community organization but naive about design, regulation, and the politics of the public review process. Unequivocal decision making, a prerequisite for an effective development, is often undermined by the board of directors, most of whom are not in the building industry, and by local political forces. Even experienced developers find it hard enough to complete a project. An unsophisticated CDC can go through several application processes, several rounds of public review, and several years of angst to win approval for even a modest project.

Finally, there is a danger that the chief merit of the nonprofits, their concern for and sensitivity to their communities and low-income constituencies, will be undermined by for-profit developers who horn in on the action. Many nonprofits are forming joint ventures with market-rate developers who took a beating in the recession of the early 1990s and are now enticed by the access to capital, the tax-exempt status of their partners, and the waiving of property taxes. For the CDC the partnership, which provides expertise in construction and a sharing of financial risk, may be necessary to create cost-effective projects in an increasingly competitive system. But architects who may have been willing to reduce fees for the work entailed in the tax-credit application process or to share financial risks with CDCs whose funding cycles may be sporadic and infrequent are less willing to be magnanimous with for-profit developers. While some CDCs welcome the experience and organizational backup, still others see the one last hope of a responsible social housing for the twentieth century being subsumed by those driven primarily by the motive of profit.

THE ARCHITECT AS POSTULATOR

If architects were arbiters of social mores during the reform era of public housing and unwitting pawns in the era of housing as public utility, they became proponents, advocates, and postulators in the age of community activism. Some of Europe's most famous twentieth-century architects deemed affordable housing an important topic. Mies van der Rohe and Le Corbusier, for example, wrote about as well as built multifamily housing. After both World War I and World War II various European cities invited well-known architects to design housing to replace devastated neighborhoods and to propose ideas that were "technically irre-

proachable and architecturally strong and forward-looking."[25] Architecture and architects were viewed as instrumental, not superfluous or ineffectual, in addressing and solving housing problems.

With the rise of CDCs and more socially responsive housing administrators, this tradition has been resuscitated, mostly through design competitions. The United States has a long and honored history of architectural competitions, and these have become a primary indicator of excellence and innovation within the profession. A competition is a means of selecting architects (or buildings) by allowing anonymous submissions of designs in response to a specific program drafted by the event's sponsor. Some of the world's most famous buildings and monuments, like the Sydney Opera House, the Centre National d'Art et de Culture Georges Pompidou in Paris, and the Vietnam Memorial in Washington were the result of such events. The device is also prevalent in housing. Its primary advantage, according to housing architect Michael Pyatok, who has won several competitions, is that it provides "a chance to reflect and invent, to fuse the best of our real-world experiences with our most idealistic projections about the future of the human community. Housing competitions can play an important role in advocating the cause of those who need and have a right to well-designed, affordable housing."[26]

Competitions are not simple events; they are costly for the sponsor and even more so for the architects who toil long hours with only a small chance of winning. If the sponsor does not have land, financing, and a management procedure in place, the contest may inspire publicity and much controversy, but no building. In the 1960s and early 1970s, for example, three major housing competitions were held for sites in New York to elicit designs for affordable housing in very high density urban contexts. The first was for Plaza 1199 in 1963, which attracted 253 proposals; the second for Brighton Beach, near Coney Island, in

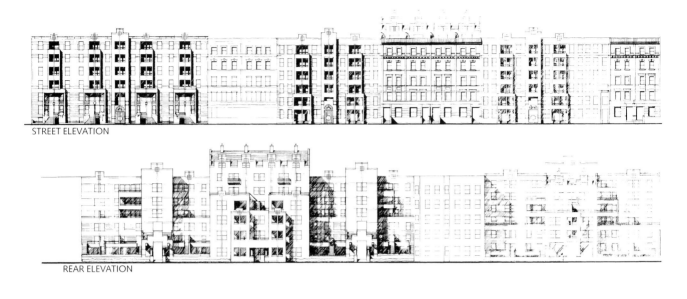

STREET ELEVATION

REAR ELEVATION

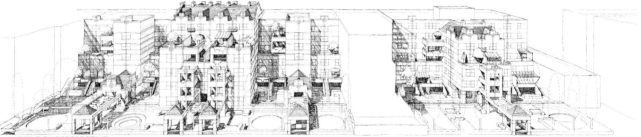

MIDBLOCK PERSPECTIVE

FIG. 6. New York City Infill Housing Competition winner (1985), by Michael Pyatok, as seen from midblock and the city street, knits buildings around courts and mews while reinforcing the existing street grid.

1968, with 88 designs; and the last for Roosevelt Island in 1974, which yielded 268 submittals.[27] The jury report for the Brighton Beach competition was typically enthusiastic ("the solutions expressed the state of the art of architecture today and the experimental nature of the young architects as applied to housing problems"),[28] and the submissions for all three events attracted much publicity in both the popular and professional press. But only the one for Plaza 1199 produced a building—and that took eight years and a wholesale alteration of the winning proposal. Political pressures and economics doomed the other two projects. Nonetheless, these events left an important legacy; many young designers whose names are found in the published record of the entries went on to produce excellent affordable housing.

The Roosevelt Island competition, with its program for one thousand dwellings, schools, and shops, signaled the end of such large-scale events for the design of high-rise public housing. Once the superagencies and government institutions were out of the housing game, the scale of both the competitions and the projects diminished. Attention turned from high-density high-rise developments to modest infill projects. For example, in 1985 New York was the site of the Infill Housing Competition, which requested proposals to build four hundred units of infill housing on several sites in Harlem, all in mid-rise buildings (i.e., no higher than seven stories). The winning design, by Michael Pyatok, reinforced the existing pattern of frequent entrances, stoops, and porches along the street (fig. 6). Behind these perimeter blocks, and perpendicular to them, he proposed an alternating series of buildings and linear courts. The front courts were pedestrian mews from which one entered the dwellings, while the rear courts formed areas for protected play and quiet respite for seniors.

In the 1980s, a bleak time for affordable housing, theme competitions served to highlight new talent and to keep architects' concern and interest alive; they also allowed for the exploration of new markets, occupant groups, and technologies.[29] The New American House competition (1984), sponsored by Minneapolis College of Art and Design and the National Endowment for the Arts, proposed to build six units that would "explore the needs of non-traditional, professional households in architectural terms" by providing space for parents to work at home (fig. 7).[30] The design by Troy West and Jacqueline Leavitt, chosen from among 346 entries, underwent the trials and tribulations of shifting sites, politics, and economics and was never built. In a poignant reminder of the obstructions faced by unusual affordable projects, as well as other plans that win national competitions, Leavitt remarks, "The New American House provides several lessons. Paramount among them is that it is very difficult to introduce innovative ideas into housing development. There is no place for the faint of heart or those who desire immediate gratification."[31]

In 1989 the small city of Colton, east of Los Angeles, saw the proposal to construct one hundred affordable apartments for seniors as an opportunity to bring prestige and attention to the community. The city's national competition attracted 137 designs. Of these, five were selected, and their design teams were paid to refine them for a final round. The winner, Joseph Valerio's eccentric design for Colton Palms, presents not only a very enjoyable place to live but also an intellectually and conceptually artful, playful, and exuberant architectural statement, one that received two national design awards (see Chapter 5).

Would Colton Palms have been built were it not for a competition? No. It took a town wanting a project that would elevate it to prominence, a developer willing to take some risks, a special group of citizens willing to listen and learn about design, and a selection panel of articulate professionals who could interpret the special qualities of

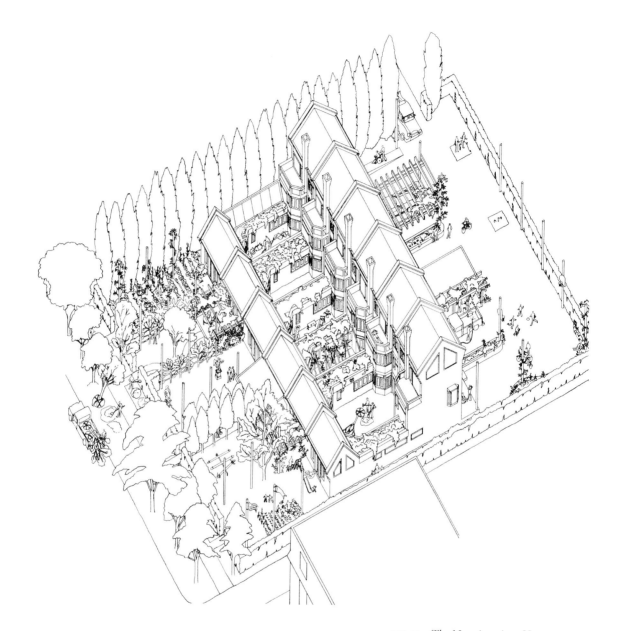

FIG. 7. The New American House
competition winner (1984), by Troy West
and Jacqueline Leavitt, is based on a
conventional rowhouse with the addition
of an integral workplace. The one-story
office faces the street and is connected to
the living quarters by a kitchen wing. The
three components—office, kitchen, and
living quarters—form a private courtyard.

the design latent in the graphics. As juror Rob Quigley suggested, the panel liked the idea that even though the project was senior housing, it did not have one foot in the emotional grave.[32] The design is full of life, optimism, and powerful architectural articulation and clarity. The competition generated civic pride and excitement—an unusual context for the planning of affordable housing.

SOCIAL HOUSING AS COMMODITY

Architects' ambivalence about how to respond to technological advancements in housing is well illustrated by the history of the industrialized building of housing. Industrialization has been a siren song for supporters of affordable housing and for architects. The modern movement in architecture had its social rationale—the anticipation that industrialization would make well-designed housing accessible to all—but also its beguiling aesthetic. There was optimism in the belief that technology could answer all needs, particularly those that called for quick, repetitive, high-quality production, like housing. The early proponents of mass-produced housing felt that this new process demanded, even compelled a new image for its product. Efficiency of manufacture had to be manifest in unadorned and futuristic building. Buckminster Fuller's Dymaxion 1 House of 1927, a gleaming space-age saucer, was one of the prototypes that emulated automobile production. Some thirty years later Disneyland built the Monsanto House of the Future, a cross-shaped, smooth plastic-and-glass capsule that showed off new products, such as ultrasonic dishwashers.

It is ironic that the early efforts in industrial production proffered new images for the single-family house. While anticipating the dominance of the most conservative type of house, some designers were suggesting very bizarre forms, totally closed systems that allowed no individual variation

and no personalization. They were faithful manifestations of their process, not of the lifestyles or inclinations of their intended inhabitants, many of whom sought housing that fit a conventional, middle-class image.

Other architects, however, saw both the need for variation in the mass-produced product and the wisdom of not perverting the conventional image. Of these, Carl Koch was most successful. His Lustron House was actually a kit of factory-made parts that could be assembled in many configurations. Koch also anticipated what others had not—that, like cars and other products, factory-produced housing needed a network of financiers, sellers, and maintenance support to be successful in the market.

This network of factory-to-consumer support is what has made the mobile home industry the only sustained effort in affordable factory-produced housing in the United States. But mobile homes, though they provide a significant number of low-cost housing units, are a low-density solution. Furthermore, they are perceived by many as inferior products and are isolated by zoning from desirable locations. The perception of the quality, while somewhat unfounded, is exacerbated by the massive devastation wrought by hurricanes and tornadoes on mobile home parks.

In the early 1970s the mobile home industry, continually denigrated by architects, attempted to improve its image by sponsoring a series of national design competitions for new mobile homes. The architects responded with better, more interesting, and more diverse products, but the industry was slow to accept the innovations they suggested. Their efforts were much like the concept cars at automobile shows: they draw crowds, receive TV coverage, and drum up interest in the industry, but they are not for sale.

As recently as 1991 the magazine *Progressive Architecture* sponsored an affordable housing competition based on the Lustron model, intended both

FIG. 8. The Abacus Architects design for a factory-produced affordable housing competition in 1991.

to awaken the profession to the pressing need for housing and to demonstrate, yet again, the benefits of mass production. The Abacus Architects prototype (fig. 8), built on a site in Cleveland, Ohio, and manufactured in Pennsylvania, was a handsome conventional building, but only one manufacturer in the region was willing to take it on. The final lesson of the competition was how complicated even a simple house can be to produce remotely and apply to a site.[33]

Unlike cars, houses cannot be built in one part of the country and shipped easily and efficiently to another. The product is large, and in many ways each one is unique, fitting into its individual site differently than the next. Codes and restrictions, while becoming more universal, are subject to local variation and application. Moreover, the very

nature of the housing construction industry in the United States precludes treating houses like other consumer products. The industry is composed primarily of small businesses that are supported by the products of larger companies. Of the approximately 47,500 builders of new dwellings, both single- and multifamily, most average less than fifty units each year, fewer in a recession.[34] These builders are localized and draw their labor force from the region in which they build.

Consider home builders as a fleet of small sailboats. They follow the same general tack, being influenced by the environmental conditions and by local rules and culture, as well as by one another. The speed of each will vary depending on the skill and goals of its crew. Every so often one boat will find a favorable current or wind and break away from the cluster. Probably as often another will fall behind, caught in a calm. Occasionally a unique craft will appear, faster and more technically advanced than the others. If they are able and willing, the others will emulate the newcomer.[35] In contrast, an ocean liner, which represents a large home-building entity, is not nimble and cannot change course quickly, but it can accommodate a lot of people. Its route determined by corporate headquarters, it heads inexorably toward its destination. Local concerns or minor variations in conditions will not affect it much.

Throughout the century many have tried—architects among them—to convert the home-building industry from a sailboat fleet into an ocean liner. Government programs have tried as well, most notably Operation Breakthrough in 1969, which sought to encourage the big-industry assembly-line model to make housing. They optimistically trusted in new technology, innovative management methods, and centralized control to reduce costs dramatically, thereby solving the problem of housing affordability while stimulating the country's industries, above all the automobile manufacturers. But these attempts had only modest success, for they failed to consider the independent sailboat nature of the industry.

Moreover, the home-building industry is subject to dramatic fluctuations. The cost of financing, the weather, the availability and cost of labor and materials, and the political climate for new housing all influence the timing and amount of construction. In both its local nature and its cyclical aspect, the building enterprise does not allow for the required market share that would justify the capital costs of mass production. Factory production reduces some of the vagaries of building, such as bad weather and the need for skilled on-site labor, but not enough of them. Local design expectations and development politics are still substantial factors, undiminished by factory or centralized production.

Most attempts at industrialization, like the mobile home industry, have emphasized detached houses, partly because of market forces but also as a result of the recurring precept that a house is a consumer product. Once the concept of factory production is extended to multifamily and higher-density houses, the issues become even more complex. While multifamily housing may be less customized than individual homes, making it seemingly more amenable to repetitive assembly-line approaches, each project must still be specifically designed. Every development is different, catering to the requirements of the site, the local market, the anticipated occupants, and the physical environment. Variation and uniqueness are the bane of centralized factory production; the more variation, the fewer economies of scale.

The desire for factory production, for the quality control and efficiency it yields, and the need for a product that is transportable on the roads between factory and site have led to various forms of component buildings. Component and panelized building recognizes that while a certain amount of site work and customization must occur, parts of the construction enterprise can best be done in factories. Components, which can be whole rooms, walls and floors, or major structural elements, have insinuated their way into conventional building, and they can have an impact on housing cost, if not form. (These approaches are discussed in Chapter 3.)

Industrialization as a means to increase production for multifamily housing has had its successes, mostly in Europe. The destruction of so much of the housing stock in World War II required rapid rebuilding, and several systems, many government-subsidized, emerged. Heavy concrete walls and slabs produced in temporary factories at the building site were lifted into place with large cranes. Like the house forms whose size and shape are restricted by what is transportable on roads, these designs were determined by the capacity of

FIG. 9. Manufactured housing based on technology from the space program.

the cranes and the limitations of the concrete molds. Few of these three-dimensional puzzles were significant architecturally, and few were imported to the United States. The systems allowed only minimal variation, and occasional variations in facades; rather, they relied on the efficient stacking of walls. Sometimes distinctions emerged from what was removed, rather than what was added: for example, taking walls away from a structure to make courts or to create diversity in form was often the only design option available. In some of these countries industrialized building continues to thrive, largely as a result of several factors that are generally nonexistent in the United States. These include a centralized regulatory system, little national variation in culture and aesthetic expectations, and often a very short building season that demands fast construction.

By the late 1960s a few of the best architects in the United States had become involved in designing factory-produced buildings, a signal that factory-made housing was indeed a worthy design

pursuit. Paul Rudolph, a dean of the architecture school at Yale, designed affordable housing using stacked trailerlike boxes and even proposed a massive high-rise version for New York, wherein these boxes, upon arrival at the site, would be expanded and then lifted into a three-dimensional framework. Charles Moore, who followed Rudolph at Yale, also designed low-cost housing using factory-produced boxes for a rural New England town. Even the Frank Lloyd Wright Foundation, the protectors of the master's tenets, created mobile home designs.

In 1969 HUD launched the ill-fated Operation Breakthrough, intended to combine the best of American know-how with government subsidies to jump-start a massive factory-produced housing effort. HUD secretary George Romney, who had been head of American Motors, once again cited the automobile analogy—the assembly lines and network of sellers and servicers throughout the nation—as the answer to increasing production and guaranteeing that the product would find its way into the marketplace. The industrial model for manufacturing, Romney proclaimed, could be wedded to new technology. Hard on the heels of the race to the moon, consortia of high-tech firms, many heavily involved in the space race or in defense contracts, collaborated on new housing products, methods, and systems.

Well-known architects who had been working in factory-produced housing, like Paul Rudolph, were poised for Operation Breakthrough and submitted proposals for the initial demonstration projects. But the federal program was directed toward innovative techniques of production and new materials, and architects were given a backseat to product engineers, scientists, and management teams. The clearest example was the proposal by Aero-Jet General for a filament-wound system, designed for the Department of Defense using technology borrowed from the space program (fig. 9). Huge mandrels were rotated as fiberglass filaments were wrapped around them into room-sized tubes. These tubes were then cut to length, windows were excised, and the rudiments of a house, albeit without the recognizable distinctions of walls and roof, were left.

Operation Breakthrough was no breakthrough. A few demonstration projects were constructed, but the collaboration of high-tech industries and management systems did not create a sustained housing market that would encourage industries to invest in housing-manufacture facilities. By oversimplifying housing into a production problem, Operation Breakthrough did nothing to address housing as a complex issue with a critical social component, nor did it motivate any significant architectural designs.

THE ARCHITECT AS MEDIATOR:
PRODUCTION VERSUS LIVABILITY

Obsession with production leaves housing without a social imperative. Producing more units of low-cost housing is both politically wise and morally defensible, but just as making more cars does not reduce transportation problems, making more units does not solve housing problems. If the housing is not suitable, if people do not want to live in it, if it does not fulfill expectations or aspirations, it is soon abandoned, or at least resented. Faith in technology and manufacturing alone beget uninspired, grim, and unwanted housing. As many architects have argued, technology, manufacturing, and new materials must accommodate the social and cultural aspects of housing rather than presuming that people can and will adapt to any housing circumstance.

In *Housing without Houses* Nabeel Hamdi makes a distinction between a provider paradigm and a support paradigm for housing.[36] The provider paradigm emphasizes centralized control to increase production, and regulation to ensure standards and quality. Operation Breakthrough was a model of the provider paradigm. The support paradigm recognizes the dispersed nature of the nation's building enterprise and finds management and resource allocation methods to reinforce this system. The CDCs, particularly volunteer-driven housing groups like Habitat for Humanity, are models of the support paradigm.

The hope is to find a balance, some combination that achieves sufficient production, but does so in a way that allows significant individual control in design decision making. Many theorize about this balance, focusing on the difference between housing infrastructure and the dwelling itself. Some, like John Turner, a housing consultant and advocate, emphasize the social and economic infrastructure of the support paradigm, its encouragement of community action and redirection of subsidies to CDCs and small builders.[37] Others, like John Habraken, an architect and theoretician, focus on the technical infrastructure, the physical structures to which dwellings are applied. Habraken posits a coalition between producers, with their technological approach, and supporters, with their social and small-scale approach: the producers and large builders are responsible for the context, but the small builders and individuals are responsible for their own home.[38]

This compelling and primarily architectural approach was proffered by futuristic groups such as England's Archigram and Japan's Metabolists in the 1960s. For the past thirty years there has been growing recognition that the housing problem can be divided into several solvable components, with each level of solution suggesting a different level of production and technology and yielding a degree of self-determination to the occupant. For most of our housing history only the detached, single-family house was deemed fit to answer these needs, but it could not reconcile them with the demands of high density and cost efficiency.

The framework, or plug-in, approach devised by architects seemed destined to answer both sides of the equation. Dwellings could be unique and separately designed, while the framework into which they were applied would be universal, like a city's infrastructure. But few such structures were ever built, and those that were, such as the demonstration projects for Operation Breakthrough, were so architecturally ungainly that whatever promise they held was undermined. Several projects emulated the approach architecturally, such as Ralph Erskine's celebrated Byker Wall complex in England (1968–82),[39] where individuality is exuberantly expressed through the projection of balconies and bays on a multistory serpentine mass, or Davis, Brody & Associates' Riverbend in New York (1968), where two-story townhouses, complete with front stoops, are set upon a frame.

Of all the approaches that rely on technology or factory production but still recognize the need for a high level of individualization and amenity, Habitat in Montreal is perhaps the best known and most architecturally significant (fig. 10). Built

for the 1967 World's Fair, this demonstration project captured the imagination of those still mesmerized by the producer mentality and those who saw housing as a social and humanitarian undertaking. As Moshe Safdie originally envisioned it, Habitat was a framework system into which his individual houses were to be placed. But the structural needs of the dwellings were so significant, both for their erection and for their own integrity once in place, that the framework was seen as redundant, and the boxes were stacked directly one on the other. The result is a startling image of industrialized, modern housing that has the feel of an ancient hill town with views, open space, and privacy. The product of two housing imperatives, social and technical, Habitat proved that the combination could generate significant architecture. *Architectural Review* commended the completed project "as a visually stimulating exhibition item; as a means of opening the visitor's eyes to the possibilities in the way of planning, designing, and constructing dwelling houses and showing him how many alternatives there are to what he is used to; as a means of testing the validity of new prefabrication techniques."[40]

A quarter century later Habitat is a healthy, fully occupied development. It is a success as architecture and as housing. It was not, however, a successful model of affordable production. Only 159 units were constructed, not nearly enough for economies of scale, and these were highly subsidized as part of the Expo exhibition. For a decade after its construction Safdie tried several similar factory-produced schemes throughout the United States, which were also successful as architecture but not as new modes of production. Like others before him, he had come to realize that mass production yielded relatively minor savings in the total cost of housing. Land and financing were much larger components. Only one-third of the cost of construction, he estimates, is embodied in

FIG. 10.   In Montreal's Habitat, by Moshe
Safdie (1967), the technological imperative
yields humane housing.

the enclosure, where mass production is most effective. Structure, mechanical systems, and interiors account for the rest.[41]

In a thoughtful reflection on Habitat's twenty-
fifth anniversary, Safdie concluded that the technological imperative is a device not just for increasing production or even lowering overall costs,
but also for achieving needed amenities at high
densities, amenities allowed by his stacking technique.[42] Habitat represented a humane approach
to apartment living, one that made the type appropriate for families. Other prominent architects,

including Mies van der Rohe and Le Corbusier,
favored apartments and designed famous housing
complexes. Le Corbusier's Immeuble Villas, also
designed for an international exhibition, suggested
individual villas aggregated into a high-density
high-rise form, and his Unité d'habitation placed
houses in a tower, each one a floor-through, two-
story unit. But Habitat represented an alternative
not to the suburban single-family house but rather
to the high-rise, high-density apartment block.
There penthouses embody the best of urban living, but whereas they are limited to the tops of

FIG. II.   Habitat's outdoor terraces are as large as living rooms.

structures, Habitat made it possible for everyone to have the equivalent of a penthouse.

Habitat was also a definitive statement about the relationship of building technique to architecture. The large-scale boxes could have been closely packed, simply stacked one on the other in a regular pattern. But because of the desire to create large terraces, and because the system allowed for a more irregular aggregation, the overall form could be far more diverse and intricate, without being more costly. Proportion and composition, heretofore important ingredients in making significant architecture, were so inconsequential to the design that conventional elevation drawings were never produced. The geometry of the room-sized pieces and the rules by which they were connected determined the design, just as in the indigenous architecture of hill towns and seaside villages (fig. 11).

Habitat is the closest anyone has yet come to combining technology with the desire for humane high-density housing that is architecturally exciting. It was fundamentally an architect's response to the social and technical complexity of housing, but one that cannot be replicated by closed manufacturing systems and centralized production. That it exists today as a wonderful place to live is testament to the strength and wisdom of its social intentions.

The form of housing is strongly influenced by politics, regulations, desires of the client, the needs of the user, and the expectations of the community. Throughout our social housing history, each element has taken its place at the top of the list. But now all the exigencies of housing must be satisfied by the architect's design. In the process, the architect makes hundreds of decisions and judgments that are ultimately manifested in the physical form. But managing these elements is not enough. The architect must imbue the work with a spirit that elevates the structure from a building to a home. Housing that lacks spirit, dignity, and intellect, that caters only to regulation and production, saps the vitality and degrades the values of its inhabitants.

THE PROCESS: THE LONG AND WINDING ROAD

Notification laws, community participation, and the many levels of building-approval bureaucracy are the legacy of the 1960s. Slum clearance, the displacement of the less-than-powerful through oversized, unfriendly, and cumbersome urban renewal projects in nearly every American city led legislatures to require that proposed projects solicit input from a broad spectrum of people affected, not the least of whom are the immediate neighbors. Environmental impact procedures, design review boards, and citizen participation have joined planning commissions as common elements in the development process. Each phase may entail public hearings and votes of commissioners, and each such exchange can alter the size, nature, and quality of a project, for better or for worse.

THE FIRST MEETING

The small conference room is stifling, even with air-conditioning, as the meeting moves into its third hour. Forty people, representing both the opponents and proponents of a thirty-six-unit affordable housing project, are present. It was clear almost from the outset that they would reach no agreement, no consensus. There would be only hostility and frustration.

California law stipulates that everyone who lives within three hundred feet of a proposed housing project's boundaries must be mailed notice of a public hearing. This evening's get-together is an informal meeting arranged by the developer in preparation for the public hearing. The developer wants to gauge the neighbors' concerns, to find out who objects to what. This night the developer gets an earful.

The sponsor of this thirty-six-unit project is a community development corporation (CDC), a nonprofit organization whose charter is to develop affordable housing in Davis, a small community just west of Sacramento, California. The corporation was created by the city as an independent entity, eligible for city seed money and planning support, to meet the state requirement that every jurisdiction have an affordable housing plan and a development strategy. This CDC, like its counterparts throughout the state, has a board of directors made up of local citizens. At the meeting this evening are two board members who live in the neighborhood in which the new project is to be built.

The inadequacy of the notification law has generated the most heat in the room. The neighbors feel suspicious

FIG. 12.   Using this detailed model for their Tuscany Villas project in Davis, the architects try to convince the skeptics.

and betrayed. Some have not received notices, even though they live near the project, and most feel that an earlier project in their neighborhood has not lived up to the developer's promises for open space, amenities, and traffic mitigation. Two women stationed at the head of the conference table are the most vocal opponents. They sit erect, with arms crossed, responding quickly and tersely on every topic. It is as if they see the project as a nasty pest that must be eradicated and are using the no-tification law as the bug spray. Their complaints and the responses of Keith, the CDC's project manager, and Ike, a representative of the city's staff, take up the first hour of the meeting.

A simple strategy would have been for Keith to agree with them that the law should require notification of a larger segment of the community—but that in any case this community-based developer should have done more than the law provides—and that all of them together should ask the city council and planning commission to expand the notification provision. Instead, Keith digs in, telling the neighbors they are being unrealistic, that

the CDC has done what the law required, and that is that.

To some degree this hard line serves a purpose. First, it focuses on an issue quite apart from the specifics of the project. The CDC, knowing that the planning commis-sion had zoned the project for affordable housing three years ago and that hearings about land use have already occurred, is confident that this argument about notifica-tion or concerns about land use, density, and environ-mental mitigation will not affect the planning commis-sioners' votes. Second, planning commissions know "NIMBYism" when they see it. It is big, bold, and only partly camouflaged by issues such as notification.

A balding man with a French accent who has been trying to sell his home next to the site wants data on the property values in areas where such housing has been built. To the surprise of many, Keith cites a recent Cali-fornia study that found little evidence that property values are affected.[1] Others wax poetic about the qual-ity of the area and its history relative to the development of California, and intimate that there are wildlife *habitats, if not in this immediate location, then certainly nearby. All the classic arguments used to fight affordable housing are raised: the diminution of property values and the quality of life; the increases in environmental hazards, noise, and traffic, along with obstructed views; and the incompatibility of the scale of the building.*

An hour into the meeting the architects, Sam and Lisa, rise to present their project. They gamely describe the buildings, pointing to elaborate models sitting in the middle of the conference table (fig. 12). It is the height of arrogance for them to feel that their good works will turn the tide and convert the skeptics, but in their blind optimism they harbor that hope. They emphasize that the plan calls for thirty-six units—rather than the allowable forty-two—in order to minimize the visual impact of the project and also to create more generous courtyards. The buildings are modestly sized, with no more than five or six dwellings in each. Most of the dwellings are townhouses, with individual front doors and ground-floor living rooms, dining rooms, kitchens, and fenced patios. The courtyards provide an amenity for residents while also focusing the noise and activity of the project inward, away from the neighbors. Appealing residential details embellish the buildings: awnings, tile roofs with deep overhangs, and a recessed entry for each dwelling. The architects express their desire to make the project look not so much like apartments but like houses. There are no large structures and no balconies, exterior stairs, or visible fire escapes.

While the neighbors are attentive during the presentation, they are disinterested in the design. That, in their minds, will come later—and only if they lose the big battle.

The meeting is over. Small groups huddle to plan their strategy for next week's hearing.

INPUT AND THE DEVELOPMENT PROCESS

Developers bemoan the substrata of regulation and fight hard to avoid, finesse, or circumvent the system. But they are rarely successful, and when they are, future projects suffer for it. This thirty-six-unit project in Davis is a good example. A large market-rate project had just been completed.

Its developers were required to include affordable housing, but rather than build it themselves, they donated the adjoining parcel to the CDC. The neighbors were angry that the large, uninspired project had been built and angrier still that they were scheduled for yet another project.

REQUIRED INPUT

Input for a project falls into two general categories: required and expected. Required input usually involves formal hearings and testimony from the public. Planning commissions, design review boards, and city councils hold hearings, many of which are televised by cable to the entire community. The format of these events is routine: a board of commissioners or council members sits on a dais, listening to audience members who are invited to make comments from a podium in front, and the board then deliberates and votes to approve, deny, or demand stipulations for approval.

While the system is the same for all types of buildings, affordable housing projects are most vulnerable, because they are the most controversial. No one wants an affordable project next door if given a choice, and every stage of the approval process offers opportunities for a battle royal. Even if opponents lose and the project proceeds, there is ample opportunity along the way to alter the scope and design by wrenching concessions won in the individual skirmishes. Often even community-based CDCs are forced to redesign, downsize, or abandon a project. In one such case, only a few miles from this thirty-six-unit project, neighbors were so upset by the prospect of poor families living nearby that they compelled the sponsor to redesign the two-story townhouses intended for families into one-story duplexes for seniors. (Low-income seniors are always seen as more tolerable than families.) This reconceptualization delayed the project and increased the cost substantially, in addition to reducing the number of units.

Hearings and reviews often yield conflicting information for the architect. For example, courtyards, which contain the noise generated by the development and the increased activity from cars or people, can be seen as a positive attribute for the neighbors. But police and public safety officials, who must also be consulted, object to them because they hinder drive-by observation and access into the project.

Before public testimony is invited, city staff make a report and a recommendation to the panel. This report covers the rudiments of the project, the applicable zoning, and past decisions regarding the project, from both this panel and perhaps others. For example, if a project is appealed to the highest body, the city council, the staff will report the actions of lower bodies, like the planning commission or the design review board. If a previous decision has been made on the zoning of the land, this too will be part of the staff report. Staff will render opinions on why a variance is requested and the likely impact of granting it.

Thus, while the public hearing is paramount, it is but one component of the required input. The developer and the architect must first present project data and the design to staff, with whom they must remain on good terms. Undermining staff or not disclosing the true and complete character of a project is wholly counterproductive, although succumbing to the often conservative whims and desires of city staff usually leaves the design insipid. City staff are happiest when projects move through the system easily and are built without controversy. They hate fielding calls from irate citizens once a project is under way or after it has been completed. These circumstances often militate against unusual, irregular, innovative, or interesting designs. Even something as seemingly ordinary as color is scrutinized by staff. In one project, also in the same town, the brick-red stucco finish enraged local homeowners whose houses had not

even existed when the development was planned, reviewed, and constructed. City staff were so shell-shocked by the fusillade that they began recommending that subsequent projects be only in pastels and whites.

For developers and architects, the best strategy is to consult with city staff early on, when the project is in initial design phases and various options and alternatives are open. It is also helpful to allow staff to choose among some of the options, so that they have a stake in the decision making. The more involved the staff feel, the harder for them to make a negative report afterward.

City staff for the various commissions must in turn solicit input from other segments of city government. Each project will have sidewalks, curb cuts and driveways, utilities, and fire protection systems. Public works and building departments must have their say, and on-site building inspectors may refute or modify their decisions.

Some elements of a project's design seem so rudimentary that they could hardly be subject to public scrutiny and controversy. Not so. Trash pick-up is one example. The neighbors of a new apartment project do not want dumpsters next to their yards; they want them deep within the new development, out of sight and earshot. The architect, on the other hand, wants to distribute the dumpsters so that the residents of the project do not have to carry their trash over long distances. The developer wants the dumpsters at the heads of driveways by the street, so that large garbage trucks do not traverse the site, putting increased loads on parking areas and requiring their frequent resurfacing. Refuse-removal companies also want the trash near the street and balk at designs that require their trucks to turn around or even back up. As in all aspects of a project's design, everyone has a different agenda. The secret is to find the correct balance, which often means a compromise. For trash, the compromise is usually to disperse the dumpsters but enclose them in sturdy, concrete-block fences that can be surfaced with upgraded materials and then lavishly landscaped. The developer may pay more but saves in driveway maintenance costs; the architect is confronted with a modest design challenge; the refuse collectors minimize their driving; and the neighbors acquiesce.

If a housing project is large enough, innovative approaches can be cost-effective. For garbage, a relatively large and expensive on-site trash compactor limits the need for individual dumpsters. An on-site maintenance person with a small vehicle makes rounds several times a week, delivering trash from small, scattered cans to the main compactor. Noise throughout the site is reduced, and all occupants have convenient access to trash cans.

Like trash collection, the setup for mail delivery, the addressing of buildings, and the placement of utility meters all require input and entail design decisions. Each such decision influences the others in a ripple effect. While such individual items seem mundane and inconsequential, dealing with them takes time and money. Thoughtful solutions, however, create a better environment for residents and reduce community resistance.

The system of approvals, hearings, and negotiations has become so complicated that a whole new profession has arisen to confront it: the expediter, or wheel-greaser. For a fee, an expediter guides the project through the various hoops, keeping current on the decisions and decision makers. In places like New York, where the building code has grown to over four thousand pages, an expediter is nearly a necessity. The entire process is like an exercise par-course. As a proposal completes each stage, it gets stronger. If it finishes the entire course, it is either robust and healthy or emaciated and withered. If the architect and developer are experienced, each subsequent trip through the course becomes easier; if not, it is unlikely they can or will make a second try.

The required input is not limited to that prescribed by law and by a city's regulatory environment. Lenders and funding agencies, and even the CDC's board of directors, have their own requirements and regulations. They too expect to be kept current on the project's development and design. If a lender or state agency agrees to fund a project, that agreement stipulates the number of units, their sizes, and their type. If any of these changes during the public review process, the funding source may pull out.

EXPECTED INPUT

Expected input, an increasingly normal part of the approvals procedure, is not required by law, but wise developers and architects will solicit it. They will contact neighbors before a public hearing and meet with regulatory officials before there is a completed design. Public bodies, like a planning commission or a city council, are loath to consider a project that has not been previously reviewed. Like city staff, they abhor surprises. Developers and architects are publicly admonished from the dais if the panel feels the citizenry has been neglected or, worse, hoodwinked. CDCs that want to create affordable housing cannot risk such ill will if they wish to succeed in their mission.

Another reason to voluntarily solicit input is purely economic. If the developer and the architect are adept at handling meetings and can gain the confidence of the neighbors, they will have smoothed the way for the public hearing. If they can get even one or two neighbors to speak favorably for the project, they have saved time and money, obviating design revisions. Given their druthers, public officials want to vote for affordable housing, but they don't need much of an excuse not to, and they need even less of an excuse to require design changes, reductions in allowable zoning, or delays. All these cost money, much more than it costs to hold a few community meetings. If a city council or a planning commission asks for changes or for more information, it may be several months before the developer or the architect can get back on the agenda. Such delays play havoc with construction schedules and, furthermore, can push the developer past the deadline imposed by lending agencies for spending their subsidies.

A third reason to voluntarily solicit input is that neighbors and others may have ideas or preferences that will improve the project, and in the process of participation they develop a personal stake in the design. A community organization may have invaluable knowledge of the culture and life-patterns of an area. When San Francisco architect Steve Kodama was designing his Savo Island project in Berkeley, local planning authorities and architects insisted that a neighborhood store and community center be placed on a public corner of the project to tie the new project into the community. The neighbors, however, many of whom intended to live in the project, resisted this idea, claiming that it would instead attract outsiders and undesirables. They prevailed, and the community facility was placed within the project, not on its periphery. Kodama is convinced that this was the correct approach, an opinion bolstered by the success of the project, and particularly of its community center.[2]

Similarly, in a proposed renovation of a 733-unit public housing project built in 1939 in the Hunters Point area of San Francisco, Marquis Associates had anticipated segmenting the project into mini-neighborhoods, each with its own character and focus, to make the project more manageable, provide more open space, and create more definable territory. This plan entailed removing some buildings to reinforce the concept. Here too the occupants resisted, fearing that such division would foster unwanted internal competition and encourage turf wars among gangs within the de-velopment.[3] The architects heeded the residents' concerns.

Had the architects not solicited the information, their designs would likely have been less successful. In both cases the architects and their sponsoring agencies benefited from going beyond what the law required and drawing more people into the process.

WORKING THE SYSTEM

From many vantage points, particularly that of the general citizenry, this system of inputs, hearings, regulations, and bureaucracy is protective and beneficial. It has made the large, heinous block-busting project more difficult to develop. But others see a well-intentioned system that has become cumbersome, costly, and inequitable. It can easily be misused by malcontents and can ultimately have a dampening effect on the production of affordable housing. Some estimate that the system in California adds as much as $20,000 to the cost of a house.[4] In a modest-sized multifamily project of thirty units, the approval process, even if well managed and fair, can cost as much as an entire unit, and there are no additional amenities or improvements in quality to show for the expenditure.

The most recurrent criticism from developers and architects is that the process is unclear, uncertain, and unevenly applied. Each community has its own set of rules, and each has its administrators, who interpret even the common regulations and processes differently. Parking is a good example, since it takes up so much space in the project and is the cause of so much community concern. Some communities require a specific number of parking spots for each type of unit: a three-bedroom unit may need 2.5 spaces on average. But this number, and the percentage allowed for compact cars, can vary depending on the jurisdiction. Some municipalities allow surveys of car ownership among tenants of comparable projects to guide their requirement, while others negotiate the allocation in each project.

The land entitlement and building-approval process are becoming increasingly complex. The most obvious hurdles are the public hearings. But lurking behind these events are the rules, regulations, commissions, and meetings. At the core of it all is NIMBYism, a powerful force. People are fearful of change—change in their lifestyles, change in their property values, change in their level of security. They are afraid of the unknown, particularly of their new neighbors, who they are sure will bring crime, drugs, and noise, because they are poor. Most people will agree that there is a need for good affordable housing, but they do not want it near them. No matter that the project may have an excellent design, that the tenants are carefully screened by the CDC, that there is an on-site manager, or that there are strict rules for tenant behavior. No matter that their current neighbors can let their houses run down, leave old cars parked in the drive, paint their houses horrendous colors—all without public hearings or scrutiny. No argument can ward off the NIMBYs' fear, and the approval process has become their forum for fomenting greater fears. For developers and architects, allaying these fears requires time, money, an understanding of the process, a knowledge of the culture and politics of the local development, and more than a casual acquaintance with the people who make decisions.

THE COMPENSATORY APPROACH

One approach to the approvals process is to overdesign a project, knowing that the process will erode it: submit an initial proposal for fifty units, and let the neighbors barter it down to forty and think they have wrung out a victory. This devious strategy can be adapted to almost any aspect of a project, including color, the number of parking spaces, or even the location of dumpsters, as long as the anticipated fallback positions are tolerable and economically feasible. Thus, the design must be flexible and resilient enough to withstand continued assaults and still have clarity and integrity at the end.

A similar, but more subtle, approach could be called the compensatory strategy. A basic premise of the approval process is that all projects have negative impacts and that the procedure will identify them in order to compel the developer to limit or mitigate the potential damage. The compensatory approach, while it may include mitigation, is based on the idea that a project can have benefits for a community that more than compensate for whatever deleterious impact it might have. Thus, the project includes amenities that the neighbors could not likely afford on their own, such as sports facilities, day-care centers, or open spaces.

For Arlington Farm, a 9.4-acre, 138-unit development in Davis, the developer, John Whitcombe, intended to build a large project of two- and three-story apartments, 20 percent of which would be affordable. The site was in the middle of three existing neighborhoods. On the east was a moderate-density duplex development, all one-story attached units; on the north an upscale neighborhood of single-family homes; and on the west an apartment complex. (To the south was agricultural land.) Whitcombe determined that the homeowners on the north were the most politically powerful group and that the least powerful were the apartment dwellers on the west. To appease the homeowners he agreed to build a park along the northern border, with open space and tennis and basketball courts, which were scarce in this part of town. He also agreed to build a day-care center in the park, another amenity needed

Existing single-family homes

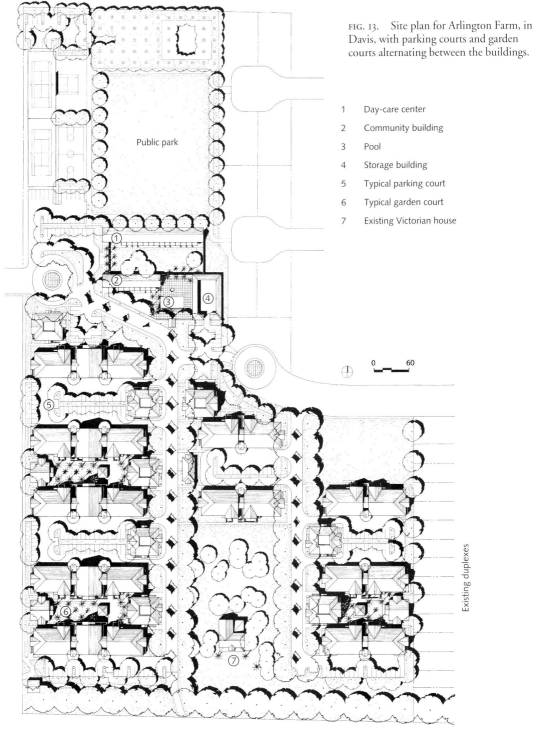

FIG. 13. Site plan for Arlington Farm, in Davis, with parking courts and garden courts alternating between the buildings.

1   Day-care center

2   Community building

3   Pool

4   Storage building

5   Typical parking court

6   Typical garden court

7   Existing Victorian house

Public park

Existing apartment complex

Existing duplexes

0   60

FIG. 14. One of Arlington Farm's garden courtyards.

in the community (fig. 13). One may see these as magnanimous gifts of a public-spirited developer, but they were clearly factored into the overall cost of the project. The day-care center was even presumed to be a profitable component, since it would be leased to an independent operator, much like a commercial retail operation.

These enticements notwithstanding, the duplex owners were not mollified, but they were also not very powerful. Many did not live in the neighborhood; they rented out their units. But knowing that they could delay the project, Whitcombe

asked the architect to offer them two benefits. First, the design, which featured a series of alternating courtyards (fig. 14), one for parking and one for residential use, was adjusted so that relatively few units, sharing one pair of courtyards, were placed next to the duplexes, while the majority were placed against the existing apartments. This transitional zoning preempted the duplex owners' complaint about increased housing density, since the new units closest to them would have a density per acre comparable to that of the duplexes. Still, Whitcombe had a final card to

FIG. 15.   A lane with large, Victorian-like houses, each with four apartments, in Arlington Farm.

play. He agreed to donate to each duplex owner along the shared eastern border an additional twenty feet of backyard, and to build a fence, of the type they selected, on this boundary. They were happy.

These changes were anticipated in both the economic and architectural plans for the project. The buildings were relocated without sacrificing their attributes and amenities, and the various audiences approved of the disposition of buildings and courtyards. Nonetheless, the project had to appear

twice before each of five commissions or boards. At the last of the public hearings, with some city council members still unsure, Whitcombe gave his "I'll just go fishing" speech. He recounted the history of the project and all that had been done to satisfy the various constituencies. He summarized the elements of the plan and the architecture that made the project suitable for the site: parking that exceeded the city's requirement and was hidden in courts and garages, lavishly landscaped courtyards that focused the apartments inward and away from neighbors, the details of the buildings that emulated those of the existing historic building retained on the site (fig. 15). All that could be done had been done, he said, to design the best project for the site. "I have plenty of other projects and other things to do. You can turn it down, and I'll just go fishing. But you will never have as good a plan for this site if you deny us." It passed.

THE BULLDOG APPROACH

Often developers and architects have little choice but to design a project as they see fit and then mount an intensive, aggressive campaign to push it through the approval process. Either the expense of holding the property or, more likely, the time requirements of the funding sources force a project to move more quickly than public opinion or the system normally allows. Although it is not unusual for even modest-sized projects—those of fewer than fifty units—to take three years or more to emerge from the hearing and approval process, funding sources ignore these scheduling realities and force affordable housing developers to run roughshod over the community. The risks for the CDCs are high but unavoidable. If they are to gain access to the money that allows them to fulfill their mission, they must move a project quickly, even if they incur the wrath of the community in which they must continue to operate.

One reason funding agencies maintain pressure on CDCs to spend the funds is that no one is sure how long the money will remain available. Legislatures are hard-pressed to set aside money for any social programs, let alone housing. And recent newspaper exposés increase the pressure to spend the money, identifying huge caches of federal funds sitting idle because the regional government agencies and housing authorities are too poorly managed to distribute them.[5]

So the CDCs have to choose between working the system for three or four years or incurring

some hostility that is likely to dissipate once the project is occupied. The latter is sometimes selected as the most economical course. If a CDC decides to bulldog the project, it almost certainly must opt for a design that conforms to all local zoning codes and respects local precedents. A proposal for a project in an urban rowhouse neighborhood should continue the pattern of front stoops and walk-up units. To save time, the design must be nearly completed, and even documented for construction, before it is presented to the public. Elaborate models, renderings, and color selections help the mostly lay commissioners understand the project and may impress them enough to sway their votes. Of course, this expensive undertaking can also backfire, particularly when presenting a completed design is seen as snubbing the approval process.

How much long-term ill will is generated from the bulldog approach depends on whether the project lives up to its description and expectations. Since the design moves so rapidly, late changes may occur, either because of oversights or because costs could not accurately be forecasted. If these changes are perceived as a breach of promise, later projects and the reputation of the development team will suffer. If a project exceeds expectations, perhaps the recurring resistance to affordable housing will diminish, along with the rigor and length of the normal public review process, thereby saving costs and producing more housing.

GRASSROOTS EFFORTS

If a community group whose members need housing initiates a project, and if this group has or can create a political base, then the housing will evolve in its image. The growing homeless population has stimulated some successful grassroots efforts, among them James Lee Court in Oakland. After six years of protest by the Union of the Homeless, who continually and aggressively publicized their

FIG. 16.   James Lee Court, a grassroots effort by a homeless coalition in Oakland.

needs by occupying government buildings, the city's homeless shelters were enlarged, and the union, with the assistance of Dignity Housing West, a local CDC, developed their own building for twenty-six families (fig. 16).

Since the homeless were their own clients, they generated a housing program to fit their needs, including social services and day-care. They also chose their own architect, Michael Pyatok. The planning called for townhouses around a court-

yard for families with children and second-story units for seniors who wanted security and privacy. The union and the architect together embellished the design with different ethnic themes representing the residents: bright tiles depicting a frog, a West African symbol of prosperity, adorn the exterior, and Asian spirit houses (fig. 17), small shrines that Buddhists believe house those spirits displaced by a new building, are placed throughout the complex.[6]

FIG. 17.   One of the spirit houses that adorn James Lee Court.

For such a grassroots effort community resistance tends to be less of an obstacle than institutional qualms about the experimental nature of the project (and its organizers) and the intricacies of the funding mosaic, which may include local, state, federal, and private funding. Nevertheless, the grassroots approach has the potential to create sound housing services and provide training in various skills for the participant-residents.

BUILDING BY CONSENSUS

Many architects who work in affordable housing insist that nothing can replace direct participation by the community and representative future tenants (if not the actual future tenants, then surrogates). Building by consensus entails several sessions in which groups of people actually design the project. The early meetings generally focus on establishing the design values and priorities. Image, desired amenities, and absolute necessities are identified. As the sessions progress, physical attributes of the architecture are discussed. The later meetings often seem like an adult preschool; they are noisy, lively, and messy, as teams work on models, using anything inexpensive and convenient, like Cheerios to outline parking areas and driveways or broccoli stalks to represent trees. While the meetings may seem disorganized, the architect or a consultant facilitator orchestrates and directs the activity, recording the results on large sheets of paper, complete with photographs. After each session the architect codifies the decisions and prepares more definitive architectural drawings to represent the range of options and choices that the teams suggested.

For building by consensus to work, architects must sublimate their egos; this is not their building, but one designed by many. They must also be able to interpret the will of the group in ways that make architectural and structural sense. Furthermore, they must be gregarious and outgoing, able to stimulate lay people to think three-dimensionally and in architectural terms. Finally, they must be nimble thinkers, able to see clarity and potential in inchoate, often nebulous ideas that arise in highly charged meetings.

Many argue that the consensus approach does not, and simply cannot, generate distinguished architecture. But others feel it is the only legitimate way to create housing that befits the occupants. San Francisco architect Robert Marquis is among this second group. His extensive experience in this process has convinced him that the aspirations of residents are related to their economic level, a seemingly obvious observation that some architects do not appreciate. For him, "a rich man's amenity may be a poor man's necessity"; for example, parking in or near the dwelling is a selling point in market-rate housing, but in affordable housing, particularly in urban areas, it is a necessity for the security of both the residents and the vehicle. Conversely, elements as simple as security screens over windows, which housing administrators feel are necessary safety provisions, are often seen by residents as prisonlike.[7]

Marquis cites the example of an affordable project in San Francisco that was developed on the site of an abandoned brewery. The architects retained one of the large vats as a play structure because they liked the form and because they felt it made an intriguing historical reference to the site's previous use. But the residents hated it; they found it demeaning to have junk in their playground, while market-rate housing had new, real play equipment.

Some architects feel that building by consensus is critical in affordable housing design, because it removes the often well-meaning but detached board member or community representative from the process. These third parties, who act in behalf of the affordable housing tenant, often see their responsibility as ensuring there is no risk and, consequently, no innovation in the design. People in the community do not fear such risk, as long as they are confident it is a means of fulfilling their needs.

Each community has different values and aspirations, and no single guide or source can reveal them. In Marquis's renovation of the 1939 Sunnydale Housing, the consensus process was extended through construction. One of the buildings was constructed as a prototype, and the community was invited to evaluate its components before the remainder of the project was built.

In order to leverage these sessions into the approval process, city officials, neighbors, and funding agencies are invited to send participants, who have a hand in shaping the results and go on to make favorable pronouncements for the housing at the public hearings. Some architects encourage the participants to write down their concerns, in order to supply a clear set of principles in an informal contract with the architects. Unfortunately, this type of consensus building takes time, and the opportunities to employ it are increasingly rare. The funding deadlines, the cost of holding the land, and the staff time involved for architects and sponsors often preclude it.

Each of these four ways of working the approvals process involves an understanding of the political context and how it relates to the project at hand. When neighbors are motivated by personal interest to preserve what they have, the compensatory strategy can work, although some people expect compensation that amounts to extortion.[8] A conflict of values is much more difficult to negotiate. When neighbors view new construction as a crime against the environment, developers have but one potent response, and that is to co-opt the moral argument by making a stronger case for the housing need and community's obligation. To do this, building by consensus or grassroots strategies can work. Finally, while all these strategies benefit from good public relations, the bulldog approach requires it. Knowing when and how to release information, knowing how to respond to vitriolic public attacks and hysterical fliers, and knowing how to handle the constant pressure of the news media is essential.

THE PLANNING COMMISSION HEARING

During the four days between the informal meeting and the planning commission hearing, the neighbors organize, albeit loosely, an attack on the project.

At the commission hearing the tension is palpable. The protagonists gather in the lobby to review last-minute strategies; they cast furtive glances toward their opponents. The commissioners take their places, hang their name plates in front of their microphones, and run through a few minutes of housecleaning items from previous meetings. They then announce the opening of public testimony for the project under consideration.

The purpose of tonight's hearing is the final plan development approval for the affordable project's thirty units of family rental apartments and six units of senior apartments. The staff begin by reviewing the issues and reiterating that the zoning for affordable housing has been in place for three years. This evening's objective, the staff announce, is merely for final approval of the project as designed. This interpretation is, of course, ignored by the forty people about to speak, who will hold forth until around midnight. (Several hours into the meeting, people who have already spoken begin to approach the podium for another shot. They have either thought of something new or simply thought of a new way of saying the same thing. It is clear that the commission chair will let them go on until they exhaust themselves.)

During the four hours of public testimony, several issues are raised. The first is notification, but that is quickly dispatched by the commissioners, who agree that the law should be broadened and promise to pursue the matter, but at another time. Next, wide-ranging concerns about the environment are aired. The property was once part of the Pony Express Trail, one citizen affirms, the implication being that it is historically sensitive and sacred land. The Swainson hawk hunts field mice on the site, another citizen testifies, and the project will limit its habitat. A lively exchange ensues between the speakers and city staff about the sufficiency of the environmental impact report and the project's compliance with the state's fish and game regulations. The staff are well versed and convincing, and the assault fizzles. But while they're on the subject, an equestrian who boards her horse nearby demands access to neighboring fields for riders.

Subsequent arguments are less specific and in many ways more passionate. The mostly older residents worry about their property values, as well as the increased traffic and decreased security that the affordable housing population will bring. They freely admit that their arguments are selfish, but they are close to retirement, have all their assets tied to their homes, and have few

options. Although there is no evidence that their fears are realistic, these speakers are very effective and the audience erupts into applause after each speaker leaves the podium.

The most cogent arguments come from the professionals, led by Bonnie, a lawyer from the neighborhood. They attack the language of the staff report and the zoning guidelines, hoping to defeat the project by turning the city's approval mechanisms inside out.

The history, documentation, and administration of a project are never tidy and unambiguous. This is partly because city procedures, staff, and elected officials constantly change; planning and development are fluid processes subject to ongoing pressures. Here it was no different. Early in the zoning process, when the neighboring for-profit three-story apartments were approved, the owner had suggested, and the city council had reinforced the notion, that the affordable component, the three-acre parcel adjoining the market-rate apartments, be forty-two duplex units. This specific language never made it into the zoning ordinance, but remnants of the idea were present in such allusions as "the backyards of the affordable duplex units will be fenced."

The specific zoning for the site allowed three stories of garden apartments. City staff and the CDC worked under the assumption that any dwelling type within the size restrictions was appropriate. The zoning and city requirements also called for amenities such as tot-lots and ample open space for recreation, none of which would be possible if only duplex units were built.

During the zoning hearings three years ago, each constituency had worried about the relationship of the affordable housing component to its neighbors. The market-rate apartment developer wanted a project compatible with his; the neighbors wanted housing more like their own. Compromise language was reached, but no one considered what it meant for the design. The demands were mutually exclusive: the affordable project was to be matched to both the new three-story apartment development on its south border and the existing single-family and duplex neighborhood on the north. The final zoning approval actually required that the affordable project include some three-story elements and, in other language, that it be of a residential quality comparable to that of the existing homes.

Norma and Bonnie, two neighbors who had attended the first meeting, have studied the zoning and the minutes of previous hearings, and they seize on these ambiguities. They do not entirely fault the CDC, but they excoriate the commission and city staff and demand that the blameworthy commissioners reject the project.

But their arguments are inconsistent and flawed. Norma, a most articulate speaker, hammers at the duplex issue, emphasizing the expectations of the residents, some of whose realtors had assured them when they bought their homes that only duplexes were planned for the end of the block. She can conceive of, and even tolerate, three-story duplexes. Others, however, undermine this plea by insisting that the character of the neighborhood be preserved. For them three-story units are intolerable, regardless of the building type.

Sprinkled among these serious arguments are the silly and profane. More than one speaker denigrates renters and those with low incomes as people who just "hang out and drink." Several of the commissioners reproach these speakers, but such crude prejudices lie at the heart of most of the arguments made. These people do not want this project.

In the four hours of public testimony, only one person in the audience speaks in favor of the project. He is a local for-profit developer who has come for a hearing on his own project. Clearly, that can no longer take place this night, but he has stayed on and now recounts his own experience. The CDC and these architects have just built a project next to one of his, and while at first he feared that the affordable project would be of lesser quality than his development, he is very favorably impressed by the buildings, which are now complete and occupied. He feels that the quality of materials, design, and workmanship is equal to that of any housing in the city.

When Keith, the CDC project manager, and Sam and Lisa, the architects, are finally invited to speak, it is well past midnight. Their short presentations do not directly respond to the myriad issues raised earlier. Instead, they restate the zoning requirements and how they are met by the project, reiterate that this property was zoned for affordable housing several years before they became involved, and emphasize that the city staff had been informed about the nature of the project and

had continually encouraged them to proceed.

The architects, as they had done in the earlier meeting, unveil the elaborate models, which a few of the commissioners have already seen. The models are effective because they are so realistic, so definitive, and so concrete after an evening of wide-ranging emotional pleas and ambiguous discussion, little of which is focused on architecture.

Each of the commissioners praises the design but nevertheless asks several questions that suggest compromises in the position, height, and form of the buildings. The architects patiently respond that each of the suggestions is indeed possible, but that they will be costly and will not ultimately satisfy the desires of the neighbors. To a commissioner who suggests splitting the four-unit buildings into separate duplexes, the architects explain that this would simply move the units apart, creating an unusable shaded alley between the buildings and spreading them across the site, thus reducing the courtyard spaces. They also mention the increased costs for foundations and exterior walls and the delays for redesign.

Tim, the director of the CDC, is invited by the commission to have the last word of public testimony. He takes the hard line. The city wants, even demands, affordable housing; his CDC has followed all the rules, has designed an excellent product, has a good track record of building sound housing, a good record of selecting responsible tenants, and the support and encouragement of city staff. What else can the CDC do? They have spent a lot of money getting to this point and have adhered to all the rules the city has set up.

The public testimony is finally closed, and the board deliberates aloud. They praise the citizens for their concern, passion, and participation and encourage them to remain involved. Most of the board members, however, emphasize the need for affordable housing; the effort to distribute it throughout the city, not just in this neighborhood; the fact that the property was properly zoned for this use; and the excellent qualities of the project. Still, a few of the commissioners are clearly dismayed by the ambiguities in the zoning ordinance. They also know that whatever happens, the losing party will appeal to the city council, letting the commission off the hook.

The project passes 4 to 2, with few stipulations about design changes. It's on to the city council.

FIG. 18.   Parkview Commons, beset by controversy, set a standard for affordable housing in San Francisco upon completion.

WHITHER NIMBYISM

NIMBYism is endemic to American society. Americans pride themselves on self-determination, independence, and self-reliance, traits that manifest themselves in tenacious protection of their communities. Housing patterns in the United States reinforce these values by encouraging single-family home ownership. The majority of Americans own their homes, and ownership is the aspiration ingrained through a century of government incentives, tax breaks, and financing. The subtle but persistent message is that those who rent, those who live in apartments, and those who need subsidies to do both are second-class citizens.

The tenacity with which people fight against affordable housing in their neighborhoods almost defies belief. In Berkeley, for example, the local CDC purchased a motel along the city's busiest commercial street and planned to convert it into affordable housing. The neighbors fought the project, claiming that the increased residential density would harm the neighborhood, and demanded an environmental impact report. The run-down motel was occupied by transients and frequented by prostitutes; it was to be completely upgraded and renovated for housing. But that made little difference to the neighbors, who said they already had their share of low-income housing.

In San Francisco, the abandoned Polytechnic High School became the focus of a similar fight when Bridge, Inc., one of the state's largest nonprofit developers, acquired the site and began plans for Parkview Commons for-sale affordable housing (fig. 18). An excellent design by San Francisco architect David Baker that included 75 percent market-rate and 25 percent affordable units generated a long and bitter fight over density and parking, with Bridge eventually prevailing. Here again the neighbors' arguments seemed irrational. Was it better to have a desolate, abandoned school or new housing for sale to qualified low-income families? The completed project was an instant success, winning several design awards, and there were long lists of eager buyers. As a result, whenever Bridge targets a new neighborhood for affordable housing in San Francisco, the response is, "You can come into our community if you agree to do another 'Poly High.'"

The approval and review process is a mechanism that NIMBYs use effectively. It protects those with something to lose but is less effective for those with something to gain. Often the only voice in the process speaking on behalf of those without political might, the low-income tenants, is the nonprofit CDC or a grassroots housing coalition, and these groups must always be on the defensive against NIMBYism.

The idolization of the single-family home is not the sole culprit. The poor record and failed images of subsidized housing share the blame. The optimistic view is that the new generation of social housing will be different, that in the decades to come much of it will have been knitted comfortably into the texture of American life. But if good affordable housing is to be built, institutional intervention will be needed to overcome the strength of NIMBYism. Some states have enacted "antisnob" laws that mandate that a project cannot be rejected simply because it is affordable housing. In Massachusetts, for example, developers of affordable projects may appeal to a state board if they are rejected locally. The board is the final arbiter, and in 1991 it overturned twenty-three of the twenty-seven denials it reviewed. The board's record has compelled parties to negotiate more actively during the process and work out compromises, since communities know that if the project is rejected, the state board is likely to approve the sponsor's design.[9]

ARCHITECTS, ARCHITECTURE, AND THE PROCESS

Architects see themselves as occupying their own niche on the continuum between artist and problem solver, between conceptual genius and practical mastermind. Those who see themselves as artists, who feel the integrity of their work is sullied by the input and opinions of others, do not do much multifamily housing, let alone affordable housing. Those who see architecture as a public art, part process and part product, are more likely to work in the housing arena. Designing affordable housing requires imagining clear solutions to often conflicting ideas and input; it is the artful resolution of the multiple goals, aspirations, and expectations of many different people.

In order to work in this context, an architect needs skills and attitudes different from those used in designing houses, commercial projects, or corporate buildings where images predominate. Designing affordable housing is not a task for the egoist, the control freak, or the weak at heart. One's design comes under constant assault, not just from those who don't like it but also from those who insist they have a better solution. Any sign of equivocation during the heat of a meeting or public hearing may be seized upon by neighbors, commissioners, or council members as indicative of a lack of resolve or knowledge.

Most of all, the architect needs to be committed to the cause. Fees for affordable housing are usually comparable to those for other buildings, but the extensive process erodes the fee, and since the funding sources dole out money sporadically, it is not unusual to go unpaid for long periods. The exigencies of the process can be trying; the constant starting and stopping, hurrying and waiting, and designing and changing test everyone's patience. Architects who do not believe passionately that affordable housing is a crucial venture will either drop out or lose interest and settle for mediocre work.

Donald Schön, in his work on the education of professionals, suggests that designers must be nimble in thought and have the capacity for reflective action.[10] The design and approval process for affordable housing is arduous and cumbersome, and it is getting even more so. Schön believes that architects are well equipped for these conditions because their education prepares them to confront the confounding, and they must use judgment and reflection to construct whole, clear, and sound solutions.

The cumbersome approval process militates against architectural innovation, and this is a two-edged sword. On the one hand, affordable housing residents should not be the subjects of experimentation. They have little choice about where to live, and an odd design serves only to further stigmatize them and to undermine their desire to fit into the community. Historical typologies like the bungalow court or the urban rowhouse are respected and tested housing forms. Their use is legitimate, both for their contextual attributes and for their livability.

On the other hand, hard-and-fast conservatism dissuades talented architects from venturing into housing and proposing new ideas or contemporary translations of these proven types. Until now, housing innovations have come from the market-rate side. The resuscitation of the single-room-occupancy hotel, the creation of live-work housing, and the renovation of lofts have been brought about by developers who identified new housing markets and were willing to take some risks.

It is difficult to see how such bold moves can be made in affordable housing design. Government intervention is unlikely to stimulate new ideas. Rules and regulations only tend to hinder innovation. State agencies, however, could do more to sponsor awards programs and competitions and to entice cities and CDCs with extra funding for design excellence.

The public hearing process, particularly over real estate development, is largely ceremonial. It is like the suspense movie you have seen several times: you are compelled to watch, even though you know the outcome; in some bizarre way, you feel there is a possibility that it will end differently. By the time a project reaches the city council, the final administrative remedy before litigation, the contenders have made ample efforts to lobby, cajole, negotiate, and compromise. Each member of the city council has heard all the arguments several times over. The votes are decided. But city council members hate having to make development decisions, because no matter what they do, they will alienate some constituency. They much prefer it when a resolution is achieved outside of council chambers and then blessed at the hearing.

In the month between the planning commission and city council, all the parties were active. The neighbors became more organized and lined up behind Bonnie, the lawyer, and Lance, her contractor husband. While the two of them claimed not to be leaders, she had drafted the appeal and thereby officially became the "appellant." As in any ad hoc political coalition, the group had moderate and radical factions. The moderates wanted to eke some design changes from the developer, particularly along their street, and the radicals wanted the entire project killed. The internal dissension made negotiations difficult, both within the group and between it and the CDC.

The major assault was on the design and building form. It focused on two interrelated issues, one perceptual and one technical. Earlier city council decisions about this site referred to a design of "lower residential density." The neighbors took this to mean what they currently had: attached one-story duplexes on separate lots. Their logic was that building form and density were inseparable, so that if you perpetuated the duplex form, you automatically had a lower residential density.

At a gathering of the CDC and the neighbors, the mayor, exasperated by the range of issues and the neigh-

bors' inability to focus their concerns on how to improve the project, gave them an ultimatum of sorts: find a solution. The more moderate neighbors, those who claimed no opposition to low-income housing, felt the design issue was the most potent. Since the project was going to proceed, as was clear from the mayor's admonition, they would seek to exact compensation in the form of design changes.

A more cynical view is that this group knew that substantive changes to the design, such as a new building type, would entail costly delays that could kill the project. But suppose it survived. The project had already completed its construction bid process, and the costs were approximately 3 percent higher than the budget. Scrutiny of the bids and specifications was already under way. What the neighbors did not understand is that any changes they exacted that increased costs but did not stop the project could denigrate the final product. If they were successful in changing the building type, the architectural embellishments would be sacrificed to pay for it; for example, the tile roofs would be downgraded to asphalt shingles. Then no one would be happy.

As a lawyer, Bonnie knows that the project will be approved, that litigation would be costly and pointless. Her fallback is to get whatever concessions possible in the residential character. She also admits privately that she has little problem with the project's design or its existence but is upset by the process and the lack of consideration for the neighbors' viewpoints. Lance, being a contractor, is mainly concerned about the materials selected.

Several nights before the city council meeting, Lance and Bonnie, Tim and Keith from the CDC, and Sam, their architect, meet to negotiate the design. The CDC offers to switch the two five-unit buildings on the street with the two four-unit buildings that were planned for the back of the site. The cost of the change is estimated at about $15,000, most of which would be needed to alter the drawings. The neighbors have little understanding of what it takes to change a set of one hundred drawings and how a seemingly minor revision ripples through these documents. In this case not only the architect's drawings but also the civil engineer's work, which entails grading and parking plans, and the landscape architect's work, which includes planting and irrigation, would need to be revised.

The architects had placed the five-unit buildings on the street for two reasons (fig. 19). First, these buildings contained only townhouses, each with an individual entry, and thus seemed more residential in character. They would be eighty feet long, covering only 40 percent of the site's street frontage. The four-unit buildings, each seventy feet long, had two townhouses and two apartments, one of which was for physically disabled tenants. Since the disabled unit had to be entirely on the ground level, these buildings could not be made up of two-story townhouses that emulated private houses. The other reason for placing the shorter buildings in the back of the site was to allow some additional open space next to them, and away from the street, for the picnic area required by the funding source. Considering that this amenity could produce noise, the architects thought it should be far from the neighbors.

Once these reasons are revealed, in the quiet and relative privacy of this negotiating session, both Lance and Bonnie agree that keeping the longer buildings along the street is fine. Bonnie quips, "The difference in the length is only two of me lying down." The discussion then moves on to the townhouse entrances and how to make them more individualized. Since the CDC will not be spending $15,000 to alter the drawings, the developer offers to allocate this money to the entryways or to landscaping.

Sam and Lisa have anticipated this next request, since they were confident their planning rationale would be compelling. Thus, they have prepared several options for embellishing the entryways of the five-unit buildings, including awnings over the doors—the most modest proposal—or porticoes with balconies above. The discussion of the porticoes unveils a set of issues about which the neighbors had been misinformed. The most important among them is the streetside setback. Bonnie and Lance worry that the porticoes, while architecturally satisfying, further reduce the street setback. They are under the impression that the setback is already the minimum that the building code allows, fifteen feet. The neighbors are upset about this, because their own houses have twenty-foot front-yard setbacks. But the project's design has always called for twenty feet, and because of the angle of the street, the setback is twenty-two feet at the point closest to the neighbors.

Bonnie and Lance are prepared to present the pack-

FIG. 19. Tuscany Villas site plan.
Buildings with four or five units in each
form courtyards.

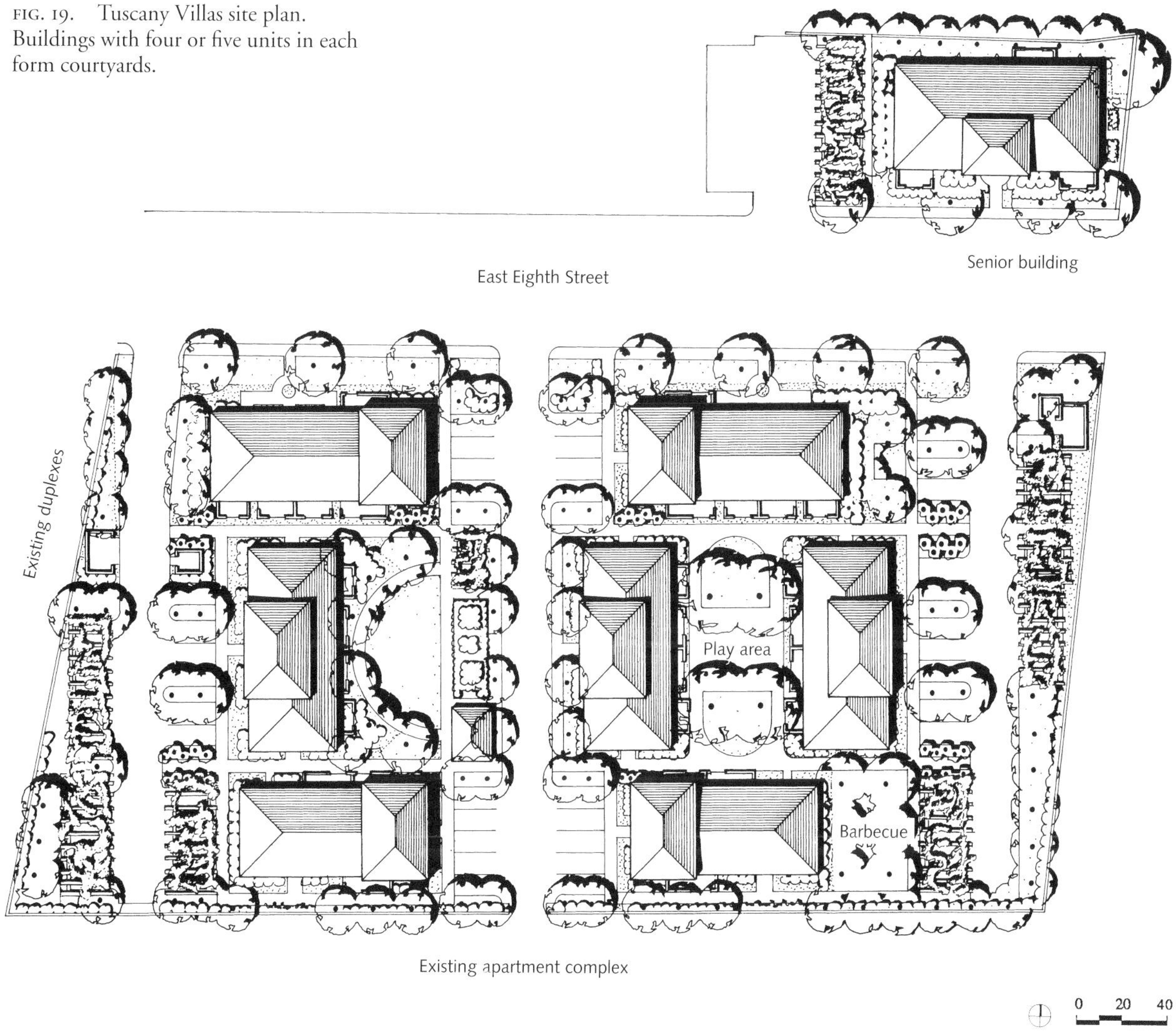

Senior building

East Eighth Street

Existing duplexes

Play area

Barbecue

Existing apartment complex

0   20   40

age to the neighbors—the agreement for the improved entries, larger trees along the street, and perhaps landscaped hedges—and to give them accurate information about the setback. But Tim tries to close the session with a hard line: either the neighbors drop their appeal to the city council, or what has been negotiated this night is off the table. Bonnie and Lance offer to deliver the message but add that they doubt they can persuade the neighbors group to give up on the appeal.

In the next few days Sam and Lisa set about seeing what a scheme of duplexes would look like and cost. Building codes require that an imaginary property line be placed between buildings, even if they are on the same site and in the same development, and operable windows must be ten feet from that line. The result is architecturally abominable and costly: too many buildings, too much unusable space between them. The architects also study the impact of switching the five-unit and four-unit buildings and then splitting the shorter ones into two duplexes along the neighbors' street. This is feasible from a planning standpoint, but it makes the buildings proportionally awkward, and because the code requires side yards between them, the buildings are pushed far apart, giving the impression of more building along the street, rather than fewer.

The day before the council meeting, someone puts out a scare sheet, and someone else places an ad in the local paper. Both are incendiary and filled with misinformation:

> Once again East Davis is a dumping ground for illegal, high-density projects which will negatively and adversely impact our traffic and environment.
>   LAST CHANCE TO PROTECT YOUR NEIGHBORHOOD!! WE NEED YOUR HELP NOW!!!!!!!!!!!
>
>   What's Happening? Davis Community Housing (DCH) is attempting to force high-density housing in an area which is zoned single-family. The City is approving all of this despite the fact that it is illegal. Here's why it's illegal:
>
> MAIN ENVIRONMENTAL ISSUES:
>
> 1. No Environmental Impact Report has been done.
> 2. Illegal building permits on untested soils that may be unstable and/or toxic.
> 3. Extreme disregard for our rare and threatened Swainson Hawks (Fred, Ethel and babies).
> 4. If you think our traffic is overwhelming now, you ain't seen nothing yet.
> 5. And there's more
>
> MAIN LEGAL PLANNING ISSUES:
>
> 1. Illegal zoning from single-family to highest-density multiple housing allowed in Davis.
> 2. Inadequate notice to residents (not even within the City's own 300-foot radius requirements).
> 3. Noncompliance with City's ordinance.
>
> Despite all these problems (and more), the City is still moving ahead with these illegal projects. They never expect opposition from East Davis residents. Let's give them a surprise—here's how you can show them East Davis residents will not be duped. Come to the City Council meeting—we need your body.

THE CITY COUNCIL MEETING

The flier notwithstanding, the atmosphere at the city council meeting is less angry and less anxious than at the planning commission the month before. This is partly because the players and the issues are known, and time has dampened hostility into either frustration or determination. The council chamber is full, but this time both sides have phalanxes.

The mayor announces a tightly controlled format. She has accepted a list of speakers from the neighbors and is adamant about a three-minute maximum for each; she instructs the clerk to use a timer. After the initial round of speakers, she will allow others from either side to speak once for three minutes.

The opposition ultimately narrows its attack to three fronts: the lack of clarity and communication in the rezoning process, the adequacy of the environmental impact report, and the design. The city staff, both the present members and their predecessors, take the brunt of the criticism on the process issue. The neighbors insist that city employees have misinterpreted earlier city council decisions and policies and have poorly drafted the zoning ordinances pertaining to this project. The council, they conclude, must stop the project and rectify the errors.

Of course, the staff disagrees, and the staff report, which was distributed before this evening's hearing, disputes each of the appellant's points. This refutation is reinforced by the city attorney's written analysis and testimony at the council meeting. She reiterates that the rezoning occurred three years ago, and that the time for appeal was within ninety days of that hearing, not now.

The neighbors' attack on the adequacy of the environmental impact report is also rebuffed by both staff and the city attorney. The EIR is the lightning rod of development politics. The law, written somewhat loosely, indicates that the potential presence of a hazard or a possible detriment to the environment, not just a known or actual problem, is sufficient to trigger a full-scale study. When the property was rezoned three years ago, an environmental impact statement was prepared for this part of the city. The required mitigation measures for the entire long-range plan for this area were undertaken; individual sites within are not required to take additional measures or to undertake their own analysis. In such a case the individual site is granted a negative declaration, which relieves its owners of the obligation for a full-scale environmental review.

The neighbors argue that new information—about the Swainson hawks and flood control—that was not known at the time of the original environmental impact study is sufficient to trigger a new EIR for the site. Here again, however, both staff and the city attorney have cogent rebuffs. Both the hawks and the flood control issues were addressed three years ago, at the time of the rezoning, in the original EIR. No new information has been produced, and no new EIR is required.

After the reports of city staff and the city attorney, the mayor opens the public hearing and asks the fourteen neighbors on the list to line up behind the podium. They have prepared their presentations so that each speaker addresses a distinct argument or issue. Bonnie, the appellant, begins with an impassioned legalistic oration about the process, its inconsistencies and vagaries. She refers several times to documentation and minutes of previous councils and commissions. She concludes by saying that the arguments they are about to hear are not motivated by NIMBYism, referring to the planning commission's accusations. The neighbors, she claims, are not against low-income housing.

The subsequent speakers take their turns at the microphone. There is little of the impromptu passion that marked their presentations a month earlier. They are well-prepared but emotionless, and the relentless march of speakers, fourteen of them for three minutes each, has a dulling effect. At one point a council member interrupts to suggest that perhaps the project's proponents be interspersed in order to simulate more of a sense of debate and give-and-take. But the march goes on: duplexes, residential look and quality, Swainson hawks, increased traffic, lack of notification, diminished quality of life, and loss of horse trails, recreation, and farm land. There is no mention of the Pony Express.

Finally, Kathleen, who has been retained by the neighbors as an advocacy consultant, summarizes on their behalf. But her summary contradicts much of the previous testimony, which argued that any development is inappropriate because of the serious environmental problems. Instead, Kathleen contends that the critical issue is the design.

Two hours into the meeting, the mayor asks the president of the CDC's board of directors to present. Leslyn, a resident of the neighborhood where the project will be built, begins by saying what a difficult situation this is for her. These people are her friends and neighbors, and she cares about their feelings, but they are wrong. She also is shaken by the scare sheet, which she views as a serious breach of ethics and goodwill. She takes each of the issues on the sheet and refutes them in order.

Between her testimony and that of Tim, the CDC's executive director, all the architectural and site plan issues are reiterated: the lowering of the allowable density from forty-two units to thirty-six, the relatively small buildings of six units or less, the twenty-foot setback, and the architectural details. Leslyn admits that there is a difference of opinion on what constitutes residential quality, but she argues that the project achieves that quality by not looking like conventional apartments. As Leslyn continues, Sam begins pinning up an elevation study of the alterations that resulted from the negotiating session the week before with Bonnie and Lance. Tim, backing down from his previous stance, states that these ideas are still on the table.

The public hearing continues for another hour, with speakers from both camps. Several people support the CDC's effort, praising its good projects in other parts of town and its careful management of these projects. Basically, no new information is forthcoming.

After a brief adjournment, the council members begin to discuss the legal and administrative questions raised about the process. Now the staff and the city attorney deliver their final salvo: the process, while imperfect, has fully addressed all the legal and administrative requirements. It is obvious to everyone in the room that the council has anticipated these answers, and all the members are favorably disposed to the project—except one.

The newest council member, a young artist named Julie, is attentive to the neighbors, and several slip notes and whisper to her throughout the evening. Her agenda is environmental, particularly the issue of the hawks and site drainage, but she is summarily rebuffed by the city attorney. She persists, however, and the other council members, the hour growing late and the questions tedious, squirm.

The most powerful pronouncements from the council members come from the two who were in office when the rezoning was approved three years ago. They remember the debate clearly, particularly the issue of duplexes and residential quality. There was never, they say, a requirement that the project be duplexes. The council requested that the look be "lower residential density," as a protection from a commercial-looking design, but this was never a condition. The issue of the architecture arose during rezoning, they recall, only because the previous mayor did not like the design that the for-profit developer had suggested for the affordable housing parcel. But the for-profit developer never intended to build this parcel; he intended to donate it to the CDC, which he did, and it was to hire its own architect, which it did. The language about density was included to dissuade the CDC from accepting the for-profit developer's suggested design.

Four of the five council members praise the CDC and the design. One remarks that the project has been portrayed as some heinous "high-tech, super-dense project," but in fact it calls for townhouses with individual entries.

The neighbors are going to lose, but the council does not want them to go away empty-handed. They stipulate that the project must incorporate larger trees and additional landscaping at the street, as well as more elaborate entryways for the units facing the street—all the items that were negotiated a few nights before.

The project is approved unanimously.

THE FINAL RESOLUTION

Ten days after the city council vote, the mayor convenes a meeting of a few representatives from the neighborhood, the city, and the CDC to mediate the final design elements. The city council's stipulation that the entrances be more emphatic, highlighting the individual quality of the units facing the street, and that the landscaping be embellished seems to be the only outstanding item. But a week of informal meetings among the neighbors and their newly retained consultant and the CDC have expanded the list. Keith and Tim want to

cure whatever ill will has developed within the community, as long as the project's design does not suffer and as long there are no increases in cost or time. Many of the items are minor—about scheduling, noise during construction, and ensuring the plants on the fence that divides the property from the working stable are safe for the horses.

After an hour of conciliatory discussion on these smaller issues, the main design matters are at hand. Sam begins by assuring everyone that he and Lisa had thought about many of the issues that concern neighbors and that they had sound reasons for the choices they made. While the process has been adversarial to this point, he reminds the group that the purpose of this meeting is to make the buildings better.

Sam and Lisa have prepared several add-on elements for the entries, including porches, awnings, and trellises. Small cut-out drawings of each are taped onto the model or a rendered elevation. Through their two representatives—a young woman named Sarah, who says little, and Joy, the neighbor who had spearheaded the opposition—the neighbors reveal that they do not want the porches that had been negotiated with Lance and Bonnie. They feel these encroach too far into the setback. Quickly the trellises become favored, much to the relief of the architects, who had included trellises in other parts of the design.

The landscaping issues are noncontroversial, particularly in regard to the trees along the street. B.J., the advocacy consultant retained by the neighbors to represent them in these negotiations, has more than a rudimentary knowledge of plants and has several suggestions. Again, neither the architects nor the CDC has objections, since the list of city-approved street trees is already quite restrictive. The decision is quickly made with the help of a brief visit from the city's landscape administrator.

The neighbors want individual walkways from the sidewalk to the dwellings. The current design has a single walk from the sidewalk toward a planter, and then individual walks from the planter to the units. The architects explain their reasoning: first, that individual walks would result in more paving than the neighbors would like, and second, that the rounded planter against the rectilinear buildings was intended to

FIG. 20. Tuscany Villas courtyard.

soften the architecture. The representatives agree but cannot commit without checking with their constituents. So the item is shelved, with the understanding that the model will be available for neighbors to view.

The most difficult issue, one that has been anticipated by the CDC and the architects but was never mentioned in any of the public hearings, is color. The orange-brown building color, intended to reinforce the "Tuscan" design, is unilaterally and unanimously disliked by the neighbors. B.J., who proved knowledgeable about landscape issues, also claims a knowledge of design (her brother is an architect) and pulls out a stack of

magazines to reveal what should be done. Although color selection was not among the stipulations of the council vote, the architects know that the upcoming design review process by city staff will look at the question, so they might as well address it in this setting.

They are prepared to take a hard line. The darker base color with lighter, contrasting trim and details is not a negotiable item; Tim and Keith concur. The darker color will be more recessive, making the buildings seem smaller; a lighter color would make the tile roofs, which everyone likes, feel ponderous and large. Sam also emphasizes that viewing color indoors under

FIG. 21. Tuscany Villas from the street side.

fluorescent lights is unfair; the meeting and the model move outdoors. The neighbors' contingent is not appeased. It is fall, and there are several dried leaves on the ground. Sam begins collecting them and placing them against the model, suggesting that building colors in this range would be fine. This demonstration works, and a set of "official leaves" is distributed.

Sam reiterates his and Lisa's desire to have a range of color samples, those represented by the leaf collection, applied to the buildings when construction is nearly complete; a final selection can be made then. This plan allows the project to proceed without further hassle; it also suits the architects, who intended to use this procedure even without the controversy.

The final item is the neighbors' plea to have more

landscape, lattice, or detail elements on the facade, both to further emphasize each unit and to cover some of the dark color. They had earlier suggested decorative shutters, and the architects have prepared some stick-on shutters for the model. The added detail mollifies the neighbors, while the architects see it as a suitable embellishment within the spirit of the design.

By January 1993, five months after the initial meeting with the neighbors, construction of Tuscany Villas began (figs. 20, 21). Funding requirements had forced the CDC and its architects to take a bulldog approach to the approvals process. Fortunately, the project's design was sound enough and the political support in city government was strong enough for the fast-track approach to succeed. Shortly after its completion in October, the project won a design award for housing. But the final test is yet to come: whether the project will be a success, both as housing and as part of the neighborhood.

WHY AFFORDABLE HOUSING ISN'T

Affordable housing often costs at least as much to build as comparable market-rate housing. This may sound illogical, inappropriate, or wrong, but it is true. A modest study conducted in California compared assisted projects—those that received some type of subsidy—to similar suburban and rural garden apartments that received no assistance.[1] Both per-dwelling and per-square-foot costs for the subsidized projects were higher. A subsequent, more disciplined study compared pairs of affordable and market-rate projects and found that some subsidized projects cost less and others more than non-subsidized housing. This study concluded that "most affordable projects in the study sample were equivalent to their market-rate counterparts in terms of development costs."[2]

How can this be? Why spend so much on the poor? Are subsidy programs grossly inefficient? Are these programs just hotbeds of abuse? It is politically embarrassing for affordable housing to cost as much as or more than market-rate projects to construct. When the excess lies in administrative costs, there are recurrent calls for welfare re-

form. When the excess can be attributed to better or more interesting architecture, the arguments turn toward the efficacy of providing "luxury" for the poor.

The attitude that subsidized housing should not look or be too good or should not cost too much is persistent. Low-income or social housing has long been considered a temporary way station for people who will eventually get on their feet and move into the market sector, and a way station for poor transients need not provide more than basic shelter. But poverty and economic hardship are not so easily overcome, and the tenancy for these projects has become more or less permanent. We need to recognize that these dwellings are long-standing homes, not way stations or warehouses.

If we want affordable housing that fits comfortably into the community, that bestows pride and a sense of self-sufficiency on its occupants and helps them assimilate into that community, then we cannot continue to build the stripped-down subsidized projects that we have come to accept as low-income housing. The deterioration and abandonment of subsidized housing, much of it less than twenty years old, has proven this approach unworthy and unwise.

THE COST OF DESIGN

DESIGNING THE BUILDING

Nonprofit CDCs and other developers of affordable housing need to spend at least as much as their market-rate counterparts to ensure that affordable housing looks good and will remain attractive. The expense is necessary to overcome the public's grim perception of affordable housing. For-profit developers often sell their project and therefore may be less concerned with its image in perpetuity. When confronted with choices for finishes, particularly exterior materials, affordable housing developers select long-lasting, easily maintained options, such as stucco rather than wood, which does not weather as well and needs extensive maintenance. For roofs, tile or shingle that has a thirty-year guarantee are preferable to lighter, lower-quality materials. Embellishments like decorative grilles, flower boxes, and awnings are included to make the housing friendly, dignified, architecturally distinctive, and acceptable to neighbors. When funding sources like HUD disallow these selections, regarding them as frivolous, CDCs still find the means to include them. For example, architects and CDC project managers will identify awnings as energy-saving devices, which is only part of their function. This often surreptitious manipulation of the budget is necessary for good design, and local agencies that want a proposed project to be accepted by the community will collaborate in the deception.

Appearance and maintenance affect only part of the building design budget. Design decisions based on the intended occupant groups also lead to increased costs. Affordable housing is often for families with children who require three or more bedrooms, but market-rate projects are more often one- or two-bedroom units. And while additional bedrooms are relatively inexpensive compared to kitchens and bathrooms, which require plumbing, cabinets, and water-resistant surfaces, they make the affordable units larger. Larger units have more walls, doors, and windows than smaller dwellings. On a per-unit basis larger units cost more, but on a per-bedroom or a per-person basis they cost less.[3]

To provide the character and amenities of traditional houses, an appropriate form for families with children, affordable projects may incorporate rowhouses and two-story townhouses with individual entries and patios. The living areas are on the ground floor and the private areas on the second floor. This plan has several advantages for families, and the type can easily be fitted into existing neighborhoods. But it also requires more floor area than the conventional apartment, partly because of the space needed for the interior staircase, and it is therefore more expensive to build.

Affordable units are relatively small on a per-person basis, and a private outdoor area is a means of extending the space both perceptually and functionally. Private walled patios are a relatively inexpensive solution, but they still add to the cost. This amenity, which is common in market-rate housing, dramatically increases the livability of the unit, creating a transitional space between public and private on the site and providing a real sense of retreat and security for the occupant. Contrary to both popular and bureaucratic belief, private patios are not luxuries but necessities in affordable housing. For those who can afford market-rate housing, eating out in restaurants provides entertainment and brings variety to their daily patterns. But for those who spend a substantial portion of their small incomes on housing, dining out is a rare treat. Barbecues in the patio are a welcome option, as is the extra private space, even if usable only in moderate weather.[4]

Many other items that seem luxurious and were therefore disallowed in government-financed affordable housing are really necessities. Families with many children in a three-bedroom dwelling need larger water heaters or those with quick recovery, which of course cost more. A compartmented bathroom, perhaps with two sinks separated from the toilet and bathtub, is a feature often seen in market-rate housing but viewed as excessive in affordable housing, where in fact it is more necessary. If there is only one bathroom in a unit shared by a family of six, separating the fixtures serves a real purpose.

Long-term operating costs are also a primary concern in affordable housing. Awnings or trellis-covered patios that extend the interior space and embellish the architecture do cost additional money, but the shading they provide reduces the need for air-conditioning and so cuts down on energy costs.

PLANNING THE SITE

The often contentious processes of land entitlement and building approval can add to the cost of affordable projects. The hearing and approval process may take three or four years and require endless meetings and design changes, all of which add to the cost of the project. Arguments over density also increase the cost of affordable housing. To win approval, these projects often call for fewer units per acre than local zoning allows. Assisted projects in one of the California studies averaged only seventeen units per acre, while the comparable unassisted housing averaged twenty units per acre.[5] This factor alone could represent a 5 to 10 percent difference in costs.

While lower densities are in part politically motivated, they are also a function of the type of occupant. Since dwellings for families with children are generally three-bedroom, fewer fit per acre, relative to the two-bedroom units more often found in market-rate projects. Compared to apartments, two-story townhouses have more of the

qualities of single-family houses. There are no exterior stairs, access balconies, or fire stairs. But stacked apartments can share the entry staircase and the access to all units, making them more efficient in both size and cost. Furthermore, since each townhouse typically occupies a piece of ground by itself (although it is possible to stack townhouses over flats), the number of units possible on the site is lower.

The total number of units is also affected by required or desired site functions. Zoning codes generally demand 2.5 parking spaces for each three-bedroom dwelling, and this applies to low-income housing even though the extra bedrooms are occupied by children and the tenants tend to have fewer vehicles per household. Funding agencies, as well as responsible design, require playgrounds for the children. The land is gobbled up by these nonhousing uses, and the density diminishes.

Making the buildings compatible with existing neighborhoods, designing them for families, and providing ample amenities further increase costs. For example, not only do the required tot-lots use site area, but their equipment and resilient ground surfaces can add $30,000 to a project. More mature landscaping, necessary to make the project blend into its neighborhood immediately upon completion, likewise increases costs.

In addition to having fewer units per acre, affordable projects often have fewer units per site than their market-rate counterparts. This is partly a function of the site amenities and parking, as well as the larger unit sizes, but it also reflects the inability of many CDCs to aggregate larger plots of land, to arrange for financing, and to manage bigger projects. The affordable projects analyzed in one of the California studies averaged 89 units, whereas the market-rate developments averaged 385.[6] This smaller project size means a loss of economies of scale.

Land acquisition has many components that affect design and ultimately costs. Often sites for affordable housing are the castoffs of other projects. For-profit developers required to have an affordable housing allotment would rather donate or assign land to the local CDC than create the units themselves. This land, rarely the prime cut, is more likely at the edge of another development, with an odd geometry, and subject to utility easements or other restrictions. Making efficient site plans becomes difficult and costly. To avoid neighborhood resistance, many CDCs seek land in areas previously used for industry or perhaps agriculture. But the cost of investigating the development potential of these properties, including the analysis of likely toxins in the soil from chemicals or fertilizers, cannot be easily borne by affordable housing developers. While the land may be donated, it is not always free.

If, for example, a for-profit developer donates a three-acre triangular corner for affordable housing, the parcel may, under local zoning standards, be able to support sixty units. The developer gets full credit for the required affordable allocation, but once the zoning setbacks, parking requirements, and lot coverage restrictions are determined, there is really only room for forty units. The buildings may have to be smaller still, with fewer units in each, in order to fit into the irregular site. The overall efficiency of the project is sacrificed, even though the land was free.

Often a for-profit developer will identify several sites for the affordable housing allotment, not wanting a single large project within the development to be identified as low-income. This also suits neighborhoods and even CDCs, since there is less resistance to smaller projects. But this scattered-site approach, even if the building designs are consistent, and even if the construction occurs simultaneously, adds costs. The civil engineering must be undertaken for individual sites, construction supervision is more expensive, and the design

and drawing phase is more complex, since each site must be separately documented.

The design decisions by architects and developers of affordable housing increase costs, but they also increase the quality and livability for the occupant. These decisions may have been forced on the affordable housing supplier by politics and the circumstances of the site, but they nevertheless place the supplier on the horns of a dilemma; neither the expense nor the results have been traditionally acceptable in the United States.

THE COST OF CONSTRUCTION

The characteristics of the home-building industry in the United States have both obvious and subtle impacts on affordability. Few technical advances have had the effect of substantially lowering construction costs, and those that have are prevalent in both affordable and market-rate housing, a fact that further muddies the distinction. Furthermore, most construction advances are slow to make it to the marketplace.

As pointed out in Chapter 1, the industry comprises many small builders who are supported by larger companies that supply materials and products. These small builders see their work load rise and fall abruptly, depending on the economy, natural disasters, weather, the availability of labor, and local politics. As the hearings and approval process play out, builders must cool their heels, unable to budget a project that may not get under way for months or even years. In the case described in Chapter 2, the wait, though it was only four or five months, added $48,000 to a $2.8 million project because the cost of lumber rose. This is only a 1.7 percent increase, but it represents the cost of an important amenity, like a tot-lot. The cost must be exacted from sacrifices elsewhere in the project, such as using sand instead of a resilient play surface for the tot-lot.

Most small builders run independent operations that rely on a network of subcontractors and suppliers. This bare-bones approach provides the flexibility needed to counteract the cycles of the industry and its vagaries. It fits well with the traditional methods of home building, but it also perpetuates these conventions, even if they are not efficient.

Multifamily housing of the garden apartment or townhouse type now preferred for affordable projects is usually either "stick-built"—made with studs and sheathing—or masonry construction. The choice between the two is regional and has much to do with aesthetic expectations, local building culture, and available labor. In either case, the common characteristic is the highly labor intensive, on-site placement of relatively small elements, either studs or bricks. Large equipment is not required, and floating pools of laborers move from job to job, from builder to builder. Small contractors can enter into this system without high start-up costs or an extensive in-house labor force. They are basically managers and agents who facilitate construction. It is also possible for them to leave the industry just as easily as they enter, and they often do.

In stick-built wood construction, building processes and methods have evolved and become streamlined. The lumber industry that supports this construction mills and manufactures boards and sheets in standard sizes and configurations; power nailers replace hammers; construction adhesives, premanufactured connectors, and premade windows (called "nail-ons") that are simply nailed over openings in the building's exterior are all available to save time and money.

This evolution has industrialized and standardized conventional construction without forcing it into the factory and without changing the nature of the end product, thereby allowing the continued existence of the small builders. A balance is reached between, on the one hand, the desire for cost efficiency and quality control and, on the other, the recognition of the nature of the building industry that precludes the high capitalization needed for full factory production. This evolution is continuing, leading to various forms of component and panelized building construction. Component and panelized building recognizes that while a certain amount of site work and customization must occur, parts of the construction enterprise can best be done in factories. Although factory production of whole houses has proven less than successful, this experience has not ruled out the use of prefabricated major building elements, if they are easily transportable, manageable without costly equipment or on-site labor, and available to small builders. These components can be categorized into three general types: whole rooms, wall panels, and spanning structural elements.

PREMADE ROOMS

Bathrooms and kitchens are the most technically complex and the most expensive rooms in a dwelling. They have fixtures, appliances, cabinets, and wall or floor surfaces that must be easily cleaned and impervious to water. Many suppliers and subcontractors are needed to create these relatively small rooms, so on a square-foot basis their cost is substantial. Since they are complex, relatively small, and costly, they are prime prospects for factory production. The concept of the factory-produced kitchen or bathroom, delivered and inserted into the nearly completed dwelling, is one of the most enduring images of industrialized housing. But there are few such models on the market in the United States, for reasons similar to those constraining factory production of whole houses (see Chapter 1).

For the multifamily housing architect, designing an efficient unit plan, aggregating it with other similar plans, and making room dimensions and proportions comfortable is like fitting a puzzle together. A small adjustment for one purpose sends ripples throughout the dwelling plan. Moving a door, shortening a cabinet, or altering the dimensions of a room are common and expected moves in design, even in kitchens and bathrooms. Fitting in a large component with little tolerance for adjustment or alteration is a difficult proposition. Designing around it, particularly if the component presents relatively minor savings in cost, means sacrificing other needs and functional requirements. It becomes a case of the tail wagging the dog. Furthermore, the sequence of conventional construction allows for bathrooms and kitchens to be completed after the shell of the dwelling is up, and the work proceeds simultaneously. But premade components must be inserted before the dwelling is enclosed. Without a proven product—one that can fit easily and comfortably into all projects and dovetail into traditional construction processes, one for which delivery is readily available and model variations are real options—there simply is no sustainable market for room-sized components.

As the size of the factory-produced component is reduced, its availability and its model choices increase. In the bathroom, for example, several bathtub and shower components are available, one- or two-piece fiberglass elements that include the full enclosure, often with options in color and configuration. Compared to the cast-iron tub, which requires tile or impervious sheets to surround it, the fiberglass unit is quick, easy, and inexpensive. One could argue that it is of lesser quality than traditional tubs, that it scratches if not cleaned properly, or that it may feel less substantial, but the cost is low enough and the quality high enough that these units are in general use and are a good example of the evolution of industrialized production in housing. These products are available from several manufacturers; they are lightweight, making them accessible to small builders without heavy equipment; and they reduce the number of building trades (they do not require tiling) and time needed on the site. They can be installed in the normal sequence of construction, without special scheduling. Other widely used premade components include modular cabinets for kitchens and bathrooms, combinations of kitchen appliances, and even some of the components hidden within walls, like plumbing lines.

PANELS AND SECTIONS

Sectionalized and panelized building components do for the structural aspects of the dwelling what the plastic inserted bathtubs do for the bathroom. An expensive aspect of the construction, the building's exterior wall, is produced in the factory. Walls require the work of several building trades and include interior and exterior finishes, electrical outlets, windows, and insulation. The efficient factory production of walls would certainly be an advantage. But panelized and sectionalized building has seen only limited use, usually in areas of high population and active multifamily housing construction.

Here the restrictions are administrative, rather than physical. As major enclosing and structural elements, panels must meet strict building codes and pass various inspections. In conventional construction, a building official comes to the site periodically to check the work, but how can a local inspector ensure the quality of major components produced in a factory? If the factory is not in the same jurisdiction as the site, who does the inspecting? The panels can be approved by an underwriting laboratory, but this cost would have to be borne by the manufacturer and ultimately passed on to the buyer.

A second drawback in the use of panels or sections is fit. In conventional construction, small errors and inaccuracies in the foundations can be remedied in the wood framing. Corrections can be made as needed throughout construction. But in panelized or sectionalized construction, the accuracy of the site preparation and foundations is critical. If panels are delivered to the site and do not fit, they must be returned, which causes delays, or adapted. In either case costs go up, negating whatever economic advantage factory production had yielded.

A third problem is that in order to maintain a continuous construction schedule the factory production of panels must begin before building begins at the site. The panels must be finished and delivered when the foundations are ready, or else one of the great advantages of their use, reducing construction time, is lost. A factory will demand 10 percent of the payment up front before beginning a production run.[7] In the conventional construction and financing of affordable housing, payments are made as the work progresses on the site, and funding sources have regular meetings, sometimes called "draw meetings," at which incremental payments are doled out. Substantial up-front expenditures do not work well within this system.

There are also architectural limitations in the use of panels—the building must be laid out on a regular grid, for example—but these constraints are not onerous. If the project is large enough, factory production can be adjusted to the design, rather than the other way around. In some larger projects a mobile factory is set up at the construction site and relocated as the project progresses. In smaller projects the design limitations imposed by panels, while tolerable, do have an important impact. Panelized systems cannot accommodate structural cantilevers more than a few feet long, making architectural features like projecting bays problematic. Alterations for special conditions— for example, at the ends or corners of buildings— increase costs much more dramatically than in conventional construction. If the overall cost savings of panelized walls were substantial, these re-strictions would be outweighed, even at some sacrifice to the character of the architecture. But they are hardly less costly, and the risks are high. Several phased projects, those built in increments over time, have used panels in the early phases but reverted to conventional construction when the savings did not outweigh the design limitations and administrative difficulties.

SPANNING ELEMENTS

Structural components like roof and floor framing are also prime candidates for industrialization. Lightweight, premade trusses for floors and roofs are a common building element that can be custom-designed and -engineered, factory-produced, and trucked and hoisted into position by inexpensive mobile equipment. Their evolution is a result of three factors. First, engineering for residential construction has become increasingly exact, aided most recently by computer techniques that are easily translated into production systems. Second, advances in the science of wood products have made it possible to use composites and combinations of products both safely and efficiently. These save money by reducing the lumber dimensions and therefore the amount of wood required. Finally, the making of trusses on site is time-consuming, takes space, and in the case of composites, must be done under controlled conditions. The truss itself is relatively light and can be easily transported and placed, making factory production and transport feasible.

Like other aspects of industrialized production, factory-produced trusses and structural elements are most economical if repetitive. Again a balance must be attained between the conflicting desires for recurring parts and for a diverse architecture.

The industrialization of buildings has been something of a quiet revolution. Although unions and code officials have been slow to accept some products, fearing either a loss in wages or a reduction in safety, the manufacturers of these products have prevailed. In many cases the newest products are better, sturdier, more energy efficient, and easier to maintain; the aluminum nail-on window is a good example. With an eye to increasing quality while reducing on-site labor, manufacturers have developed products that are flexible, varied, and open, products that can be applied to many different circumstances, even within the conventional building process. This is a far different course from the initial vision of industrialization as the manufacture of closed systems of large components.

But lumber, bricks, and mortar cost the same whether used in affordable or market-rate housing; the construction techniques, methods, and standards are similar, and similarly expensive. Construction accounts for 60 to 70 percent of the total cost, excluding land and financing. Of this figure perhaps about a third may be in the enclosing and structural components, the aspects most amenable to the new techniques. Thus, while new methods may help hold the line on some costs and improve overall quality, they are no godsend for affordability. And because these techniques are useful in all types of housing, they do not give affordable housing any edge over market-rate housing. The difference is that in affordable housing even modest savings in construction costs can be applied to carefully selected embellishments that effect major improvements in the architecture.

CONTRACTORS

Most new affordable housing is conventionally built with stick-framed or brick walls. Contractors are experienced with the type and are in control at the site; there are few surprises, and any planning errors can generally be rectified with a little resourcefulness. The innovations discussed above are available to them, but they are optional. This is not to say that without use of these techniques the quality of their work or the product is lower than it could be or that there are no efficiencies available within a traditional method. Quite the contrary. As hammers are replaced by power nailing guns, so paintbrushes are replaced by compressed spray guns, and drywall taping devices combine the paper and paste in one motion as the worker applies the mixture to the joints.

In Chapter 1, I described the building industry as a fleet of sailboats that loosely and independently follow the winds and currents. As the captain of one of those sailboats, each contractor has an opinion on how to get things done. But in conventional building practice the design is completely documented, with the materials and their expected installation specified before contractors are brought into the process. They then bid against one another for the right to build the project. If the architect has made selections and decisions with which a contractor is unfamiliar, if there is a limited number of subcontractors in the area to perform that work, or if the materials specified are difficult to acquire, then a contractor's bid will be high, the fear factor driving up the price.

One would expect the architect of affordable housing to refrain from designing elements that are unusual and may make the contractors uncertain, but what frightens one builder may be preferred by another. Housing construction is not an exact science: there are customs and traditional methods but also enormous variation within them, and new products and methods appear all the time.

Many architects believe that a building costs whatever a contractor thinks it should cost, even before that contractor actually begins to make any calculations. The construction bidding is then a self-fulfilling prophecy. This realization is critical in affordable housing, where there is so little margin for costs overruns and so little time to redesign when there are any. One searches for ways to reduce the fear factor. Some strategies are quite simple. For example, contractors are suspicious when overall building dimensions include fractions of inches. A building should be 60 feet long, not 59 feet and 3.5 inches. The dimensions have little do to with the manner of construction or its difficulty, but the fractions are a red flag to a builder, a hint that many odd dimensions will require special vigilance that translates into time and money. Errors in building dimensions can be compounded at the site, leading to problems at the top of the building, when the premade trusses arrive and do not fit.

Unusual features, and irregular and nonrecurrent elements are also red flags to contractors. A housing project that has thirty units should have only three or four different types of units. There may be minor variations or mirror images of those units, but if there are many different types, each must be carefully measured, and each is likely to have individual details, as well as different doors, windows, and fixtures. Such distinctions add to the contractor's (and subcontractors') time, care, and costs. This approach marks one of the big differences between affordable and market-rate housing. A for-profit developer may feel compelled to offer a range of dwelling choices to accommodate a wide market, but an affordable housing developer always has a long list of prospective tenants to match to whatever type of dwelling will be built. There simply is no need for variation in the type of dwelling, except as a means to make the architecture more interesting.

Structural framing is a major component of a project, representing perhaps as much as 15 percent of the cost. The contractor's ideal is that each segment of framing be identical. Trusses can then be ordered all the same length and be interchangeable, eliminating planning, thought, and the possibility of error at the site; a steady rhythm and pattern of installation will ensue. Uniformity and replication lead to contented contractors and lower

costs. Architects, on the other hand, often feel that variation in the dimensions and configuration of the plan makes for more interesting buildings, but this entails inconsistent framing. Furthermore, the odd site dimensions and configurations common to affordable housing often demand diverse building forms. The challenge for the architect, which is addressed more fully in Chapter 4, is how to balance regularity and irregularity.

To avoid the untimely surprises and disappointments that can occur in the bidding process, affordable housing architects and developers often favor a negotiated contract with the builder. In this method the contractor is retained early, before the design is defined, and can collaborate with the architect in making choices and decisions. Bringing the contractor in at the earliest point eliminates the fear factor and makes it possible to take advantage of the contractor's knowledge of the availability of local labor and material. Negotiated contracts also preclude the most disastrous outcome of competitive bidding, the case in which all the bids exceed the budget and the project must be redesigned. The negotiated contract was generally not an option in directly subsidized affordable housing, since government contracts require open competitive bidding. But CDCs are independent entities and have more flexibility in the method of project delivery.

Bringing the contractor into the creative team can not only reduce costs but also improve the architecture. For Parkview Commons, on the site of the old Polytechnic High School in San Francisco, the contractor, Bill Moffett, was confident that concrete block would be less expensive than the architect's initial design for a poured-in-place concrete base enclosing the parking area and forming the foundation for the housing above. He set about finding the masons and carefully drawing out each course of block to calculate the exact amount needed. He knew the local labor market and the availability of the product; he was less

FIG. 22. Delancey Street in San Francisco. The residents used the construction process as an opportunity to acquire marketable skills.

comfortable with pouring so much concrete, which would entail extensive use of wood forms and reinforcing steel. His inclination and legwork paid off. The block was substantially less expensive, and the architect agreed that its color and split-face texture made for a better design.[8]

This type of collaborative relationship also promotes a sense of solidarity and teamwork that can save time and money. Conventional selection of contractors through bidding sometimes brings together groups unknown to each other. The contractual agreements can force parties into adversarial relationships in which they retreat and retrench behind the written terms. When problems arise— and they always do—this contentious atmosphere hinders creative, cost-effective remedies. But if everyone has participated in the design phase, everyone has a stake in the overall mission, as well as in the design, and solutions are more likely to be found quickly without compromising the design or the budget.

There are drawbacks to the negotiated contract, however. In the absence of competitive motives a contractor may not seek out the best prices from subcontractors, who may represent 60 to 70 percent of the total contract, or fully explore options and possibilities in design and construction methods. This is the worst of both worlds: a recalcitrant team member with no incentive to reduce costs.

In some cases the relationship among client, builder, and architect is wholly interactive and cohesive. In the Delancey Street housing in San Francisco the future residents, former substance abusers and felons, entered into a cooperative arrangement with the architect, Howard Backen, and a local contractor. Backen met often with groups of tenants, and together they worked out design solutions that would require a specific skill or trade. For example, the tenants wanted wrought-iron handrails throughout, and once this detail was determined, Delancey Street members went about training themselves to produce the rails (fig. 22). In this way the future occupants obtained exactly the features they wanted, while acquiring valuable, marketable skills and inestimable pride in the results.[9]

THE COST OF REGULATION

Regulation is the Jekyll and Hyde of housing. In the nineteenth century the absence of regulation allowed for real-estate speculation and rapid growth in American cities. Although the unregulated industry provided millions of immigrant families with affordable shelter, the tenements were unhealthy and unsafe. Prompted by insurance companies, many municipalities adopted building codes in the early 1900s. But regulations also pose obstacles to affordable housing. In the words of a 1991 Presidential Advisory Commission, "The comprehensive nature of building codes, coupled with the broad discretion customarily possessed by local officials charged with code administration and enforcement, sometimes turns the codes into regulatory barriers."[10] Regulation raises costs in three ways: zoning restrictions limit where and how much one can build and often exclude affordable housing altogether; building codes specify materials, procedures, and designs; and the entitlement and approval process extends the development time.[11]

Building codes are massive documents covering all aspects of the structure, equipment, and design.

The codes try to anticipate every possible danger or hazard and then prescribe preventive measures for each. Conventional codes provide few options for meeting the desired safety standard. Newer codes, however, such as energy regulations, include both detailed prescriptions and performance standards, which allow architects leeway in meeting the goal.

New housing today, be it affordable or market rate, is generally sturdy and safe. Nevertheless, we continue to discover new maladies and problems and create new regulations to rectify them. For example, poor indoor air quality, once primarily an issue of adequate ventilation, is now known to be caused by the chemical residues in some materials installed within the dwelling. Energy codes that demand tighter buildings allow toxins that once dissipated to linger within. Several materials common only a decade or two ago, like lead-based paint and asbestos, are no longer allowed.

To understand how seemingly simple provisions can increase the cost of affordable housing and affect its architecture, let's look at fire prevention and control, which is but one of the many regulations that influence building form and cost. The codes deal with fire safety in three ways. The first is isolation: should a fire break out, containment is paramount. The second is escape: routes of travel, the number of exits, and the size of halls all play a role in saving lives during a fire. The third is access: fire fighters need unobstructed entry onto the site and into the building.

ISOLATION

Stringent code provisions intended to isolate dwellings and prevent fires from spreading have increased costs and decreased the quality of the interior. Only a few years ago it was possible to run heating and air-conditioning ducts in the ceiling between a first-floor apartment and the one above. The most recent Uniform Building Code in use in most jurisdictions, however, adopts the premise that such penetrations into the ceiling and floor structure reduce the fire separation between the dwellings, even if there is sufficient flame-retardant material above the ducts to contain the fire to the lower unit. Now the entire ceiling and floor assembly, and whatever is within it, is considered part of the required separation between the lower and upper units. As a consequence a false, or second, ceiling is needed below the ceiling and floor assembly to house the ducts. This is an additional cost of construction, and it reduces the ceiling height in at least part of the lower unit. One alternative is to run the ducts in the main ceiling and floor assembly and then install fire-closing dampers at every heating outlet. Each damper costs about $200, and since there may be eight or ten outlets in a dwelling, this alternative can add $2,000 to the cost of each unit. (Fire sprinklers for the lower unit, which may be a safer and more cost-efficient alternative, do not satisfy the code.) Another alternative is not to use a ducted heating system but to rely on radiant systems. In climates that require air-conditioning this option is less appealing, because it necessitates through-the-wall air conditioners that serve only one room.

But the lowered, or furred, ceiling is also an issue of design quality. The hallways, kitchen, and bathrooms, the usual spaces where the lowered ceiling is placed, become more cramped. Architects try to place the lowered ceilings in closets and other nonoccupied areas, but attempting to route the ducts efficiently may contort the plan. Another alternative is to make the entire ceiling of the lower apartment nine feet high, instead of eight, so that the lowered portions will still be eight feet high, a standard we have come to expect. This is costly, however, since it entails more material and a greater building volume. Or we can adjust our expectations to accept seven-foot ceilings in portions of the dwelling.

Other code provisions involving air-ducting have both cost and design implications. If the washer and dryer are included in the unit, the dryer must be within ten or twelve feet of an exterior wall. The reason is that the maximum length of the dryer vent is fourteen feet, and the vent, which starts behind the machine, must find its way up and across to the exterior. In dwellings that are already small and tightly organized on the site, the amount of exterior wall for habitable rooms is very scarce, and this ducting provision further limits its use. This code requirement may drive washers and dryers out of the dwelling and into common facilities. Central laundry rooms may be cheaper to build, but they place a burden on families with small children and on the elderly.

Also in the interest of isolation, the code regulates distances between buildings and the total amount of area within a building. These restrictions tend to determine both the size and positioning of structures. For Tuscany Villas, discussed in Chapter 2, the issue of duplexes versus garden apartments became a moot point when the architects calculated how few duplexes could be on the site, given the required distances between them. But in other cases the efficient aggregation of several units within a single building may be limited by the allowable enclosed areas. The codes provide alternatives that allow for larger areas, such as increasing the fire-resistance ratings of the building walls or between units within a building or using fire sprinklers, but these choices raise the cost.

None of these code requirements in and of itself is sufficient to make housing unaffordable, but the combination of many such provisions erodes already tight budgets.

ESCAPE

A major change in code provisions enacted in the late 1980s demonstrates how significantly a seemingly insignificant requirement can affect architecture, costs, and livability. Until recently, occupants of the third floor of a dwelling had to have two means of egress in case of a fire. Jumping from a window did not (and does not) constitute one of those means. The code required a separate stairway.

Creating this stair in a multilevel or elevator building is not so difficult, or at least its provision is so obvious and so anticipated that it becomes part of the heuristics of the form. These buildings have halls providing easy access to several stairways. But for a three-story building, particularly one made up of townhouses, the additional stairway is both an expense and an architectural problem. Allowing more than two units to share the required access reduces the cost but necessitates an awkward balcony access high above the ground, which in turn reduces privacy as people walk past the windows of others to reach the stairs.

The most recent code allows for five hundred square feet of living area on the third floor without a second means of egress. This is enough room for two bedrooms and a bathroom or a single master bedroom. In terms of unit planning, this change is a godsend. It frees space at the ground, since units can be built up rather than out, and it eliminates all the design problems associated with the second stairway. But there are still costs. If there is any third-story component in a building with more than two dwellings, the new code requires the entire building to be "one-hour," a fire-separation rating that entails increasing the interior wallboard thicknesses throughout. Similarly, the revised code also requires that any building with three stories have fire sprinklers throughout, which can add one to two dollars per square foot to the overall costs.

Herein lies a distinction between affordable and market-rate housing. The former's reliance on larger, three-bedroom units pressures the designer to provide ample ground-level open space for parking and recreational uses. This pressure forces

the buildings from two to three floors, now more easily accommodated by the code. But a careful calculation is needed to balance the costs. The higher buildings mean less foundation and roof for the amount of enclosed area and fewer stairways for the number of occupants. On the other hand, the increased fire protection, in the form of more gypsum board and sprinklers, may more than offset the savings. Affordable housing, because of the tight sites and higher densities, incurs these costs that market-rate housing usually avoids.

ACCESS

Access onto the site and into the buildings probably exerts the most influence of any regulatory issue on design. The sizes of buildings, their placement and proximity to each other, their materials, and the amount and nature of open spaces on the site are all subject to the scrutiny of the fire marshal. In suburban developments particularly, fire truck maneuvering is the major preoccupation. Fire marshals often demand that the trucks be able to turn around on the site, and this requires a vast expanse of hard paving. This space is not unusable, but its magnitude often precludes landscaping or the otherwise sound planning of the site. Here again affordable housing bears the brunt of the requirement. In market-rate housing there are more opportunities to use upgraded ground covers. Paver stones, instead of asphalt, make the extensive hard surfaces much more inviting. The larger sites and bigger projects provide more opportunity for internal road systems that allow trucks to move freely through the site without turn-arounds.

Firefighter access and parking requirements often conspire to make housing developments a sea of hard surfaces. To provide wide access for trucks and to meet the civil engineers' and local public works department's desire for wide driveways, a plan that calls for two lanes of perpendicular parking with a two-way drive between consumes a chunk over sixty feet wide—well beyond the needs of most residential lots and emergency vehicles. In many warm weather communities these paving requirements are compounded by energy codes that require 50 percent shading on parking areas. For affordable projects this means an extra expense for carports or tree-planting. Both these amenities improve a project, but their cost can also bury it.

Often affordable housing developers and architects negotiate with fire marshals and public works officials. Since data on car ownership in affordable housing indicate fewer cars per household than the code anticipates, the parking requirements may be adjusted. Allowing fire trucks to drive over landscaped areas in an emergency further reduces the costs of paving and improves the site, while risking only the eventuality of repairs.

OTHER TYPES OF REGULATIONS AND RESTRICTIONS

While fire and safety issues have been the primary motivation for building codes, other issues relating to the general welfare of the citizenry have given rise to regulation. Most notable among these are the provisions to make dwellings accessible to people with physical disabilities. Individual states have included such components in their codes for some time. In California most new housing has at least 5 percent of the dwellings designed for the disabled.

Few dispute the intention or necessity of such codes; the issue for affordable housing is how to bear their costs and what must be sacrificed in the process. Codes for accessibility have enormous influence on the planning of individual units and the costs of those units, mostly owing to the dimensions of rooms, particularly bathrooms. To accommodate wheelchairs, bathrooms have grown from a nominal five-by-seven-foot space to one that is at least five-by-nine. A hundred-unit project may have fifty bathrooms on the ground floor, where the increased size is required. At $60 a square foot, these bathrooms cost an extra $30,000, or roughly half the cost of an additional dwelling.[12] HUD estimates that the cost of disabled-access compliance is $670 per dwelling, but the National Association of Home Builders places the cost at $2,000 to $3,000, which increases rents by $25 each month.[13] For the private builder larger bathrooms are a market-rate bonus, an integral part of what sells or brings the higher rents that pay for them.

Often a CDC's desire to serve the various populations leads to conflicts. For example, in a townhouse, a dwelling type often favored for families, the bathrooms are generally upstairs, which makes them inaccessible to those who use wheelchairs or other mobility aids. There are also specific needs: for instance, a CDC developing housing for seniors may feel compelled to install more expensive roll-in showers, even though these are not required by the code.

Another layer of construction regulation and restriction comes from funding sources. Their rules are not nearly as onerous as those applied by HUD, but they have the ironic effect of increasing costs, rather than containing them. In California, for example, the Department of Housing and Community Development (HCD) has tight specification standards for buildings in order to protect the investment; these usually demand higher-quality materials. HCD requires better cabinets than many for-profit developers use in market-rate housing, and they generally cost twice as much. HCD also requires that each unit, rather than each building, have a water shut-off valve. While individual valves are convenient should a specific dwelling need repairs (the whole building will not be without water), they can add $5,000 to the cost of a small project. These regulators also demand more site supervision than contractors normally expect, which often leads to higher construction bids as contractors fear the capriciousness of the inspector or likely scheduling delays.

CREATIVE APPROACHES TO RESTRICTIONS

Everyone could be a good tennis player if there were no net and no lines; designing would be simpler if there were no regulations. Those who learn to work creatively within them, to find opportunity within them, will likely make good and safe buildings. Those who, exhausted or enervated by the codes, merely succumb to their prescriptive provisions will make safe but bland housing. Many regulations can be turned to architectural advantage. The awnings and trellises that help comply with energy codes make for lively architecture. The minimum size required for a bedroom window to aid in rescue during fire also provides more light and ventilation to that room.

Buildings can be reflections of the code, or they can be faithful to its intentions. The tower-block form, once the staple of American affordable housing, can be seen as merely a function of the allowable distance between fire stairs, the allowable extension of halls beyond those stairs (or dead ends), and the placement of efficient unit plans around this exit system (fig. 23). This code-driven scheme, together with the efficiency of structural spans, has determined the volume of hundreds of buildings, most of which are drab, uninteresting boxes. Architects who adjust the rudiments of the system while still keeping to the requirements and standards make better buildings, even within the limited type. Davis/Brody and Associates in New York, renowned housing architects, push and pull the code-prescribed envelope, giving dwellings special views and character and bestowing variations on the mass by angling the corners and off-

setting the hallways. Ben Weese's designs for affordable housing in Chicago splay the plan to provide corner windows and views for living rooms, and nonlinear hallways that have vestibules at the entries to apartments (fig. 24).

For the architect who anticipates doing the unusual, making early contact with the building department, fire marshal's office, and public works department is essential. It is possible to get agreement on the design before much is determined and much is at risk. At the least, the architect will know where the lines on the court will be drawn and how high the net will be. Good negotiating skills are helpful in this arena, but few architects learn these skills in school. After one or two encounters they discover that getting indignant, hostile, and aggressive during a meeting with a building official is a surefire way to lose. Listening to the interpretation and the logic and probing the resolve of the regulator provide the best opportunity for consensus. An unfavorable reading of a code provision can be argued or appealed if one studies the code and prepares a documented refutation. This may be a cost-saving approach, even if it takes more time.

Building-code compliance is a matter of judgment and interpretation, both the architect's and the official's, and some subterfuge is often employed. For example, loft space in a dwelling, with a steep stairway or a ladder, does not conform to the code's definition of habitable space. The architect and the developer may intend this space as a room, and they know full well that a low-income family will use it as such, but it will be identified as storage on the drawings. The drawings are approved, the cost of construction is reduced, and the occupant gets the extra space.

Zoning restrictions, like building codes, are sometimes circumvented using this strategy. With zoning it is often less a matter of safety and more one of politics. The use of in-law units (or "echo"

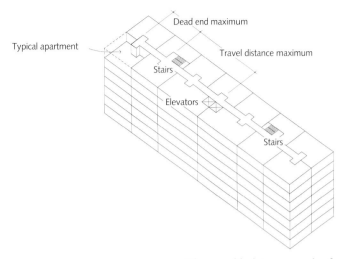

FIG. 23.   The tower block is an example of how the requirements of exit systems can determine the building form.

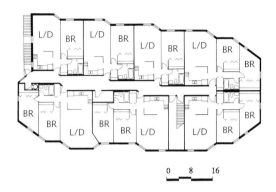

FIG. 24.   Variations in the plan form, as in this design by Ben Weese, can help improve the quality of the corridors while providing different vistas from the apartments.

or "shadow" apartments, once know as granny apartments) in low-density areas is a particularly volatile issue, one that has enormous implications for affordability. Building a small studio in the rear of a property, or an extension to a home with a separate entry, is an efficient and effective way to make a house affordable both to those who own it and those who rent the unit. It also doubles the density in a single-family house zone. Identifying the unit as a home office or not including the doorway in the original construction avoids the zoning issue.

Any evasive or deceptive tactic has its risks. Building officials are not liable for their interpretations; developers and architects are. Should a building department approve plans that are not in compliance and there is a mishap related to that aspect of the code, the architect, contractor, and developer are responsible. If there was knowledge of nonconformance, the penalties can be severe.

Since codes are always in flux and are open to interpretation, there is a thin line between creating housing that is cost-efficient, architecturally distinguished, and safe versus that which is absolutely compliant with every aspect of the code. Sometimes spending money to include universally accepted safety provisions, like fire sprinklers, a feature that is coming to be required in many jurisdictions, may be a suitable substitute for decreasing the distances between buildings.

Recognizing the vagaries and complexities of the code, some jurisdictions have instituted a simple variance procedure. The architect brings to the panel of officials the list of issues, makes the plea, and awaits a determination. In his single-room-occupancy housing in San Diego (discussed in Chapter 5), the architect Rob Quigley used this procedure in order to save costs. His proposal to reduce the number of electrical outlets in each room to only two (one for the microwave and one for the television) was rejected. He argued that the occupants had few appliances and therefore little need for the outlets. The variance board, however, figured that the occupants would be more likely to overload the few outlets. But the board did relax other provisions, as suggested by Quigley; for instance, they allowed a reduction in sound insulation between rooms and hallways but not between rooms.[14]

CONFLICTING VALUES

Regulation in affordable housing is a crucial issue, because budgets are so tight that a single restriction can make or break a project. Even the inclusion of sprinklers can add $60,000 to a small project of thirty units, or nearly the equivalent of the cost of a whole unit. The problem is not just the extensiveness and pervasiveness of the regulations, but also the inconsistent and erratic ways that local authorities interpret them. Local building culture, the lobbying power of various trades, and an unwillingness to allow for new procedures or materials not yet represented in codes increase costs and reduce affordability. The President's Advisory Commission cites the example of thwarted attempts to use plastic plumbing pipe as a substitute for iron and copper. Although many in the industry feel that plastic is in some ways superior, its use is often limited either by pressure from pipe fitters or by the lack of data on its quality.[15] Officials have little motivation to take risks on products unfamiliar to them.

In an ironic twist, the very agencies and pressure groups meant to promote and stimulate the building of good housing have also added regulations and procedures that severely limit construction. As agencies like HCD in California seek to improve the quality of affordable housing by their demanding standards, they also increase its costs. Communities that want to preserve the qualities of their neighborhoods demand lower-density and higher-quality housing, which is also more expensive. Federal agencies empowered to finance housing require that it be built in accordance with the Davis-Bacon Act, which mandates prevailing union wages, thereby reducing competitiveness even for small developments. And housing reformers, working to protect those without a powerful voice in the process, lobby for improved safety and accessibility conditions—all of which cost more. Beneficial national policies like energy conservation, which improve the quality of housing and reduce the occupant's monthly utility bills, also increase the front-end costs to the developer.

As the cost of building conformance increases, affordability decreases. And as conformance consumes more of the budget, the amenities and architectural qualities that can make affordable housing acceptable to occupants and the community must be sacrificed. Thus, some suggest that a separate set of standards be written for affordable housing. Among them is Anthony Downs, who proffers a "Hong Kong" solution. He observes that millions of people in Hong Kong, Singapore, and Tokyo live in very small but serviceable dwellings and suffer no major physical or psychological detriment. While admitting that these units are tiny and very dense relative to American standards, he believes that our cultural expectations of sound housing raise its cost by 50 percent. "Most American housing is built to standards that go far beyond the minimums required by health and safety because builders and occupants want shelter that greatly surpasses such minimums. They want amenities that are not essential to human health but are desirable for a comfortable and satisfying life in a wealthy nation." As a result, Downs concludes, we have failed to serve many people who would welcome small but sturdy housing, and the remedy is simply to "reduce the quality standards such housing is legally required to meet."[16]

From a purely economic standpoint, Downs is correct. Building smaller units would be less expensive, and several exemplary projects (such as the single-room-occupancy projects in San Diego described in Chapter 5) illustrate that minimal housing can be graceful and dignified. There are also projects with densities of thirty-five units per acre, a figure Downs proposes, that are humane and livable. But Downs's proposal could also lead to two tragic results. First, affordable housing would again be stigmatized, as would those who live in it, a tragic reversion to the mean-spirited housing of the previous generation. Second, the cost of the approvals fight for such high-density insertions in communities, even with government intervention, might well offset the construction cost advantages. Moreover, reducing the area of units would generally raise the square-foot costs. Every dwelling would have certain fixed and costly items, such as a kitchen and a bathroom, but there would be fewer square feet over which to spread their expense. Building additional area is a relatively cost-effective amenity in housing.

Others, including the architect Donald Mac-Donald in San Francisco, recommend abolishing certain code requirements that add thousands to the cost of a dwelling: double walls between dwellings for better acoustic privacy, fire sprinklers, gentle stairways rather than steep ones, and hallways between kitchens and bathrooms.[17] The easing or deletion of only a few such provisions would make a dramatic difference in affordability. One solution is to move toward a performance-based code that would allow options for conformance. In some cases increasing density on the site by moving buildings closer together could more than offset the cost of improved fire protection systems, for instance, the installation of sprinklers between buildings as well as within them. But many worry about who interprets performance and who accepts liability should problems arise.

Finally, the nature of the subsidy programs for affordable housing also drive up the costs. First,

there is the scramble for limited affordable housing dollars through an increasingly complex application process and the need to knit together many different programs, each with its own administrative costs and requirements. Most tax-credit programs, for example, are based on a point system of features and amenities—the more goodies proposed, like security systems, the more points—and this provides an incentive to make better housing that costs more. The complexity of the application process also fuels the need for expensive consultants. Second, there are the administrative cost of transferring the subsidies. Every agency, program, and bureaucratic unit has a financing cost and a budget. The staff costs for financing real-estate developments are comparable for projects large or small, and the affordable projects are generally smaller, with fewer units over which to amortize these expenses.

REFRAMING THE VIEW

If financing is not available, a site is too encumbered, or the politics are too volatile, market-rate for-profit developers can sit on the sidelines until the conditions are favorable. They can search for the set of conditions they need, even if not in their immediate locale. When they choose to build, they can select their market and the level of amenity. If the compliance cost is high, they can target a lower-end market and gear the amenities, with what money is available, to that client.

The affordable housing developer and architect have few choices. They cannot sit out the game, because it is their mission and often their obligation to create affordable housing. They must compete for limited subsidies with other worthy projects. They cannot change their market and have little choice on the level of amenity. They cannot easily go into other geographical areas, since they are essentially community-based. They can only do their best to create sturdy and dignified hous-

ing, no matter how adverse the economic and political conditions. Americans expect our infrastructure of roads and bridges, electrical lines and
sewers to be the safest, most advanced available.
We tend to see housing, however, not as part of
the infrastructure but as the domain of its occupants. If we take the broader view of housing in
our communities, particularly in urban areas, we
realize that housing is part of the public realm,
like parks, roads, and municipal buildings. Housing defines public spaces; it is something we all
must look at, and it is an aspect of the visual panorama that gives cities their unique character. If it
is poorly designed, poorly made, and poorly maintained, it denigrates everyone, not just its occupants. If it is well made, the occupants become an
integral part of the community, rather than unwanted intruders. Given this objective, everyone
benefits from high-quality affordable housing, and
the cost of this component of the infrastructure
should be borne by us all.

It is difficult to determine what affordable housing really costs. It is like trying to measure a giant,
amorphous cloud: not only does it change shape,
but it is constantly moving. In some urban areas
the cloud may appear denser and more ominous.
An affordable housing unit in a multifamily development in California may cost $65,000 or
$120,000; every component of the cost depends
on the project's characteristics and location. Is it in
a city or a suburb? How big is it? What is the mix
of unit types? Is the site flat or sloping? Is the project controversial? Does it have unusual architectural features? Is the contractor experienced? It is

also difficult to obtain comparative costs data on
projects with similar characteristics.[18] Even the
cost of regulation, which everyone assumes is bur-
densome, is an unknown. As Downs points out,
regulations vary from locale to locale, and regulation also begets benefits, such as increased safety,
sometimes to those who occupy the housing and,
more often, to those in the community.[19] How,
then, does one discern what portion is a burden
to affordable housing? The sources of expense discussed in this chapter relate to the physical aspects
of the building. It is unlikely that lowering the
cost of any one component would have a dramatic
impact on the overall cost of building affordable
housing. It would be like removing a piece of
cloud.

What we must do is refocus our attention.
Many feel we do not have an affordable housing
problem at all but rather an income problem, and
that we should either find ways to increase incomes so that people can afford housing or else increase our commitment to house those without
sufficient incomes.[20]

Research and advances in building techniques
will reveal ways to cut costs. But the real question
for the design of affordable housing is not how
much we can reduce costs; we know we can make
cheaper housing. Instead we need to ask what we
are getting for the money we spend. Is it worth it?
Do we have the resolve to spend the money? How
can we minimize the administrative and overhead
costs and put our dollars into sound and humane
affordable housing?

DESIGN: THINGS BIG AND SMALL, FAR AND NEAR

How do architects begin to design an affordable housing project when confronted with the myriad rules and regulations, stringent budgets, and unrelenting politics? How do they contain, control, and prioritize the range of issues and demands for housing, and then ensure that the result is not just building but architecture? Many affordable housing architects begin by determining the desires of the residents and then interpreting these into a design. Some start with a set of principles for essential housing characteristics, which they develop into physical form. For example, Moshe Safdie, the architect of Habitat in Montreal, believes that every dwelling should have an outdoor area equal to the enclosed living area.[1] To accommodate this goal in high-density projects, he looked to industrialized production and efficient building techniques. The principles or underlying values from which architects derive affordable housing designs are often shaped by what they view as the locus of housing: the individual dwelling, the aggregation of units, or the community.

THE INDIVIDUAL DWELLING

Americans admire single-family houses, and the majority of us live in them. While other countries and other cultures certainly have free-standing dwellings, they also have other housing forms that are acceptable and even favored. In the United States the detached house is an obsession, and home ownership, now at 64 percent, is an essential piece of the American Dream. Given this social context, no multifamily housing can be totally satisfactory. Thus, the affordable housing architect and developer are at a distinct handicap from the get-go. They are creating a form that is perceived as second-rate, and worse still, they are usually building rental housing. Their dilemma has been called "the house versus housing," and solving it requires a paradigm shift for housing.[2]

The two dominant building types for affordable housing in the United States have been the high-rise and the apartment complex. In each case the collective form dominates; there are minimal attempts to recognize, emphasize, or reveal the individual dwellings within the whole. But architects

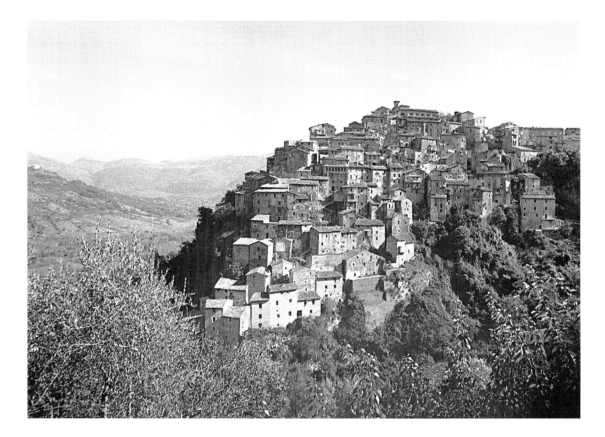

FIG. 25. An Italian hill town is an example of group form, in which individual gestures make a cohesive image.

have always been intrigued by the aggregation of a single element into a larger pattern in which both scales are recognizable and form a symbiotic relationship. This is often referred to as "group form," and the romantic images of Italian hill towns, Greek fishing villages, or pueblos continue to be seductive visions of collective housing forms (fig. 25). Thus, one recurrent approach to affordable housing is to treat multifamily housing as though it were an agglomeration of single-family houses, each with the appropriate amenities.

Succumbing to the popular perception that a detached or identifiable house is the only accept-able housing perpetuates an expensive and ineffi-cient building type; nonetheless, there are sound reasons that the form is so enduring. People invest much of their identity in their dwelling, and the individuality of their house reinforces their own self-worth. Houses also serve as a retreat; they separate the public domain from the personal one and reinforce both the connections between the two domains and the sanctity of the individual within the collective. The archetypal house, with its sidewalk, yard, porch, front door, and foyer, clearly defines the territory of the individual, as well as the transition from public to private space.

Moreover, a house is flexible and expandable, and can survive generations of use as families change.

Architects of multifamily housing strive to create the perception of individual houses at increased densities by connecting individual units, creating a houselike form with several dwellings within it, or designing simple structures and embellishing their facades to reveal the individual dwellings behind them (fig. 26).

ATTACHED HOUSES

If individual houses are ideal, why not make them but just push them closer together? The venerable urban rowhouse does just that. Most of the amenities of the detached house are retained, as is its discrete character. Densities of rowhouses can be quite high—as much as fifty dwellings per acre—and Habitat showed that higher-density high-rise housing is certainly possible. The rowhouse's collective form is the consistent city blocks of buildings that shape the community spaces and streets between them. In Habitat the aggregate form is more that of a hill town.

In the absence of an urban pattern in which to fit the housing, the question for the architect is how close the houses have to be to create a recognizable aggregation (a collective or group form), and how far apart they have to be to reveal their individuality. The architect tries to find a balance, so that up close each dwelling is identifiable, but from a distance the dwellings appear to be an integral whole.

In order to achieve the romantic images of the pueblo and hill town, maximum variation in both the dwellings and their staggering is necessary, whereas consistency and repetition are far more cost-effective. By their very nature, these historical images cannot be held up as the ideal for affordable housing. Hill towns were not built at one time; the forms accreted from structures of different sizes, designs, and orientations. Nor were they

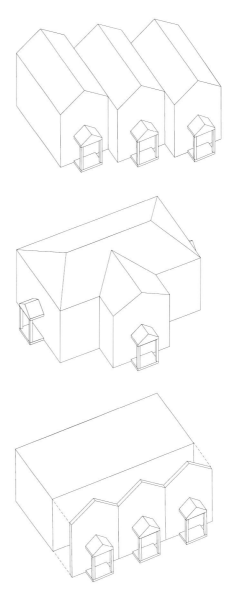

FIG. 26. Three approaches to the individualization of housing: attach individual units; place dwellings within a large, houselike form; or embellish the facades of an otherwise simple building to reveal separate units.

FIG. 27.   Staggering units can add to costs, while not sufficing to define the units as separate dwellings.

FIG. 28 (*opposite, top*).   "Monopoly-box" houses in San Francisco, by Donald MacDonald.

FIG. 29 (*opposite, bottom*).   Donald MacDonald's Two Worlds is a scattering of houses atop a concrete deck.

constrained by parking requirements or the building code. More often than not, efforts to emulate this style result in a series of similar blocks slightly staggered or offset from one another, without due concern for the assemblage (fig. 27). It is a timid approach, one that provides little individuality for the dwelling and none of the distinctiveness of a recognizable collective form.

Technical difficulties also increase the cost of building staggered attached houses. Some believe that if the dwellings are repetitive, the cost of the staggering is inconsequential. But others argue that the expense of the additional perimeter walls, jogged foundations, and complex roof flashing is excessive, particularly given the minimal benefits. If the units are identical but their position relative to each other is offset, the efficient locating of plumbing cores that is possible when bathrooms and kitchens are placed back-to-back against common walls is also sacrificed. And if the units are stacked—perhaps a townhouse over a flat—the sharing of entry stairs among the offset dwellings becomes more complicated.

Still, the lure of the single-family house is so great that many continue to search for ways to employ the type, even on top of parking decks or commercial space. Among them is Donald MacDonald, who proposes the "Monopoly box" as the most efficient, cost-effective, and appropriate of all housing types (fig. 28). For his Two Worlds project in a suburb of San Francisco, built on a concrete deck above parking and retail space, these simplified, archetypal houses are seemingly pitched across a table, coming to rest at odd angles (fig. 29). Since the boxes are identical, MacDonald believes their relationship to one another must be varied for the approach to be effective.

Another strategy is to combine similar dwellings in a very regular pattern, perhaps just two at a time, and then repetitively offset this combination. In this way some of the efficiencies of the recurrent use of a unit are retained, but so too is the

FIG. 30. In Russell Park Student Family Housing in Davis, what looks like a large house is a building of eight apartments.

perception of separate dwellings. This is the basis of the Pajaro solar condominiums discussed in Chapter 5.

BIG HOUSES SUBSUMING LITTLE ONES

The grand apartment houses along Central Park West in New York City are testament to the power of the idea of big houses supplanting individual ones. It is no mystery why these are called apart-ment houses, not apartment buildings. Their grace and distinction obviate the desire for a single house by providing residents with a stately manor that they happen to share with others.[3] Although capable of achieving very high densities, as much as one hundred units per acre, the large house approach is most effective at moderate scales in suburban contexts. As with attached houses, the architecture must emphasize the collective form but still retain vestiges of the individual dwelling. The solution favored by the architects of early apartment houses was to design emphatic entries and public areas at street level and to use domestic-scale windows with bays above.

In affordable housing the use of a recurrent building type is needed to achieve some construction efficiency. For example, Russell Park in Davis, California, designed by Sam Davis Architects and Shen/Glass, is a project of two hundred units. Although placing these units in two or three buildings would have offered the greatest efficiency, the scale would have been too massive. The next most efficient approach is to use the same building type repeated several times. Here each building contains eight units, and there are twenty-five such structures. In these numbers the potential for unrelenting monotony is high, unless there is sufficient variation of forms within the recurring building. Ordinarily such variety might be costly, but since the building is replicated, the efficiencies are retained. Putting eight units in each structure also allows for symmetry along a center line, with each half of the building identical to the other, which again permits efficient construction.

In this example the symmetrical structure has two entry areas, each accessing four units (fig. 30). With only four dwellings sharing an entry area, the residents easily come to know one another, forming small, cohesive clusters throughout the overall complex, and gain a sense of privacy and security. As increasing numbers share entries, corridors, courtyards, or stairways, the sense of neighborliness diminishes.

Since the resulting "big house" is repeated several times, how each structure relates to the adjacent one is critical. Here the roof is the important architectural element. A roof that turns and descends, that has gables and hips, ridges and valleys, can make the building seem like a large, rambling house, instead of either one big apartment building or eight small houses. Obviously a complex roof can be more costly, but since it is repeated

often and can be constructed of premade trusses, construction efficiencies are possible. Even if the disposition of the buildings on the site is very regular, the inherent diversity of the large house form militates against dullness. Rather than seeing each building as a static piece, one views the ends of buildings forming diverse patterns, depending on one's orientation and vantage point.

A similar approach is to connect a few rowhouses but vary the end units, perhaps by stepping them from two floors to one, so that the overall pattern is that of a single larger house. For example, four identical rowhouses are connected into one building, each with an entryway, living room, dining room, kitchen, and patio on the ground floor and two bedrooms and a bathroom upstairs (fig. 31). The building is symmetrical around the center, with the two units on each side sharing an entry porch or portico. In order to vary the form, to give it a more houselike character, an additional bedroom and bathroom are added to the lower floor of the dwellings at each end. This provides for both two- and three-bedroom units within one building, a high level of replication and efficiency in plans and construction, and a varied building mass that can be repeated without tedium.

Another advantage of the big house incorporating several units is the potential for a variety of unit types and sizes within the single form (fig. 32). If a project needs one-, two-, and three-bedroom dwellings, it may be possible to accommodate the mix without making different structures. In the example of the building with eight units, the four lower-level units have a total of eight bedrooms. These might be distributed by making two three-bedroom units and two one-bedroom units. But it is also possible, by locating the interior walls differently, to make all these units two-bedroom dwellings. The buildings are essentially the same, with consistent roofs and foundations.

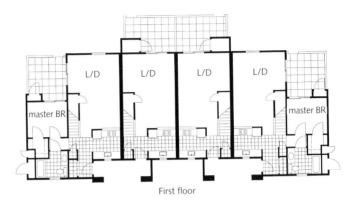

First floor

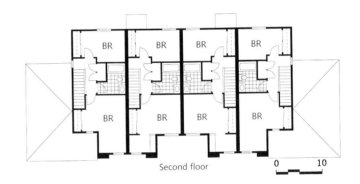

Second floor

0   10

FIG. 31.   Rowhouses linked together for efficiency can be altered at the ends to vary both the unit types and the overall form. The plans of these four units are similar, but two end units have a first-floor master bedroom suite.

FIG. 32 (*opposite*).   The building plan for Russell Park allows different unit types within the same form. The end units can be three-bedroom and the middle one-bedroom apartments, or all the ground-floor units can be two-bedroom apartments.

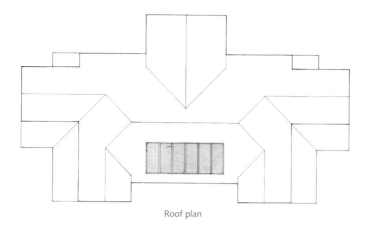

Roof plan

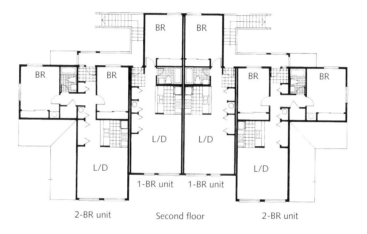

2-BR unit   Second floor   2-BR unit

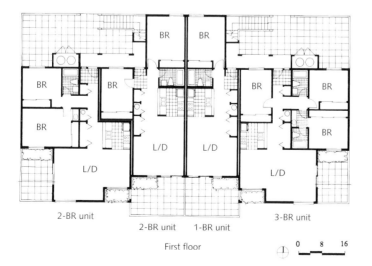

2-BR unit   3-BR unit

2-BR unit   1-BR unit

First floor

0   8   16

FIG. 33 (*left*). John Mutlow's zones of inhabitation create a varied set of spaces and forms. The pavilions and gates (*top*) constitute the most public area, while facade projections, stairs, and patio walls (*middle*) are semiprivate realms.

FIG. 34 (*above*). Gates, courtyard walls, trellises, and awnings enliven housing with texture, shade, shadow, and color.

FIG. 35 (*opposite*). Bickerdike in Chicago shows how large roofs and slight variations in color and form can turn mundane boxes into attractive housing.

THE EMBELLISHED BOX

Obviously, the most efficient structure is a simple form without variation, jogs, or complex roofs. Bare boxes are anathema to architects and to anyone who lives in them. Yet most of what we perceive of a building is its facade, and with some careful and judicious manipulation of the facade in an otherwise simple plan, one can accentuate the individual quality of the dwellings and also achieve some valuable amenities.

John Mutlow, an affordable housing architect in Los Angeles, conceptualizes this approach as zones of inhabitation.[4] The outermost zone is the public space, defined by the buildings and filled with landscaping, gazebos, play areas, and parking. As one moves closer to the structures the zone becomes more private, encompassing patios and the entries to the dwellings, often emphasized by free-standing garden walls (fig. 33). Farther in is the facade of the building, which he conceptualizes as a zone thirty inches thick. Within this zone the simple manipulation of a few elements distinguishes each dwelling, while providing special spaces for the occupants. For example, on the interior a bay is an inhabited space that extends the room, perhaps a small study or sitting area of a bedroom; on the exterior it identifies an individual dwelling, casting a shadow on its facade, and provides covered protection for the dwelling's entry.

Objects and forms in front of or attached to buildings enliven the housing both visually and functionally. Fences, trellises, and porches are parts of the architecture that people see, feel, and use (fig. 34). They go a long way in humanizing a dwelling and giving it an understandable and ap-

FIG. 36. A 1922 conception of courtyard housing.

COLLECTIVE FORMS

proachable scale. Because these features are not expensive, their use need not be consistent or recurring. An occasional variation in window sizes, a few projecting elements like awnings and bays, and even permutations of color and materials are simple gestures that embellish an otherwise mundane box.

In their Bickerdike housing in Chicago, Weese, Langley, Weese Architects incorporated several simple variations in material to adorn what are otherwise plain brick boxes of affordable infill housing. Limestone windowsills, a strip of limestone between a course of bricks, and a few lines of bricks in alternating colors enliven the mundane boxes (fig. 35). According to Cynthia Weese, these small gestures, together with a few bays projecting above the entries to units and the big, encompassing roof, are inexpensive options for elevating an institutional box form into a humane residence.[5]

Architects who see the locus of housing as the individual unit may begin by attaching small dwellings, by making "big houses," or by embellishing simple forms. But many affordable housing architects feel that the grouping of the buildings on the site, not the character of the individual units, is the essence of housing. For them the important principle is the creation of a sense of security, group identity, and shared collective space, and the courtyard is their recurrent theme.

Courtyard housing has been a prevalent type throughout the world, and its use in affordable housing in the United States dates back to the earliest social housing efforts. In their classic 1922 text on planning, *An Architects' Handbook of Civic Art,* Hegemann and Peets illustrated several versions of what they called "cheap" or "inexpensive" housing that included courtyards (fig. 36).[6] Nowhere has the idea been so salient as in California. In *Courtyard Housing in Los Angeles,* Polyzoides,

Sherwood, and Tice discuss the fertile conditions in the early part of the century that led to the regional adaptation of the typology of the housing court.[7] With the Spanish influence in California came a mission-style building that used courts to create a comfortable and secure community in an unfamiliar context. Later these courtyard buildings proliferated both because they made sound housing and because they represented an enduring heritage for the state's thousands of new immigrants. The rapid settlement of the region required an affordable low-rise housing type that could foster an instant community among the newcomers. The openness of the landscape and the mildness of the climate further encouraged a form that at once provided sufficient densities to be efficient and shaped a common usable area.

Even in colder climates, the notions of focusing housing on a commonly controlled functional space and distinguishing that space from the world outside are relevant objectives. Oscar Newman's appeal for "defensible space," in his 1972 book of the same name, is best satisfied by a courtyard, particularly if access to it is restricted and the residents can look out on it from their dwellings. Likewise, Clare Cooper Marcus's plea for safe, observable, and accessible outdoor areas for children is best answered by the housing court.[8]

The emphasis on the court does not mean that the individual units are unidentified. Indeed, early bungalow courts were simply aggregations of separate cottages around a space. But it is the courtyard, serving as a foyer for the dwellings, that marks the physical and perceptual transition from the outside world to the dwelling unit, much as the sidewalk and front porch do for a house.

New affordable housing projects are generally larger than the typical southern California courtyard complex, and there is an expectation for both private and communal outdoor space. The pressures for increased project size and for more amenities have altered the sense of the courtyard from that of a common entry or outdoor living space to that of a semiprivate minipark (fig. 37). While the intentions of the court remain—it provides community focus, a safe haven for children, and a territorial boundary—its clarity in terms of both space and function is confounded. For example, where are the individual entries to dwellings? Are they off the court, as is typical of the southern California prototype, so that the court is continually active and observed, or are they away from the court, focused on the public side of the building, perhaps toward the city street? What is the relationship of the private outdoor space to the courtyard? What interior spaces adjoin the courtyard?

There are no hard-and-fast rules, since much depends on the types of occupants, the intended use of the courtyard, the relationship of the project to the community beyond, and the overall density of the development. In some cases it may be preferable to have the courtyard function as it has done historically: as entry, shared public space, and the transition from public to private domains. The individual units are all accessed through this space, then through the private outdoor space of the unit, which leads into a living area of the dwelling. But while maximizing the benefits of the courtyard, this approach can be unfriendly to the surrounding community by turning the project's back to the public street.

For those who feel that the urban context is sacrosanct, that housing must participate in a continuous urban fabric, dwellings must be entered from the street. The courtyard is then accessed primarily through the dwellings, each of which has a living area adjacent to that open space. The court becomes an extended shared backyard, but it will likely have less activity, except as a protected play area.

The courtyard buildings constructed in the early 1900s in southern California continue to influence many architects who design affordable

housing. But often their inspiration goes far beyond the southern California courtyard type to medieval Europe. In the Carthusian monasteries, which served as the precedent for Le Corbusier's Immeuble Villas, the monks' cells open to private areas, then to shared gardens, and then to public courts; the collective and the individual are seen as symbiotic. The sanctity of the individual is not sacrificed for the collective, but rather the aggregation of their individual spaces determines the collective form. René Davids and Christine Killory cite these buildings as the basis for their award-winning affordable housing. Their projects, described in Chapter 5, are modern, abstract interpretations of the Carthusian complexes.[9]

In affordable housing, when sites are often awkwardly shaped and the design constrained, the amount, quality, and nature of collective outdoor space are important concerns. Is it better to have no such space and rely on private patios alone, or is it better to eliminate the private outdoor area in favor of the court? The lessons of southern California courtyard housing seem to suggest the latter, particularly if the scale of the overall development is modest and the number of people who actually share that space is limited. When this space is carefully planned, perhaps with play equipment, sitting areas, and barbecues, it is a valuable and meaningful amenity. The obsession with the single-family house and its attached private patio or garden undermines the needs of the community and group, while courtyard housing reinforces them. The desire of CDCs and other affordable housing developers to create a community of residents has once again revived interest in the courtyard type.

When there are relatively few units on the ground floor, as in elevator buildings or even three-story walk-ups, the key question is, What is the relation of those who live above the ground level to the court, and how do they get to it? Here again the entry pattern is crucial. If the access to most dwellings is from the street, residents may have no way to enter the courtyard without exiting to the street and walking around the building. This pattern makes the courtyard basically inaccessible to most residents, and therefore less usable and controllable. A ground-level lobby area that has access to both the court and the street is a solution, but this increases the amount of interior space not associated with any one unit, raises the cost of construction and operation, and can be a security problem, particularly if many units must use it. Another obvious solution is to enter all dwellings through the court, perhaps through a secure gate, but this again means turning the development away from the city. Langham Court, discussed in Chapter 5, uses several strategies: There are streetside entries for lower-level units, community rooms and a lobby that have direct access to the courtyard, an internal circulation scheme that allows upper dwellings access to the court without going to the street, and several walk-up units that adjoin the courtyard.

THE COMMUNITY

For much of the past fifty years planners, architects, and housing administrators made housing choices that sacrificed urbanism. The general public has viewed most of the resulting high-density housing for those with low incomes as the modern equivalent of tenements and slums. Those who could afford to do so abandoned the cities for the suburbs, with their clean houses, clear territories, and low densities. But as the affordability of single-family houses diminished, the garden apartment, cluster housing, and the housing courtyard complex became suitable and acceptable, if interim, choices for many people.

For decades the only housing model proposed for cities was the tower in the park. Cities, after all, had parks, and the image of bucolic landscapes shared by all, with new, tall housing detached physically and socially from the maladies of the streets below, seemed like a viable solution. But the towers yielded few of the amenities that people desired, particularly for families and their children who had to rely on elevators and unobserved hallways to go to and from their apartments. The park land below was not a park, it was a no-man's-land—unsafe, dreary, and uninviting. The new housing type was the worst of both worlds—unsatisfactory for its residents and for the neighboring area alike. The urban fabric rotted. Through urban renewal or abandonment, the buildings that once formed continuous walls that defined streets, made corners, and served as the backdrop for public life disappeared, leaving gaping voids.

To avoid similar disasters, affordable housing architects who work in urban areas place a priority on regenerating the city's grid and fabric. While the sanctity of the individual dwelling and the values of the communal court often figure in their work, these architects' major objective is to make buildings that belong to their streets and neighborhoods. The city itself—its vibrancy, its diversity, its density—becomes the one great amenity missing in the suburb.

The best cities are built on a pedestrian's scale,

and they offer pedestrians choice and diversity. For example, in his work on urban patterns, Allan Jacobs reveals that the much-admired walking cities of Europe have many more corners, and therefore more choices, than modern Americans cities; a square mile in the middle of Rome has 504 corners, whereas a square mile in Los Angeles has only 171.[10] The American postwar city was designed around cars and the large spaces they require. A highly textured, pedestrian-oriented city is made up of tightly knit background structures, mostly housing, which form a diverse, varied urban environment. But Americans' fear of teeming cities, and our obsession to detach housing from urban maladies, limited our vision to high-rise building. This vision did not admit European models of humanely scaled urbanism, like the walk-up housing around public squares throughout London.

Once planners recognized that the tower in the park made for poor urban design, and that this form of housing failed to keep the middle class in the cities, they began to look to suburbia for housing models that offered some amenity and security and could be adapted for the city. The garden apartment seemed the likely candidate. Formed around a courtyard and focused inward, it created the perception of a low-density, parklike environment. In San Francisco the success of reasonably high-density low-rise housing like St. Francis Square, built in 1964, gave credence to the applicability of the type in urban areas. Today, after more than a quarter century, this affordable cooperative is still successful, healthy, and much emulated, the recipient of a Twenty-Five-Year Award from the California Council of the American Institute of Architects. But its success, attributable as much to its participatory ownership structure as to its design, has also had a negative impact.

In the 1960s the insertion of garden apartments like St. Francis Square was detrimental to urban communities, notably in San Francisco's Western

Addition, where it was located. During his twelve-year reign as the city's powerful redevelopment director, Justin Herman encouraged reconstituting the entire area into new apartments. He was confident that the only way to keep people within the city was to provide a form of housing that let them believe they were elsewhere. Although the resulting enclaves may impart that comforting perception to residents, the Western Addition as a neighborhood has suffered greatly. There are entire blocks of inward-facing garden apartments, with little connection between one block of housing and the next. The streets between the enclaves are desolate and uninhabited.

The Western Addition is a poignant example because so much housing was built in such a short period, much of it replacing delicate Victorians. Elsewhere in San Francisco, in the outer Mission district, the public housing designed by William Merchant in 1954 also took the approach of creating an isolated enclave. Merchant oriented the buildings with their ends toward the street, thereby making large voids and blank walls viewable from the sidewalk. No dwellings are accessible from the street, and while parallel lines of buildings form courts, these spaces make no territorial claims. Nearby DeCarlo Court, a new affordable design by Daniel Solomon, takes the opposite approach. This project pushes the buildings to the street, forming a continuous wall, while defining a more intimate and private court within. Solomon's buildings respect the city grid and participate in the life of the street. Physically separated by a few blocks, these two affordable projects are conceptually separated by forty years (fig. 38).

For the sake of the city, affordable housing must be seen as a continuous part of the urban fabric. For the sake of the residents, too, it must be part of something else, not a separate enclave that can be identified, isolated, or stigmatized. The work of Goody, Clancy, and Associates in Boston is particularly instructive because it relies on the conti-

FIG. 38. Two views of urban housing on the same street in San Francisco. William Merchant's 1950s public housing (*top*) ignores the street, creating voids along it, whereas Daniel Solomon's 1990s affordable project (*bottom*) completes the street with a continuous building.

FIG. 39.   William Rawn's Charlestown Rowhouses in the Navy Yard of Boston. Several forms are linked, each one particular to its position either along a street or at the water's edge.

FIG. 40 (*opposite*).   Rawn's Back of the Hill Rowhouses in Boston form a two-sided city street.

nuity of scale, pattern, textures, and materials of Boston's traditional stock of buildings. Their housing knits new with old by using front stoops, brick exteriors, and bays. In both their Tent City project, so named because homeless people once camped on the site, and their Langham Court, not far away, the tenants groups were so convinced that the new affordable housing fitted into and strengthened the community that they saw no need for the wrought-iron security gates the architects had proposed. They were right.

William Rawn, also in Boston, sees the urban design imperative as critical not just to integrate the new housing into the community but also to make the street, the traditional urban public

space, better, safer, and more vital. His projects create city streets even where none existed, streets with housing on both sides and with corners. He re-creates a building pattern and scale that encourages choice and pedestrian activity. His simple embellished boxes with relatively few architectural gestures—the bay, the stoop, the cornice, and some changes in the colors and patterns of the bricks—create diverse buildings, and equally diverse public space in front of them.

For his Charlestown Rowhouses in the Navy Yard, an area without housing, Rawn anticipates future development by setting the precedent for a new urban street. Rowhouses run the length of the street, but at the ends are different building forms

that emphasize its unique orientation or varied conditions and reinforce the size and shape of existing structures. A round building toward the water capitalizes on panoramic views, while a large, cabled structure at the opposite end of the rowhouses emulates the wharf buildings along the existing street (fig. 39). The three forms of housing are appended to one another, each fulfilling the urban obligation to its public side.

Rawn has also designed rowhouses in Boston's Mission Hill that fulfilled two important criteria of urban design (fig. 40). First, they filled a gap in the area, thus solidifying the community, but equally important, they did so by creating new streets with housing on both sides. This project

best represents the tenets of urban design that Rawn applies to each affordable housing project: it must reinforce the continuity of the street, of the existing scale, and of the existing fabric, and it must do this through double-sided streets.[11]

DWELLING UNITS

Regardless of whether the focus of the design is the individual dwelling, the cluster, or the community, the dwelling plan itself must work well. Whatever principles underlie the selection of building form and the disposition of the buildings on the site, people are to live inside them. If the units are unpleasant, inefficient, or inappropriate for the occupants' needs, the housing will be a failure.

Unit planning seems like a relatively easy task, and various manuals and guides state minimum sizes for rooms, appropriate layouts, and sizes of furnishings and equipment.[12] But they offer little advice about what makes an interior a special place. The real task for the architect is to elevate requirements into prospects. What is the prospect for someone to curl up in front of a window with light filtering through and read a book? A requirement that a dwelling's front door be in proximity to the coat closet says nothing about the transition from the outdoors, the significance of thresholds in architecture, or the simple act of entering your house carrying packages, mail, or groceries, fumbling for your keys, and setting the items down on a table at the entry, while not disturbing those within the dwelling.

The patterns of people's lives should be the inspiration for the unit plan. But in housing in which many different people will live over time, none of whom are known to the architect, this is a difficult proposition. Surveys of user needs, market research, and guidelines can be useful in avoiding catastrophic planning mistakes, like designing a living room that will not fit a couch, but they cannot substitute for an understanding of how people will inhabit the dwelling. Does the dwelling provide a sense of freedom and choice, allowing residents to move effortlessly throughout? Or does the arrangement of rooms and hallways confine movement and force residents to conform to someone else's conception of how they are to occupy their home?

A poignant example of a historical discrepancy between requirement and prospect occurs in *Public Housing Design*, published in 1946 by the Federal Public Housing Authority.[13] A section on storage space in low-income housing discusses the pros and cons of closet doors. People favor doors,

the authors admit, but they question whether the intensity of this desire outweighs the costs. After all, they claim, doorless closets will encourage people to be neat, and without door swings small rooms will function more efficiently. For a more recent example, consider a dwelling that has two master bedroom suites, each self-contained and with its own bathroom. This type of dwelling would suit many low-income households: unrelated seniors who want to share an apartment in order to reduce their living costs or simply to have companionship, or young adults who are newly employed and in need of affordable housing. But because it does not fit the funding rules, government guidelines, or conventional conceptions of subsidized housing, this type of affordable dwelling is never seen. In fact, until the recent inclusion of programs for single parents and for the homeless, any alternatives to the traditional dwelling types were rare.[14]

Sensitivity to patterns of inhabitation may yield different plans, even within the conventional unit type. Should a dwelling have two public rooms—a living room and a family room—or one large space? Because two rooms often require more space and the open plan is both efficient and flexible, the latter is most common. But families with children, or unrelated adults who share, may want separate spaces for simultaneous activities. Separate spaces can allow adults to talk or entertain while the children are studying or watching television. Or think about bathrooms. If all the fixtures—shower, toilet, sink—are in one room, only one person can use them at a time. Compartmented bathrooms or bedrooms with sinks were once common in boardinghouses, but they are rare in affordable housing. Part of the motive for one-room bathrooms has to do with cost—plumbing is expensive and needs to be centralized to be efficient—but rules, habits, and conservative attitudes have also precluded experimentation.

Rules governing space standards are a two-edged sword for the affordable housing architect. Larger rooms can compensate for a poor unit design, but most funding sources place strict limits on overall unit size. These restrictions are part of the legacy that affordable housing must not be too good or too big or have too many amenities. Rules that define minimum sizes, intended to protect occupants from meager housing, can be equally troublesome when they become the norm. For example, the stipulated bedroom for a child may be larger than needed merely for sleeping but too small for play. It may be better for children to have intimate sleeping chambers, far smaller than regulations allow, but then a larger shared space for study and play.

MAKING SMALL SEEM LARGE

There is a difference of opinion among architects and affordable housing suppliers about the cost of the dwelling size. Whether a building has 800 square feet of living space or 1,600, the developer must pay for the site, the design, the contractor, the materials, and so on. The more you build, the more cost-effective the entire undertaking, owing to bulk ordering of materials, repetition of the actions of the work force, and effective use of equipment brought to the site. If a unit costs $60 a square foot to build, an 800-square-foot dwelling would cost $48,000. But if the unit were enlarged to 1,000 square feet, would it really cost $12,000 more to build? Probably not.

Even though additional living space may come cheap, there are those who are convinced that if we can make things smaller, substantial savings will be realized. The rising cost of housing, they argue, is a result of our succumbing to the desire for dwelling sizes that are far beyond our means to pay for them. The San Francisco architect Donald MacDonald believes that the answer to affordabil-

ity is a product that allows people to buy what they want, a house in an urban area. By analyzing his market and product very carefully, he has devised a set of design rules and construction strategies, guided by his belief that we should think of housing as we do cars. When gas prices went up, cars got smaller; as affordability diminishes, houses should get smaller.[15]

MacDonald's Monopoly-box configuration is particularly efficient, because it encloses the most space for the least amount of surface material, is conventionally and simply constructed, and is easily replicated. The basic twenty-by-twenty-foot house has two floors, each with 400 square feet (fig. 41). The plan calls for slab-on-grade foundations, simple two-by-four wood-stud construction, no premade trusses or lumber larger than two-by-ten, and plywood exteriors. The unit planning is also based on cost-effectiveness. The bathroom is on the ground floor, which reduces the length and extent of plumbing lines. The bedrooms must also then be placed at this lower level. As a result the living room is on the second floor, where it can take advantage of higher ceilings under the archetypal gabled roof. The living room, kitchen, and dining area are all combined in the "grand room," generally twenty-by-twenty feet in area, but seemingly much larger by virtue of the high ceilings.

To make this grand room seem even larger, it has no interior walls. Because the bedrooms are below, there is no stair rising through the grand room; it is an unobstructed area. The kitchen is placed against the wall and has no upper-level cabinets, so as not to detract from the perception of the open volume. Even the arms of the sofas are removed to make the space less cluttered. This illusion is completed by an oversized window that illuminates the space while changing its scale and by smaller windows in the adjacent wall, to ensure that the room has no dark corners (fig. 42).

In these Monopoly-box houses the minimum

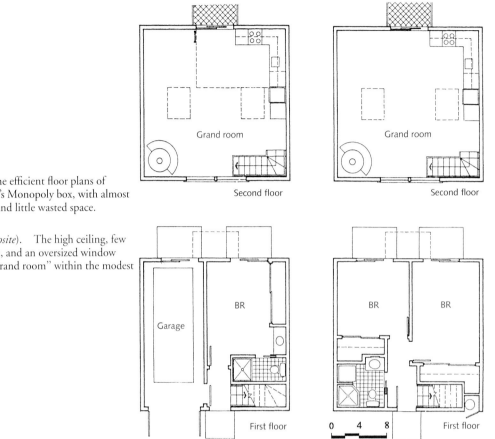

FIG. 41. The efficient floor plans of MacDonald's Monopoly box, with almost no hallway and little wasted space.

FIG. 42 (*opposite*).   The high ceiling, few obstructions, and an oversized window make the "grand room" within the modest dwelling.

is made to feel generous, and MacDonald has thoughtfully, even obsessively, scrutinized every detail to lower costs and create the illusion of more space. He has even tried mirroring the walls and baseboards. But he has been unsuccessful in providing this product as subsidized housing. Agencies, sponsors, and government regulators are suspicious of the minimal unit, and the small lot zoning that allows it to be a truly independent house simply does not exist in most urban areas. Rather than fight these battles, MacDonald develops the houses for the low end of the for-profit market, noting that the early homes in Levittown were also only 800 square feet. But the Levittown

buyer got larger sites, with space to build additions to the house, and the ability to move directly from the living room into the yard.

The issue for most affordable housing architects is how to ensure the design control and thought exhibited in MacDonald's work but remain within the rules and regulations that protect against the utterly small. In this arena mirrors will not do.

CAN SMALL BE BEAUTIFUL?

Fluid space and good lighting can make even a small dwelling seem free and open, rather than confined and oppressive. Poor use of space, par-

ticularly awkward and inefficient circulation, is the most recurring criticism of affordable housing. If one wants to make a dwelling seem larger, eliminating, or at least limiting, hallways should be a first step. Hallways are a necessary evil: they separate rooms and provide privacy for each space. But they are generally windowless and therefore dark, and not much can go on in them. MacDonald's Monopoly-box houses have virtually no hallways, only an entry at the lower level and a stairway to the living room above.

One way to limit or eliminate halls is to use functional space for circulation. The circulation space can visually expand the room without interrupting its use if the "path" passes along the edge of the room rather than diagonally across it. Passing through one room to get to another is appropriate if the room is a public area, such as a living room or family room, but not if it is a private space or a work area, like a kitchen. Having a connecting bathroom between two bedrooms eliminates a hallway but entails a major loss of privacy and limits the arrangement of bedroom furniture.

Situating the entry in the middle of a dwelling

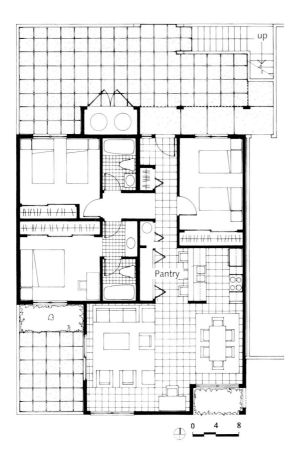

up

Pantry

0 4 8

FIG. 43.   Borrowing space from a hallway can make the unit seem larger. Here, the widened passageway accommodates an informal eating area at a kitchen counter.

is another way to limit hall space. The entry area, a transition from the outside, doubles as a means of connecting rooms to one another. When row-houses are attached, however, it is difficult to situate the entry in the middle, and the occupant is forced to move through the front space to reach other parts of the dwelling.

When hallways are unavoidable, making them large enough to be functional can make the dwelling seem more spacious. Widening a hallway, a seemingly inefficient gesture, can provide an extra nook, perhaps a study space, without much increase in cost. Hallways that border kitchens can be widened to allow room for a buffet (fig. 43). While not supplanting a dining space, this option may be particularly appealing for families with children who may not want to eat every meal at the table. Furthermore, the resulting openness makes both the small kitchen and the required hall seem larger.

Small rooms can also be made to seem larger if they look out toward the world. Views both encourage social interchange within the unit and make the housing less alienating to those outside. If one is cooking a meal in an eight-by-eight-foot kitchen, the common size in affordable housing, being able to look out to another space, either indoors or outdoors, is certainly less isolating than being completely enclosed, and it allows parents to supervise their children while they are working.

In Japanese landscaping there is a concept called "borrowed scenery." The private garden is conceived as a foreground view for the larger panorama. In this way the private space is part of a grander scheme, extending its perceived domain. This concept is useful for affordable housing, since borrowing scenery or outdoor space is a relatively inexpensive device. A small patio extends a living room, and if this patio adjoins a courtyard and each can be seen from the other, then the world of the dwelling has been enlarged.

One's perception of an individual dwelling as

part of a larger domain can also be enhanced by the character of the transitional space. In the single-family house, the transitional space consists of the sidewalk, fence, private walk, porch or stoop, foyer—all the surfaces one walks on or alongside. In multifamily housing this experience is often dramatically abridged; one merely comes to a door from a walkway and directly into a living room. There is no threshold, no sense of entering. But even in elevator buildings, a recess along the corridor, perhaps with a ledge, a flower box outside, and an entry space within, can provide a sense of transition and make small dwellings more dignified.

Vistas, outlooks, and transitions from one interior space to another and to the outdoors can make minimal spaces seem larger, but natural lighting is perhaps the architect's most salient tool for enlarging the perception of a small space. Light varies throughout the day, and as it changes it highlights different walls and surfaces, providing a diverse impression and understanding of a space. The changing patterns mean the room is never exactly the same. It is animated, never stagnant.

The placement of windows requires a delicate balance of function, costs, and architectural composition. A window in the middle of a wall makes the areas on either side appear darker and the room appear smaller. A window near the corner of a room reflects light onto the side wall, making the space appear brighter and the room larger, while projecting light deeper into the dwelling. The objective of more light, evenly distributed and balanced, perhaps from two sides of a space, often comes in conflict with other requirements. Lighting rooms from two sides becomes more difficult as housing density increases. The desire for daylight sometimes conflicts with the need for privacy or with the best placement of furniture. Windows with lower sills, for example, make a wall seem brighter and more open. If a room is on an upper floor, a lower sill makes it easier to look

down onto a yard. But if the only place in the room for a sofa is in front of the window, or if people can easily view into the window from a walkway, then a lower sill won't work.

There are also regulations that govern the size and placement of windows. For example, bedroom windows require a minimum opening for easy rescue during fires, and energy regulations may limit the amount, type, and orientation of glazing. When housing is well designed and small units are made to feel larger and dignified, the architect has organized all these considerations into a balanced composition of the building's facades.

FLEXIBILITY

If there is a single, overriding objective for the architect of affordable housing, it is to make a dignified dwelling. One aspect of dignity is choice. Choice can be something as simple as options for placing furniture in a room, or it can mean options in the form of a dwelling or the number of spaces it contains. Another aspect of dignity is known as fit, the correlation between the living patterns of the occupant and the features of the dwelling. Well-designed single-family homes have a comfortable and loose fit. When an owner's needs change, or outgrow the fit, the dwelling can be altered. Or if it cannot be suitably altered, the occupant moves. In affordable housing, though, fit can be as much a matter of luck as of planning. There are few options for redesigning the interior, and residents usually have even fewer options for moving.

The issues of choice, fit, and flexibility are recurring topics for architects and housing theorists.[16] The desire by government agencies and affordable housing suppliers for specificity and codified standards has forced subsidized housing into a tight fit, which has resulted in costly, repetitive, institutionalized, and often inappropriate housing. Design and planning strategies that attempt to loosen the fit of affordable housing fall into two categories: increasing the size and decreasing the specificity of housing, and providing devices for changing the dwelling.

When a dwelling is large, the occupants have more choices, either about where to go in the dwelling or about how to furnish and outfit its spaces. Large private houses provide a separate room for each activity, granting maximum choices with minimum conflicts. One reason loft space works so well for artists is its generous volume and incredibly loose fit. There are no obstructions, no walls—just light and space. These ingredients are essential for an artist's work, but they also offer maximum choice and freedom. The conversion of industrial loft space into dwellings, an increasingly popular urban housing type, is appealing to young adults partly because it is relatively inexpensive and close to jobs but also because it allows so many ways of inhabiting the space. You can divide the loft into conventional rooms, you can insert whole "minibuildings" that incorporate kitchens and bathrooms, or you can leave it as a large, open area.

An important dimension of unit size and flexibility is time. Life patterns, cycles, and needs change, particularly for households with children. Each newborn brings new requirements for the dwelling. As the children grow, the needs of the family change. Play space, privacy, and storage are aspects of a dwelling in constant evolution. If affordable housing is seen as temporary, only for those in transition, then the assumption is that people will move as their needs change. This is a serious miscalculation. Where will they go? Is there a suitable affordable dwelling nearby to meet their needs? The assumption that residents will move as the fit constricts also encourages transience and reduces community cohesion.

One response to the issue of evolving needs is a flexible dwelling, and it takes several forms. The first is the subdividable unit. In a version of the granny, in-law, or shadow apartment, dwellings are designed to allow for what biologists call mitosis, the separation of one unit into two totally self-sufficient entities. When a family is small and young, perhaps they need only a modest dwelling; as they grow, they subsume the adjoining space; as the children leave home, the parent or parents revert to the small space.

A second strategy is to incorporate several different types of units within a single building, so that residents can move from smaller to larger dwellings or vice versa. This strategy works well with the form of "big houses subsuming little ones," discussed earlier. While it does not afford the same flexibility as altering the size of the unit, it is an inexpensive way to provide some alternatives for residents. Obviously, the management issues are acute, but having a varied mix of units provides for longer-term residency within a development and also encourages a more heterogeneous population.

A third approach is to append space to a dwelling, expanding either out or up as needed. The dwelling starts small but grows incrementally. This growth might entail overbuilding the original structure, much like finishing a basement or attic, or simply enclosing a deck or patio.

Another set of strategies allows for flexibility through physical changes within the unit. In a loft, for example, walls can be inserted and moved without altering the structure. Privacy, variation, and fit are achieved. In MacDonald's very small Monopoly-box house, the placement of the grand room on the second floor, under the roof, makes it possible to build a loft later, if needed.

Many architects of affordable housing have attempted to create neutral or ambiguous unobstructed areas and have supplied residents with movable walls or large-scale components, like closets on casters, to divide the volume. Occupants then custom-design the space to fit their own needs, with little expense and physical effort. In some cases these ideas are quite sophisticated, requiring flexible plumbing connections and high-tech, multiuse furniture.

Creativity and experimentation, however, require research and development, as well as a risk-taking curiosity—all of which are discouraged and restricted by affordable housing suppliers and government agencies. In the case of interior flexibility, for example, code officials ask how one would assure that a heating and ventilating system or electrical distribution would be effective regardless of the configuration devised by the occupants. Financing agencies and lenders ask how they are to appraise a dwelling if the number of rooms is unknown or variable, and how movable large-scale furniture components are to be financed.

Unit alteration, on the other hand, is feasible and conforms to regulation; in fact, it is often required by code. Regulations in many states stipulate that all units with kitchens, bedrooms, and a bathroom that are either at ground level or accessible by elevator must be adaptable for physically disabled residents. This entails designing larger hallways, doorways, and bathrooms within the unit and using cabinets and fixtures that can be modified.

The simple strategy of incorporating several unit sizes within a building is constrained by management logistics. One problem is how to coordinate the evolving needs of various groups. Furthermore, the funding of affordable housing requires a set program and generally calls for larger units. Making two-bedroom units next to one-bedroom units with the anticipation that they might later become three-bedroom units poses great difficulty in developing a financing program under current programs and policies. Density restrictions also preclude it. In the United States density is often determined by units per acre, a rather inexact measurement, since it treats a small studio and a three-bedroom townhouse as equivalent. If one begins by creating three-bedroom

units in order to obtain financing but plans to divide these later into smaller dwellings, there may be a breach of the entitlements.

Further constraints are technical, although these are comparatively minor. The code requires that adjacent apartments be separated by construction fire breaks and sound barriers. If a large apartment is to be subdivided at a later date, these provisions would have to be incorporated at the outset, or they would have to be inserted at greater cost at the time of the alteration. Finally, increasing unit size, a strategy that many feel is the most cost-effective means of providing loose fit, has the negative side-effect of either forcing larger units on a site or reducing density, as well as requiring higher energy and maintenance costs.

In sum, politics, regulation, and conservative attitudes are stacked against innovation in affordable housing. The question for the affordable housing architect is, Are the battles worth waging, or is it more prudent to accept the norm and use more modest methods to make minimal spaces seem larger? Small gestures—a bay window, a nook, a patio—are space expanders and provide residents with some choices.

ORNAMENTATION, DETAILS, AND DIGNITY

Obviously, an embellished box is more inviting than a bare box; architectural details and ornamentation can add dignity to a dwelling unit. But given the acute need for affordable housing, how can architectural embellishments be a legitimate concern? How does one justify their cost? When is a detail merely an ornamental appliqué, an unnecessary frill, or the conceit of the architect, and when is it an integral and appropriate part of the design, intended to make housing more humane?

Early in this century a concatenation of architectural principles and social and political tenets yielded modernism, or the international style, which eschewed all ornamentation. For early modernist architects the promise of industrialization lay in machines that could efficiently turn out things once made by hand. The beauty of the industrial process was in its repetitiveness and exactness, and a machine aesthetic seemed both appropriate and inevitable. These beliefs were incorporated into architecture even when such processes were not used, and the modernists imbued their design choices with a moral imperative: functionalism, simplicity, and the honest use of new materials and processes were proper in a society in which the social strata were becoming blurred and in which economy of means was a sign of a healthy capitalism.[17] Heavily ornamented buildings were seen as the exclusive purview of the rich, evidence of an unhealthy attachment to a past that was inequitably opulent. Modernism was a moral force that would bring design to the middle and lower classes.

The lack of detail and the premise that any nonfunctional design element was superfluous fit well into the patronizing aspect of social housing. Utility took precedence over visual stimulation and was justified from both an economic and an artistic point of view. Modern architecture was clean, safe, and progressive, adherents argued, and the buildings fulfilled the basic needs of their occupants. But the unadorned forms were also sterile and dehumanizing. Standardization, minimal detail, and the absence of embellishment made for unrelenting sameness. Rather than elevate the residents to a higher status, as modernist proponents had optimistically hoped, the stripped-down buildings further alienated and isolated them.

It is a mistake to think that ornamentation has no function; even rain gutters and scuppers were once very elaborate. Decorative elements like filigrees, gargoyles, and friezes of older public buildings serve to make them visually distinctive. Such architectural details as changes in materials, cornices, and functional attachments, like awnings or shutters, give walls relief and cast shadows on the facades that impart a three-dimensional solidness to the surface. Smaller detailed elements give the viewer a way to relate to the scale of the larger building mass and to understand the structure. We know, for example, where to enter a building, because the doorway is scaled for our passage. This door may be modest for a dwelling, making us feel welcome and comfortable, or it may be grand and imposing for a public building, inspiring awe of the institution.

There are two types of detail or ornamentation that housing architects use and manipulate: functional elements, like doorways and windows, and decorative details, like color, materials, and appliqué.

DETAILS AND AFFORDABILITY

Part of the architect's job is to make judgments about and selections for the thousands of elements in a building. The selection of a single window entails many decisions: How large will it be? Where will it be placed to make the facade's proportions correct? Where will it go to make the room interior work well? What shape will it be? What color will the frame be? One of the principles of modernism is that these decisions can be made rationally, that design is a response to functional and scientific criteria. This, of course, is a false premise, and even in highly functional and technical designs, like those for airplanes, there are thousands of decisions based on intuition and stylistic inclinations. Buildings certainly have structural and safety requirements, but these can be accommodated in endless ways.

At the root of these decisions is architectural style. In the housing project discussed in Chapter 2, for example, the CDC requested a Tuscan theme. Discussions of style make architects uncomfortable, however, partly because, notwithstanding its failures, the lure of modernism and the scientific rationalism it implies is still very strong, and partly because buildings last a long time, and style, often equated with fashion, seems so ephemeral. Furthermore, most architects would argue that the style or look of a building should evolve from its program, site, and context, not from the sponsor's aesthetic predisposition. Architects prefer to discuss housing image in terms of a type—a building form—or an analogy. A bungalow courtyard is a type whose visual characteristics, or style, will depend on its geographical location; the form is more significant than the image. With analogies, one can say that a project is like a village or like a hill town, thereby evoking an image that does not, however, demand artificial stylistic replication, such as one might find in Disneyland.

Other architects believe that aesthetic issues supersede most other considerations. Antoine Predock's The Beach, a seventy-four-unit affordable housing project in Albuquerque (see Chapter 5), was inspired by the idea of making visual references to the mountains beyond and to the nearby commercial strip. Predock then formed mini-mountains of housing and outlined them in neon. For some architects a distinctive style is a suitable substitute for livability or amenity in housing. Ricardo Bofill's imposing complex in the suburbs of Paris makes the statement that the *appearance* of living in a castle is equivalent to actually living in one (fig. 44). Stairways are placed within immense pillars, huge archways enclose vast plazas. Never mind that there is no private outdoor space or that residents must park their cars hundreds of yards from their houses.

More often the stylistic issue in affordable housing is determined by the sponsor's desire for the project to be a good neighbor by fitting in and, of course, by the budget. There is little money for purely decorative detail and ornamentation, although sometimes a local community group or artist volunteers to embellish buildings with a mural, as happened for James Lee Court in Oakland

FIG. 44.   Grand gestures, like those of Ricardo Bofill in France, attempt to supplant convenience and amenity with a perception of opulence.

(see Chapter 2). Instead, the selection of materials, their color, and their careful combination and placement are the means for enlivening buildings. Functional elements like gutters, downspouts, and window trim take the place of friezes and cornices in providing scale, texture, and vitality.

Exterior materials have a dramatic effect on the look of housing. Plywood siding is a very inexpensive exterior material and is often used, though it is difficult to maintain. A plywood-sided building needs to have wood trim to cover the joints between the sheets for waterproofing. Trim is required at the corners of the building, around windows, and at the eaves. Although functional, this trim is also decorative. Variations in the size and pattern of the trim and the use of colors that contrast from the main building are inexpensive options for adding texture without greatly increasing costs.

Variations in the color, texture, and thickness of exterior walls are possible with all materials. Bricks, for example, come in various dimensions, colors, and finishes, and it is common to see several different types used to modulate the exterior of a set of rowhouses. Often brick patterns are used to demarcate the base, middle, and top of a building, giving it a more human scale, particularly in comparison to a building with a consistent color and texture. The insertion of a precast concrete or stone band that runs horizontally and continuously around the building, as in the Bickerdike project in Chicago (see fig. 35), creates reveals and shadow lines that make for more diversity in the facades. Sometimes this banding coincides with the windows, tying the openings together visually and adding a perceived thickness that makes the building appear more substantial.

Making a wall seem thicker and more substantial is important, because low-rise affordable housing that is built with wood, even if the exterior is stucco or brick, can have a thin appearance that makes it seem flimsy. This flatness largely results from the way common metal-framed windows are manufactured and installed; they are nailed to the outside of the building in a plane flush with the exterior finish. Older buildings have much thicker walls and custom windows with frames placed flush with the interior wall, so that the window aperture is recessed from the outside, revealing the full thickness of the wall. Although metal window manufacturers make nail-on windows that can be set within an opening rather than over it, they are costly. So architects try other, inexpensive means to achieve the same effect. For a stucco exterior it is possible to make a frame around the windows using metal strips called expansion joints (fig. 45). This frame, even if it is flush with the exterior wall, can be painted a contrasting color, which makes the windows seem more prominent.

It is also relatively easy to increase the thickness of parts of the exterior wall by placing foam inserts onto the structure before the building is covered with stucco. Setting these protrusions around doors and windows or at corners makes the wall seem more solid. Rob Wellington Quigley used the necessary expansion joints in the stucco as decorative elements in a single-room-occupancy building in San Diego. Lines made by the metal radiate from the entryway in a sunburst pattern, making the doorway more prominent. Typically these devices are used around windows or doors, aspects of the building to which the eye is already attracted. It is at these places that building scale is most comprehensible, since one can imagine people looking out of windows or passing through the doors. These areas become the important points of encounter for the building.

Giving special care, attention, and detail to the elements of a building that people actually encounter helps to create a human scale in a cost-effective way. People sit under a trellis that covers a patio and creates shade; they pass alongside gates

FIG. 45.   Thickening the wall around windows, or simply painting a contrasting color around the opening, can make the windows more prominent.

and fences that can either be solid walls or offer glimpses of life beyond; and they walk into buildings under awnings or on porches. Similarly, landscape design, an inexpensive item that often gets too little attention, can bring color, fragrance, shade and shadow, vitality and humanity to a project.

A final important element of a building is the roof. Donald MacDonald's fixation with the Mo-

nopoly box is only partly economic; he feels this shape is crucial because it is the archetypal dwelling form in the United States, strongly associated with cultural norms of good housing. Children draw this image when asked to depict a house. A roof, with its gables, dormers, and eaves, is the enveloping element, protecting the inhabitants both physically and psychologically. We are all happy to have "a roof over our heads." The modernist buildings, with their flat roofs, ignored the significance of this element.

The junction between the roof and the wall is fertile territory for architectural detail. A roof that projects beyond the walls accentuates the building's sheltering qualities. It can also make the exterior walls seem lower to passersby because it casts shadow on the higher portions, and it protects the walls from rain. Knee braces under the eaves, while usually decorative and not structural, can add yet another level of detail and interest to the facades.

It is not so much a question of whether an architect should or shouldn't add detail to affordable housing. Rather, it is a matter of seeing the necessary walls, roofs, windows, and doors as areas of opportunity for giving it vitality.

CARS

Cars, like single-family homes, are an American obsession; they too provide freedom, independence, and flexibility. But the social costs of these benefits include air pollution, the exhaustion of nonrenewable natural resources, and the construction and maintenance of an endless network of paved roads. Our twin obsessions with cars and houses have also conspired to make housing less affordable. To satisfy the desire for the single-family house, away from the ills of the city, we continue to develop land farther and farther from the urban cores, the centers for services, jobs, and efficient public transportation systems. Newly developed land needs new infrastructure, and low housing densities mean that the cost of these improvements is amortized over relatively few houses.

Although some developers have taken to building housing around commuter transit stations as a strategy to both increase density and discourage car use, it is likely too late to make a significant change in our car-oriented culture. A few courageous planners posit pedestrian pockets, small

neighborhoods that rely on housing mixed with commercial uses in suburban areas that emulate the rich walking environments found in older cities. But thus far they have been unable to attract the necessary combination of uses to make a self-sustained community. So much of American life is automobile-based that the longest, most tedious commutes do not seem to change driving habits. Unless we are beset by a sustained gas shortage, we will always have cars, and more of them.

Any discussion of the design of affordable housing must therefore include the automobile. Providing parking is a complex and costly problem. Local planning ordinances require at least one parking space per unit, and more spaces for larger units. So for each three-bedroom dwelling, a size prevalent in affordable housing, codes require 2.5 parking spaces, even though statistics of affordable housing may show car ownership at only 1.5 cars per unit. Thus, a fifty-unit development would be required to have 125 parking places. A geometrically efficient parking design, one that groups all the cars in one lot, could consume an entire acre. If the project is to be built at a modest density of twenty units per acre, the property is only 2.5 acres, and cars could cover 40 percent of the site. But one massive 125-car parking lot will not do if one thinks about the residents. Their cars are likely to be their most expensive possessions, and protecting them—from theft and vandalism, as well as exposure to the weather—is important. Like everyone else, people who live in affordable housing want their cars enclosed within their units, in their own garages.

Local planning authorities and city engineers are rarely flexible when reviewing parking designs. Maximal lane widths, few obstructions, and wide turning radii are the norm. Narrow lanes, which would reduce the amount of paving and its visual impact while encouraging drivers to proceed slowly, are rarely approved.

Faced with these exigencies, the architect has

four priorities. The first is to disperse the cars, to mitigate their visual impact. Approaching a house through a sea of parked cars is not only unpleasant but also disorienting for residents and visitors. Second is to place the parking as close to the units as possible, for both convenience and security, even though dispersing the cars into smaller compounds will mean that cars and driveways cover half the site. Third is to make the lots pleasant; landscaping and changing paving materials help. In some warm-weather communities the energy codes, in an irony that turns fuel-consuming cars into energy savers, require that half the lot be shaded to reduce heat gain and therefore energy use in the adjacent housing; placing trees between every third or fourth car satisfies this rule. Finally, safety is an important consideration. The usual approach is to locate parking at the periphery of the site, creating protected and contiguous open space within for children's play areas and for pedestrians. But this places the cars far from many units and makes them, not the housing, the predominant image for the entire development. For urban housing, perimeter parking breaks the continuity of buildings along the street.

Given the wishes of the residents, the city, and the architect, the best solution is to hide the cars, preferably within the building and adjacent to the units. But this solution is by far the costliest. Providing underground parking for three or four cars costs as much as building a dwelling above. Unless the project is very large or the land very constrained, it is not a viable solution. Furthermore, landscaping the top of parking garages—particularly planting large trees—is also very expensive.

Sheltered parking at ground level is sometimes feasible, but it requires driveways that run to each building. At higher densities the extensive paving covers almost all the land, and the facades of buildings become endless walls of blank garage doors or gaping, doorless voids. A three-bedroom, two-story townhouse of 1,200 square feet will have 600 square feet on the ground level. Storing two cars takes up about 450 square feet, leaving little living area at the ground and forcing the plan to three floors. Access to a private outdoor space or a courtyard will no longer be contiguous with the living area.

Architects covet European images of social housing from the 1920s and 1930s, with their narrow, pedestrian-oriented streets and high densities. These are humane, dignified urban structures that fit comfortably among more affluent residences or in commercial areas. What is attractive about these designs is their diminutive scale and diverse texture. But Europeans rely more heavily on public transportation, and these developments were created when cars were luxury goods. Architects who aspire to design this type of housing today in the United States cannot retain the romantic image when half the site must be set aside for cars. Ordinances on the number and required dimensions of parking spaces, the unyielding attitude of city engineers toward driveway sizes, and the need for low-cost designs militate against tightly knit, pedestrian-oriented planning.

It is easy to throw up one's hands and capitulate to the car. Or one can decide to focus on the dwellings and forgo the notion of making pleasant parking areas. But another approach, one that is relatively inexpensive, is to provide for the car as if it were a guest, not a member of the family. We want our guests to be safe and well cared for, but we do not want them to control our lives. When the guests are gone, their space should be usable for other purposes, even if the alternative use is purely visual. So one conceptualizes a parking space as an open area that accommodates cars but also provides people with something pleasant to look at as they walk around the site or gaze from their windows: trellis-covered parking, with vines that enshroud the cars, or tree islands interspersed throughout the lots.

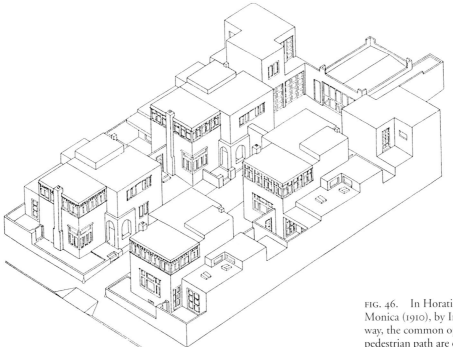

FIG. 46.   In Horatio West Court in Santa Monica (1910), by Irving Gill, the driveway, the common open space, and the pedestrian path are one and the same.

Aggressive parking schemes allow cars to intrude onto what is clearly a pedestrian space. Here the car is tolerated for those brief moments when it is moved. Anyone who has played football or stickball on the street knows how useful the space can be. Cars even serve as goal lines or bases, and the game is suspended intermittently as traffic passes. Courtyard housing often takes this approach because of the need to double the use of its meager open space. The court serves as a recreational area, a communal space, and of necessity, parking. Pavers or stones, trees, and planted areas are clues that the space is for people, while their size and distribution indicate that cars do come in there. Irving Gill's renowned Horatio West Court in Santa Monica, California, is an early example of attached houses with a shared pedestrian and vehicular access (fig. 46).

The architect Daniel Solomon's DeCarlo Court and Fulton Grove in San Francisco use aggressive parking as a means of corralling the car, getting it close to the dwelling, and protecting it (fig. 47).

FIG. 47. Fulton Grove in San Francisco,
by Daniel Solomon, features open space
that tolerates cars but is primarily a shared
pedestrian area.

Probably more important, however, he employs this strategy as a way of preserving the urban wall. By reducing the driveways and placing cars within the site, he moves the housing to the edges of the property and retains the city street front. Obviously, safety is a concern, and he makes these places so clearly pedestrian—all dwellings are entered from them—that cars become the timid interlopers.

"FROM BEST TO WORST": ACORN

The story of Acorn is instructive because the project had all the makings of a successful venture, including a design that incorporated many of the sensitivities and amenities discussed in this chapter. But while it seemed to heed the lessons of previous public housing failures, it too succumbed to the same fate.

In 1964 a competition for a large affordable housing program took place in Oakland, California. The competition called for architects to join with experienced builders to create a well-designed and solidly built development of more than seven hundred units. The program had the support of the local community, a politically potent community group, and city movers and shakers. Close to the downtown, providing excellent access to transportation and jobs, the area of west Oakland was very much in need of housing. The competition attracted some of the region's best housing architects, including Marquis and Stoller, the firm that designed St. Francis Square. The event was applauded for both its architectural and social vision. But despite Acorn's auspicious beginnings, it was a failure. After many years of neglect and decay, Acorn came under new management in 1992 and began resuscitation at a cost of $20 million. In the words of a long-time resident, Acorn went "from best to worst."[18]

The premise and promise of Acorn was that it would be its own new town—with schools, com-

munity facilities, and housing—a model for a self-sustaining neighborhood. The sponsors hoped that this bold social experiment with mixed-income and ethnically integrated residents would have a bold architecture to match. Burger & Coplans, a relatively young firm, proposed a design that seemed, at the time, a model of sound planning with a distinctive image (fig. 48). The white, cubic buildings were envisioned as a Mediterranean village. The projecting balconies, variations in building height, and judicious alterations within a recurring basic form provided an exuberant look within a modest budget.

FIG. 48.   Acorn in Oakland, as seen in 1969, presented an integrated community with a dynamic image.

Perhaps the cleverest device was what the designers called the "quatrefoil," or corner-turning building, an innovative strategy that compensated for two typically difficult planning problems. Most of Acorn's buildings were staggered rows of two-story townhouses, which allowed the larger units, those for families with children, to have private ground-level space. These basic units were formed around courtyards. The two problems with this plan are that rows of townhouses are troublesome at their ends—How can the end units address the court and still turn the corner?—and that the building type does not yield

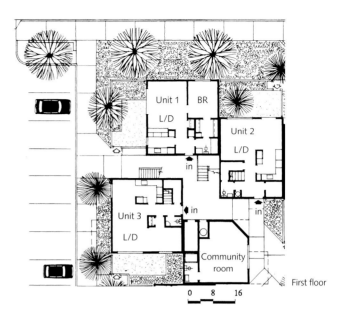

FIG. 49. Acorn's building plan combines rowhouses with these corner buildings, called quatrefoils.

First floor

0   8   16

Second floor

Third floor

sufficiently high densities. The quatrefoil was a square building, three floors high, with units in each quadrant. The interior of the square was open, with stairs rising within it to access the upper units (fig. 49). The higher building stepped up both the form and the density, and its square plan acted as a pivot between the rows of townhouses.

The overall low-rise design allowed for a high density, thirty units per acre, with no high-rise elements. Many of the competitors offered the choice of an entirely low-rise design of lesser density or a design that combined some elevator buildings with low-rise housing. The Burger & Coplans scheme had it all: courtyards, townhouses, low-rise and high density, and even a panelized construction method. Charles Moore, then a professor at the University of California and a member of the selection committee, declared, "This is either Mickey Mouse or a great breakthrough in urban housing."[19]

The sponsors hailed the mixed-income and ethnically integrated village as a pioneering social triumph. Even the architect, Ed Burger, moved into Acorn with his wife and young child, and the first wave of residents exemplified the activism and idealism of the 1960s. One of the earliest residents expressed this hopefulness: "We had been shopping around to buy a house, but when we found out about this and the fact that it will be integrated, we applied right away. It's a rare opportunity to live in decent housing in an integrated neighborhood."[20]

The distinctive architecture won praise in the local press and in the national architectural journals. It also won several design awards, including one from HUD and three from the American Institute of Architects. But the criticisms among the kudos hinted that its gleaming presence might have a questionable future. What the architects saw as a village and enclave, others saw as simply a very large housing project. What its designers intended as a collective form, a unity generated from individual diversity, others saw as sheer monotony. Above all, the design's visual characteristics that were admired by architects were seen as sterile by others (fig. 50).

The strength of Acorn's architectural image contributed to its failure. Partly to save money and partly to reinforce its hard-edged cubist forms, there were few rain gutters on the projecting sloped-roof bays and no overhangs on its extensive flat roofs. Water infiltrated the buildings and began to erode the structure. Sheets of water ran unimpeded down the sides of the stucco and into flush, trimless window frames. It did not take long for signs of deterioration to appear.

The developers were from Los Angeles, and the project was HUD-sponsored. That the two financial entities were not locally based probably exacerbated the lack of attention to maintenance. Once the problems began, they multiplied. Soon enough, the first generation of residents moved out; the incoming residents were mostly poor and mostly members of ethnic minority groups. The dream of a heterogeneous, mixed-income community faded.

When crime and drug trafficking invaded Acorn, it became apparent that certain planning decisions that had been lauded as humane, socially responsive, and architecturally clever were having disastrous consequences. The courtyards formed by the rowhouses were too accessible to outsiders, and the units that fronted them were not close enough to those spaces to provide a sense of security. At the ends of the courts the open access and stairways of the quatrefoils were out of view of any unit. And while the pattern of rowhouses and quatrefoils was relatively consistent, the entry pattern to the units was not. Visitors found it difficult to locate dwellings within the complex, and the porousness of the site plan invited the public in without supervision or control. Spread over several city blocks, the seven hundred dwellings formed a vast labyrinth. No matter where one

FIG. 50. To some, a vital Mediterranean village; to others, thin boxes with too few embellishments.

stood, the project looked the same, and what lay within was unknown (fig. 51).

Even the parking design created problems. The architects had created fingers of parking lots to reduce the overall visual impact of cars and to place the cars close to the units. But these lots were still relatively large and not easily seen by the units, and there were several means of access from them into the project. Drug transactions flourished, with dealers even escaping over the flat rooftops.

Whenever one talks about failures in subsidized housing, the conversation turns to Pruitt-Igoe in St. Louis, the high-rise project that was partly dismantled by dynamite in 1972 and then bulldozed in 1976. The finger-pointing in the aftermath of its destruction was directed primarily at its design—the repetitive high-rise chunks sitting in a desolate, detached landscape—although, as dis-

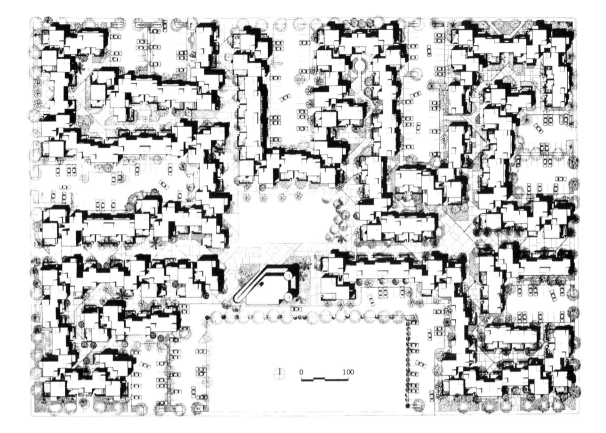

FIG. 51.   Acorn site plan. Courtyards
surrounded by low-rise buildings were
intended to make for a community on a
human scale, but the many unobserved
entries and unclear territories made the
project unsafe.

cussed in Chapter 1, uncaring management, ghet-
toization, and racism were as much to blame as
the design.

Acorn, however, is no Pruitt-Igoe. Its design
was not without its deficiencies, but the low-rise
townhouses, communal facilities, and school were
certainly the ingredients for a healthy community.
And Oakland's community-supported plan for
mixed-income housing bore no resemblance to

the slum-clearance mentality of a bureaucratic
agency in St. Louis. Nevertheless, as maintenance
costs rose, as crime and drugs took their toll, the
original vision of Acorn as a diverse Mediterranean village evaporated. Acorn became just another agglomeration of repetitive, thin boxes in a
desolate urban landscape. Windows were boarded,
either to keep vagrants and drug dealers out of
abandoned units or to protect residents within the

FIG. 52.   Acorn after thirty years.

units (fig. 52). In 1991, with roofs nearly in collapse, several units flooded and residents had to evacuate.

Buildings are like people: they require care and nurturing. And like people, buildings share certain characteristics, but each is unique. Some buildings, given the right context and physical attributes, can survive without much special attention, but others cannot. Acorn needed lots of nurturing, partly because it was so large. Most architects, including Ed Burger, feel that two hundred or two hundred and fifty units is large enough to achieve economies in construction and small enough to form a cohesive community.[21] Acorn's hard-edged design also demanded more maintenance.

It is difficult to speculate whether Acorn, if it had been smaller, had a different architectural image with more detail, and had more rain-resistant roofs or more observable courts and parking, would be healthy today. But there are several market-rate projects in the Bay Area from the same era that share several of Acorn's design features and still continue to be wonderful housing. So Acorn reinforces the lesson that design is not the sole culprit. Housing is a delicate balance: on one side is architecture, and on the other is the quality of management and the attitude of the public and the residents. For Acorn there is still hope that this balance will be restored and that its original promise will be realized.

IS AFFORDABLE HOUSING SIGNIFICANT ARCHITECTURE?

Dana Cuff suggests that in order for excellent architecture to be achieved, several conditions must exist during the design process.[1] They are *quality demands,* the concern, above all else, that the building be excellent; *simplicity within complexity,* the possibility for all members of a collaborative team (client, architects, engineers) to contribute their expertise without undue bureaucracy; *stereovision,* the confluence, rather than contradiction, of the separate visions that each principal (client and architect) has of the project; *open boundaries,* the view of restrictions (budgetary or regulatory) as opportunities or challenges, not constraints; *flexibility with integrity,* the willingness of the principals to work within a fluid process, continuously refocusing on values and visions and not on the details of a singular solution; *teamwork with independence,* the investment that all members of the team feel in the final result; and *exceeding the limits,* the willingness of all involved to commit more than originally intended to get the best building. While all of these indexes are applicable to affordable housing, three seem particularly relevant: stereovision, flexibility with integrity, and exceeding the limits.

Affordable housing is a complex endeavor, not just because of the extensive regulation and cost constraints, but also because there are so many people needing, requiring, and demanding input into the final product. The clients and the public may view the evolving product differently than the architect. For example, the developer, the community, and the architect may all want a building with a handsome exterior. The architect may propose a smooth, hard-edged stucco facade as elegant, and the developer may see the stucco facade as durable and relatively maintenance-free; these two views would be stereovision. But the community may see stucco as cold and institutional. The architect and the developer, without succumbing to each new criticism, must be able to refocus the specifics of the design in order to achieve the elegance the architect prefers, the low maintenance the client requires, and the residential image the neighbors demand. A brand of flexibility that maintains the integrity of the design is needed to resolve the conflict and produce confluence.

In some cases the varying aspirations, viewpoints, and expectations may inspire architects to new heights; they often contribute time and effort beyond contractual obligations in order to exceed the limits. Architects who work in affordable housing, particularly with nonprofits, know that the routine contractual services are not enough. CDCs are successful because they have the extra drive that results from a missionary zeal; architects get caught up in it too. Affordable housing projects are not just commissions; they have a life of their own. In James Lee Court, housing for the homeless in Oakland, artists provided murals, and the architect donated his efforts to design, construct, and install spirit houses (see fig. 17). As the architect, Michael Pyatok, explained it, the coalition became so empowered by the project that everyone involved was swept along and volunteered to add embellishments and personality to the building.[2]

The history of the architecture of social housing in the United States has been the antithesis of stereovision, flexibility with integrity, and exceeding the limits. In 1946 the United States National Housing Agency published a summary report of the status of low-cost housing. It is a revealing statement about the place of architecture in the endeavor and the government's understanding of and concern for design.

> One may feel sure that no discussion of this subject would be attempted here were it not for the direct relationship that exists between plan and what is commonly known as architectural style. The subject is highly controversial, and in any event FPHA [Federal Public Housing Authority] cannot appropriately hold opinions in the matter. . . . So far, it is safe to say that no distinctive movement in architectural expression has evolved from the program. True enough, many of the projects are stamped "public housing," but this seems due to the general use of standardized plans plus the reinforced simplicity of structural design and exte-

rior materials rather than to any inherent necessity.

Finally, there are a few projects where the architects quite evidently were seeking neither for indigenous qualities or more functional expression, but were attempting to force architectural effect into a problem which does not benefit from striving: such efforts not only have failed but nearly always laid an unnecessary burden of cost upon the projects.[3]

EXCELLENCE AND AFFORDABLE HOUSING: THE PROFESSION'S VIEW

The ten affordable housing projects profiled in this chapter have each won a design award in one of the two national awards competitions open to all building types regardless of their use, materials, budget, or location: *Progressive Architecture* magazine's annual awards and the American Institute of Architects National Honor Awards.[4] The *Progressive Architecture* awards are for projects not yet constructed but commissioned by clients who intend to build them. The winners are selected by a nationally known group of architects who evaluate the drawings, model photographs, and statements by the submitting architects. The popular lore among architects is that most *Progressive Architecture* award winners are never built, but this is not true. All the affordable housing projects that won a *Progressive Architecture* award between 1980 and 1992 were built, and they are included here. Many also won other regional and local awards once they were completed.

The other major award, the American Institute of Architects National Honor Award, is the nation's most prestigious. The winners are also selected by a distinguished panel that includes architects, a landscape architect, and a public member involved in the arts. Although the initial selection, as with the *Progressive Architecture* award, is made by examining drawings, statements by the architects, and in this case, photographs of completed buildings, the final selection is made only after at least one of the panel members visits the project.

The American Institute of Architects established the awards program in 1949 to identify and recognize excellent architecture. The early program had but two categories—houses and schools—mirroring the postwar building needs that architects were addressing. By the fourth program, in 1953, the categories were dropped, and all types of projects were encouraged.[5] A special award for "development housing" was established in 1953; still, there were only three multifamily housing winners by 1959, out of nearly two hundred awards. This trend was duly noted by the jury that year: "Unfortunately, no examples were provided to show the architect's concern for the diverse social and economic problems occurring in the redevelopment of urban centers or in the design of residential neighborhoods. Future competitions should invite submittals from the teams of architects and developers engaged in these tasks."[6] Despite this admonishment, it was not until 1964, fifteen years and 270 awards after the program's inception, that a multifamily affordable project, Marquis and Stoller's St. Francis Square in San Francisco, won a national honor award.

There are several reasons for this historical dearth of honored affordable housing projects. Most architects work in small firms with fewer than five people, and the mainstay of their practices are single-family residences. During the first fifteen years more than fifty houses had won a National Honor Award. The lack of opportunities for building affordable housing is one thing, but to do something architecturally meaningful once commissioned is another. The context, as overtly expressed by the government sponsors, has not encouraged good architecture. It is safe to say that even if the nation's best architects were doing affordable housing, they were unlikely to submit their results for awards.

But this trend has begun to reverse as the federal government's role in housing has diminished. Of the thirteen affordable multifamily housing projects that have received a National Honor Award (constituting approximately 2 percent of all the awards given since 1949), eight were bestowed since 1980, and three were given in 1993. This trend suggests two optimistic interpretations. The first is that the organizations that supplanted the federal government in housing are more likely to encourage good design, by creating the conditions for excellence that Cuff describes. Second, architects are beginning to rediscover that affordable housing is not only a socially responsible endeavor but an artful one as well.

Both the National Honor Awards and the *Progressive Architecture* awards receive over five hundred entries each year, from which only about ten or fifteen are chosen for awards. This is not to say that the award winners are unquestionably the most excellent designs, for the "beauty pageant" approach may well overlook buildings that are discreet, responsible neighbors but perhaps not so picturesque or exuberant. Nonetheless, when external and independent evaluators select a handful of projects a year, based not only on aesthetics but on context, appropriateness, and sound planning, one feels that these award winners do represent significant architecture. In fact, in 1993 the American Institute of Architects broadened the purview of their awards, with the new criteria of "design resolution," characterized as showing "exemplary skill and sensitivity in the resolution of formal, functional, and technical requirements," and "design advancement," which furthers "contemporary understanding of design by proposing new approaches to the development of architectural form."[7] There are also subcategories for technical, societal, and environmental advancement.

All ten of the projects described below are subsidized attached multifamily housing.[8] The programs and the amounts and sources of subsidies vary, but each project was subject to serious budgetary constraints and to the restrictions of the sponsoring agencies or local jurisdictions. In some cases a mosaic of funding added even more complications to the process, which in at least one project took six years to complete.

The projects are all modest in scale, ranging from 8 to 189 units. Unlike the massive projects of the 1950s and 1960s, these smaller ones fit comfortably into their contexts and do not seem "project-like." Some of them are on urban sites, fitted between, among, and around other buildings, while others stand freely on their own site. All respond clearly to their contexts, a characteristic that figured heavily in their award selection. In some cases this responsiveness is subtle, having more do to with the scale and massing of the buildings, while in other cases it has more to do with building features and the use of outdoor space. In two cases the environmental context—the orientation to the sun for energy conservation—was the primary planning strategy. The projects serve different groups: families, singles, seniors, and homeless people. The unit sizes range from full multibedroom apartments to single-room-occupancy spaces. Such variety is indicative of the increasing recognition that affordable housing is not just for families with children.

The group is also diverse architecturally, although the projects in southern California have more aesthetic similarities than those elsewhere, mostly because of their stucco exteriors and the means by which the architects detailed them. Though most of these projects have a courtyard, these too are diverse. In one case the courtyard is merely a view and a light shaft, in another a parking court, but in most cases it is an outdoor communal room, important both as a functional space and as a focal point for community identity. The architectural diversity of the group is partly a response to their different contexts, partly a result of the intended resident group, and partly a reflection of the aesthetic inclinations of the architects. That each of these projects has a unique character validates the notion that architects need not sublimate their talents or aesthetic judgments when designing affordable housing.

Only one of the projects—one of the three for seniors—is a high-rise. The other projects use one or more of the approaches discussed in Chapter 4: attached houses, big houses subsuming little ones, and the embellished box. For example, in the Berkeley Street infill housing in Santa Monica, individual rowhouses are attached, but the entries are emphasized to make an embellished box. Only three of the projects use subterranean parking; the others rely on surface parking dispersed into small lots. And all address the concept of transitional space and carefully conceived territory. In the larger projects, like Mendelsohn House and 202 Island Inn, the transition is handled through public lobbies; in the smaller projects it is typically articulated through front stoops and patios.

Most of these projects break some tenet of conventional wisdom. The light court at 202 Island Inn is too narrow by orthodox standards, and the symbolism of the mountains and commercial strip at The Beach is too heavy, according to the canon. But these heresies work, and work wonderfully, because the architects responded to what they perceived as the critical issue in some bold and unusual manner. Architecture, and perhaps especially the architecture of affordable housing, remains an act of judgment and conviction.

COLTON PALMS

Colton, California
Designed by Valerio Associates
Winner of *Progressive Architecture* award (1991) and
National Honor Award (1993)
101 units for seniors [9]

Colton is a small, somewhat sleepy town of 33,000 people east of Los Angeles. It is one of California's oldest towns, originally a mining settlement, now a working-class community from which people commute to Los Angeles, San Bernardino, or Riverside. It is an unlikely context for significant architecture. But the fortuitous combination of an enlightened redevelopment agency, an experienced nonprofit developer, and a willing citizenry has yielded just that.

At first glance, and certainly from photographs, it may be easy to dismiss Colton Palms as inexpensive housing with kitsch. Its eccentric forms interspersed with otherwise simple buildings and its angled metal details projecting from plain stucco walls invite the question, Why? But Colton Palms overcomes the viewer's initial suspicion by its intelligent planning.

The primary building element is a housing block that is three stories high with four dwellings to a floor, for a total of twelve units (fig. 53). These "houses," occasionally emphasized by a pyramidal roof, are not directly scaled to the existing neighborhood of single-family houses, but they are at least recognizable as big houses subsuming smaller ones and as a series of attached dwellings, rather than a large apartment block. The twelve-unit modules are connected either directly one to the other, with a slight reveal between them that perceptually sets them apart, or by an elaborate porch that provides shared open space for the units on each floor. Each porch includes the required exit stair but is also wide enough to accommodate patio furniture. The porches are used as

intended, as extensions of the dwellings, particularly on the frequent warm evenings of southern California.

This system of house forms and porches circumscribes the site, making a large courtyard within, but the wall of housing is interrupted at several points by special buildings—a library in the form of a cylinder, a crafts center with a conical roof (fig. 54). The housing form, consistent and recurring, is somewhat like a basic urban building, while the communal centers, unique and special, are equivalent to public buildings. These two opposing building types are carefully deployed. The housing, primarily forming a perimeter block, meets the outside of the project in a reasonably scaled and friendly pattern. The public buildings are placed with two objectives: first, they suspend the pattern of the perimeter block to signal entries and to provide visual diversity, and second, they are aligned with various vistas as one walks through the complex. Their placement draws attention to them and orients the visitor.

The courtyard within this system is, in a real sense, the public plaza for everyone (fig. 55). It contains the community building, much like a city hall, viewable from throughout the complex. Cars are allowed into this plaza, but the large circular drive that circumscribes the public green is sparsely used by vehicles. The residents have discovered that ten times around the drive is a mile, and they use it as an exercise track.

Colton Palms is thus a metaphor for a city. It has background buildings for housing, special buildings for civic functions, and a major public plaza. The danger in this approach is that this minicity, this enclave, will seem detached from its surroundings, isolated from the town—the project syndrome. The fact that all the dwellings are entered from the courtyard could reinforce that perception. But this is not the case. The public buildings scattered around the perimeter serve as doorways for the community, while not making

FIG. 53.   A system of houses at Colton Palms, each with twelve units, connected by shared porches.

the project overly inviting or porous. These entry areas allow views into the courtyard, making at least a visual connection between protected, semi-private space and the world outside it. Half the dwellings face the street, with very large windows and projecting decks. Many residents prefer these units because of their extended vistas and the connection to the neighborhood. And finally, there is a clear connection both to the Colton City Hall on one side and a lovely park across from the proj-

ect's entry, making a sound compromise between security for occupants and friendliness to the neighborhood. The residents feel neither isolated nor confined by Colton Palms.

Several seemingly small gestures further humanize this project. The corridors that slide through the house forms at each level connect the open porches, threading the entire complex together. They also connect to the elevator, making everything accessible to the disabled. As the corridors

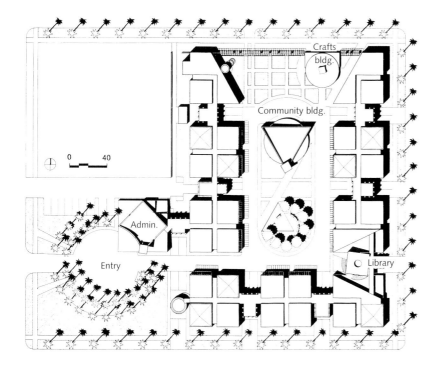

FIG. 54 (*above*). The Colton Palms site plan reveals a small city, with a public plaza, background buildings, and civic structures.

FIG. 55 (*left*). The courtyard provides some parking and service access, but it is really a pedestrian plaza.

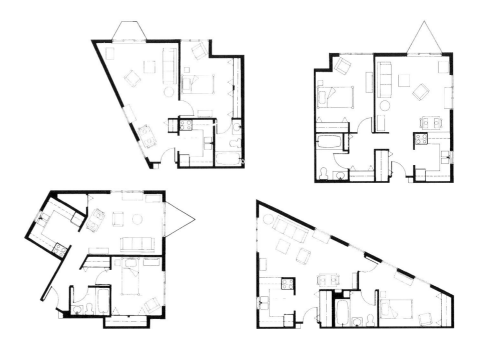

FIG. 56. Colton Palms' unit plans generally repeat, but special layouts occur when the housing pattern is disrupted by the civic buildings.

move throughout the housing, going in and out of the housing blocks, they are never far from natural light or from vistas of either the neighborhood or the courtyard. One is always connected visually to the context. The corridors also expand slightly at the dwelling entries to make a small transition, complete with a shelf that can hold a plant or can be used to set packages down while a resident opens the door.

Inside, the mostly one-bedroom units of approximately 500 square feet are efficient and filled with daylight. Because each "house" has only four dwellings on a floor, each dwelling has a corner, providing most living rooms with two large windows. The recurrent form permits construction efficiencies, yet wherever it is interrupted by entries or by public buildings the form erodes, creating ir-

regular unit types, each with a unique view or plan feature (fig. 56).

The odd metal details that support the balconies and overhangs—which cost only about $2.50 per square foot—and the strangely shaped public buildings are two aspects that the *Progressive Architecture* jury thought were perhaps nervous and overwrought. But these are of little concern to the residents. When asked about them, they either seem not to notice their unusualness or to equate them with modernity, newness, a result of simply "living in the nineties."[10] Features that might be seen as stigmatizing the residents by calling attention to their homes are instead looked upon with some pride, a constant reminder that this is a special place to live.

MENDELSOHN HOUSE

San Francisco, California

Designed by Herman Stoller Coliver Architects

Winner of National Honor Award (1992)

189 units for seniors [11]

The Yerba Buena area of San Francisco has had a tempestuous recent history. It was once the site of single-room-occupancy hotels and less-than-elegant streetscapes. But in the late 1960s San Francisco had determined, like many other cities, that there must be a higher and better use for the land just outside the main city center. In the name of redevelopment, many blocks south of Market Street were leveled, and more than fifteen hundred units of housing were destroyed. The people displaced by the bulldozers formed Tenants and Owners Opposed to Redevelopment (TOOR) and mounted a vigorous and ultimately successful assault on the redevelopment plans.[12] The city and TOOR reached an agreement in 1973 that the city would build affordable units on four assigned sites. Mendelsohn House, named for one of the original activists, is the third such project, built nearly twenty years after the bulldozers had departed. Today Yerba Buena is the heart of a bustling district that includes new arts buildings by world-renowned architects and a huge convention center.

A strange aspect of the bulldozer in urban renewal is what becomes of context. Does the new housing try to emulate the moderate massing and continuous street frontage of what is now gone, or does it respond to the new context, which bears little relation to the old neighborhood? Mendelsohn House makes gestures to both. Knowing that the building would be seen against the new civic structures, the architects designed a respectful, low-key street-oriented building, with a consistent height for much of its street frontage and a clear entry (fig. 57). The recurring bay windows and

elegant but sedate facades belie its status as affordable housing. The new building, prominently displayed to visitors to the area, is very much in the spirit of the grand apartment house.

Although it is dense, elevator-supported housing, several features overcome the dark hallways and anonymous circulation commonly associated with the type. Many of the hallways are single-loaded, that is, they have apartments on only one side. The other side has windows that look out toward the city (fig. 58). The single-loading not only provides daylight and views to the hallways but also, by means of a window from the dwelling into the hallway, brings daylight to both sides of the dwellings. Residents can look into the circulation space, see people go by, and look beyond to the city. But the main orientation of the dwelling is to the courtyard, the primary social space of the complex (fig. 59). The hallways are also inset at the entry to each unit. The combination of this slight transition and the corridor windows makes the hall feel like a friendly pedestrian street with front stoops, rather than a conventional, dark, narrow hall.

The units, one-bedrooms and studios, each have a light-filled bay window. The kitchen is placed near the center, not far from the windows, so that it too receives daylight, and the resident does not feel isolated while preparing meals. The one-bedrooms have a recessed balcony, while the studios have a shallow ledge, large enough for plants, accessed by a sliding door that is much like a French window.

The type, placement, and orientation of the public spaces are also responses to the history and context of the site. There is a recognition that Mendelsohn House is a private place, but one that does not want to barricade or isolate its occupants. Exercise areas and a community adult day-care center are at streetside, buffered from the sidewalk by an arcade, but clearly visible. These spaces look both to the city and back to the courtyard, mak-

FIG. 57.　Mendelsohn House, San
Francisco, viewed from the city street.

FIG. 58.   The single-loaded corridor provides views of San Francisco and balanced light to the apartments.

FIG. 59 (*below*).   Mendelsohn House site plan, with the court oriented to the south.

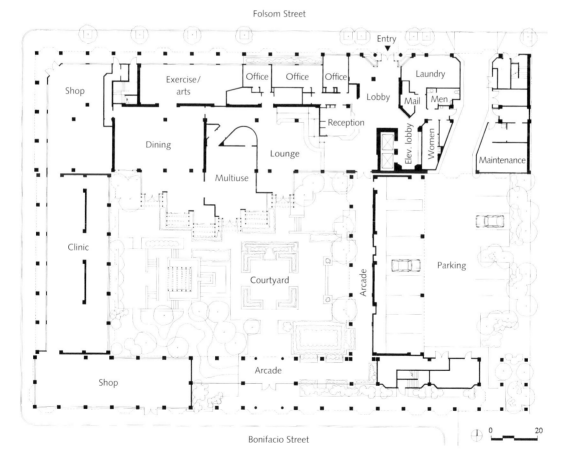

Folsom Street

Entry

Shop

Exercise/ arts

Office   Office   Office

Laundry

Lobby

Mail   Men

Reception

Dining

Lounge

Women

Elev. lobby

Multiuse

Maintenance

Mabini Street

Clinic

Courtyard

Arcade

Parking

Shop

Arcade

Bonifacio Street

0   20

FIG. 60.   The courtyard is the heart of Mendelsohn House, and all the public functions adjoin it.

ing a connection, visually and philosophically, between the public and private realms. The architects felt so strongly about connecting the building both to the city and to the history of the area that they created a "memory wall" in the public area, detailed in traditional wood paneling, that displays photographs of Yerba Buena before urban renewal.

The courtyard is both the conceptual and communal heart of the project (fig. 60). The stepped building mass and the narrow building footprint, partly a result of the single-loaded corridor, yield their own amenities, such as the daylit corridor and roof decks, and also allow a sunnier and larger courtyard. The court is the functional focal point, with all the public areas adjoining it and some actually projecting into it. Parking for only fifteen cars, on grade and partially tucked under the building, is also adjacent to the courtyard.

The architect, Robert Herman, sees the court as not just a communal space but also a contemplative one. He believes that the architecture of senior housing must reveal life cycles. Changes in light, seasons, and climate are important, because these variations express the passage of life and its relation to places, sensibilities that Herman believes seniors possess more fully than younger people.[13] The courtyard at Mendelsohn has a variety of plants, colors, shadows, winds, and sounds, all meant to emphasize the quality of time and intensify the understanding of the place.

Following the negotiations between the city and TOOR that gave rise to the project, many felt that a study should be undertaken to ensure that the future occupants had a say in the nature of the housing. Tenants and Owners Development Corporation (TODCO), the nonprofit CDC formed to develop the housing, initiated the study by asking seniors to respond to photographs of various housing elements. Among the findings were that modern housing was favored over more traditional images, since it implied that seniors were not left behind; that lobbies at the ground floor were important both for security and for their social function; that public areas, such as convenience stores, should be located along the ground floor; and that sunny, protected spaces, such as roof decks, were essential.[14] Herman participated in several of the workshops. His ability to listen to the future occupants, together with his concern for revitalizing this part of the city by creating transitional spaces that bridge public and private realms, has made Mendelsohn House a humane and urbane place.

LANGHAM COURT

Boston, Massachusetts
Designed by Goody, Clancy & Associates
Winner of National Honor Award (1993)
84 units of family housing

Langham Court is a story of salvation, both for architecture and for a community. Boston's South End suffers from the maladies that afflict many cities—crime, drugs, prostitution—and this site had seen it all. The redevelopment agency envisioned the project as the catalyst for neighborhood improvement. In an earlier era local authorities might have pushed for more demolition and construction of high-density monoliths. But lessons were heeded. The combination of architects Goody, Clancy & Associates and their nonprofit sponsor, Four Corners Development Corporation (FCDC), a group from within the community formed just for this purpose, was auspicious.[15] The architect brought affordable housing experience, the requisite will and persistence for what was to be a six-year process, and a concern and appreciation for the building type and the scale of the neighborhood. The nonprofit group brought spirited activism, motivated by a need and desire to reclaim their community and restore its architectural traditions. Often buildings reflect the compromises that the long struggles and complicated financing exact; years later one walks by and wonders why some bizarre or unusual feature exists. But Langham Court looks as if it belongs, and will belong for some time.

While the obvious features, such as the brick exterior and bay windows, are in clear deference to the traditions of the neighborhood, there are subtle planning and massing decisions that are equally important. Langham Court is actually two building types carefully knitted together. Traditional rowhouses face similar buildings along Worcester

FIG. 61. Langham Court's apartments along Shawmut Avenue in Boston.

140   SIGNIFICANT ARCHITECTURE

FIG. 62.   Langham Court's rowhouses along Worcester Street. The apartments also have front stoops and bays.

and West Springfield Streets, but a higher-density, elevator-supported apartment type stands on Shawmut Avenue (fig. 61). This combination serves two purposes. First, the rowhouse, which may have been the preferred form, could not yield the required density. Second, the project's mix of units, from 300-square-foot studios up to 1,300-square-foot apartments and duplexes, would be nearly impossible to accommodate within the limitations of a walk-up townhouse. Because the two building types share many features, they form a seamless perimeter block design that blends into the neighborhood. For example, the apartment block does have elevator lobbies, but the units that front the street share walk-up stoops, just like the rowhouses (fig. 62). The stoops compliment those of neighboring buildings and emphasize the importance of streetside entries, not just for the convenience of the occupants but also as a friendly urban gesture.

The dwellings on the upper floors that use the elevators have ground-floor lobbies adjacent to the courtyard. Both the court and these lobbies are accessed from the side streets through arched entryways (fig. 63). This entry sequence activates the court, provides a level of security for the lobbies, and allows for the architectural feature of an archway that masterfully joins the two building types and creates a larger, more urban scale for both the apartment block and the courtyard. The archways signal a transition in scale, from the side-street rowhouses to the apartment building. But they also serve as transitions between the public side of the building and the more private courtyard.

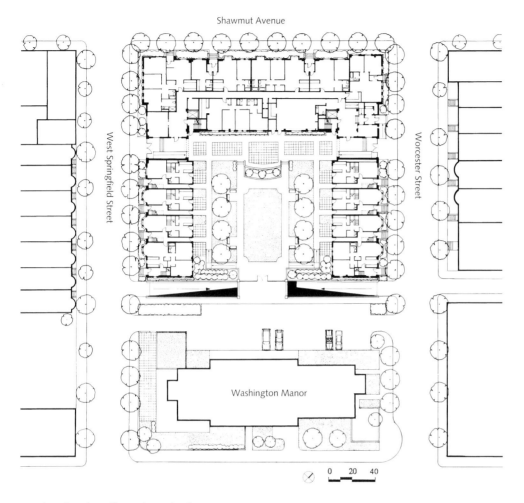

Shawmut Avenue

West Springfield Street

Worcester Street

Washington Manor

0   20   40

FIG. 64.   Langham Court, lower-level
plan. The public green is defined both by
the new buildings and by the existing
Washington Manor, affordable housing for
seniors. Parking and ramps partly disrupt
the continuity of the green.

Within the arched entryways are ramps that
provide wheelchair access to the level of the court
and the lobbies, which is slightly above street level.
The change in level is necessary both architecturally and practically. Lifting the first level of housing a few feet off the street creates the stoops and
grants additional privacy and security for those

front doors. It also reduces the amount of excava-
tion and the length of ramps required for the underground parking.

Unlike the courtyards of Colton Palms and
Mendelsohn House, Langham Court's is more of
a public green, in the British tradition (fig. 64).
Although the few community rooms are placed

directly on the court, its use is less associated with a specific function and more related to its urban context. For example, the court is open to the existing senior housing that adjoins it and completes the block. Thus the space acts as a connector, as a public park, rather than the exclusive province of Langham Court. This was a risky gesture, given the concerns for security in the area, but the community organizers and the architects were convinced of the need for continuity in the neighborhood.[16] The courtyard in fact enhances security, because the rowhouses have private yards that are contiguous to it, and the lobbies for the apartment block are adjacent as well. This arrangement populates the court, allowing the residents to keep a vigilant eye on it. Even the unit plans reinforce the "eyes on the street": kitchens and dining areas of the rowhouses overlook the court.

The only aspect of the planning that is susceptible to criticism is the double-loaded corridor of the apartment block. Single-loaded corridors, like those at Mendelsohn House, would have let natural light in. But the double-loading was necessary for two reasons. First, it meets the code requirement of two means of egress from the upper floors. Without the corridors and their stairways, this access would have had to be external, a difficult architectural proposition. Second, without the corridors and their stairs, those first-floor units that face the street would not have had easy access to the court. The residents would have had to exit to the public street and walk around the building, through the archways, to enter the open space. The corridor system gives everyone a back door to the collective backyard.

The materials and the architectural embellishments, such as the mansard roof and bay windows, are in deference to the textured and dignified buildings in the neighborhood. They also serve the important function of establishing a comfortable building scale. The emphasis on the windows, the use of both slightly projecting sills and a clear lintel, diminishes the building's perceived size. The distinctive cornice at the third level, topped by a mansard with dormers, continues the massing of the neighboring buildings and reinforces the consistency of the streets. The bays are in two forms: one of brick, which reaches from street to cornice, and another of a lighter material. Both reduce the scale of the building by identifying a smaller entity, presumed by the viewer to be a single dwelling (actually some apartments have two bays), but more important, their recurrent use in slightly different dimensions and positions architecturally unifies the entire complex while providing visual diversity.

With the overall impression of continuity and consistency, there are variations in details as well, such as slight changes in brick patterns, more prominent bay projections at the corners, and a minor change in the configurations of the dormers. A few careful and judicious moves, even within a whole block of building that is basically a set of boxes, is more than enough to provide richness and diminution of scale.

202 ISLAND INN

San Diego, California
Designed by Rob Wellington Quigley
Winner of National Honor Award (1993)
197 rooms in a single-room-occupancy building [17]

Millions of Americans lived in single-room-occupancy (SRO) or residential hotels in the early 1900s, but by the middle of the century this type of housing had been nearly eradicated.[18] Even though the wealthy inhabited elegant hotels on a permanent basis, housing reformers disdained any type of dwelling that did not reinforce the nuclear family. Apartments were bad enough, but residential hotels, mostly units without kitchens and private bathrooms, were beneath contempt. Privacy and the family meal, cooked by the wife, were the critical elements of a worthy life; neither was possible in residential hotels. This attitude had two important repercussions. First, people who lived in this type of housing were ignored by planners. When redevelopment plans were drafted, no effort was made to relocate residents of SROs. The struggle undertaken by TOOR in San Francisco that led to Mendelsohn House was in response to this attitude. Second, this prejudice was translated into regulations. The housing codes enacted in the late nineteenth century in New York, which were adopted throughout the country, virtually eliminated the SRO as a legal building form. All new dwellings had to have kitchens, and people had to reside "independently." These regulations were extended to government financing guidelines, thereby restricting funding for anything but conventional apartments and houses. Old buildings were lost; new ones were disallowed.

The near extinction of a whole species of housing was of little concern until only recently. The attitude has changed for two reasons. The first is the epidemic of homelessness, which has prompted reconsideration of any solution that can mitigate the crisis. Second, housing advocates are no longer in thrall to the social determinism that dictates housing type as a way to worthy citizenship. The notions of tolerable lifestyles and acceptable housing types have broadened. As Robert Campbell has suggested with some irony, the Victorian era, with all its social determinism focused on housing, still had more types of suitable housing for more different populations than we do now.[19] Rooming houses, single-room-occupancy hotels, and hotels for working women were prevalent housing alternatives at the turn of the century. Working-class single people, one of the fastest-growing household types today, are only now being recognized as an unmet market for new housing.

Given this history and political context, it is remarkable that anyone would attempt to build SROs, and even more admirable that good design be part of the agenda. After encountering and overcoming some bureaucratic resistance, the developers Chris Mortenson and Bud Fischer, together with the architect Rob Quigley, have now done several such projects, 202 Island Inn being the most impressive. As with many of the projects discussed in this chapter, site considerations played a prominent role in its success (fig. 65). Because the site was L-shaped and needed to knit itself around or between other buildings, one of which was historically significant, Quigley chose to make what seemed like several buildings rather than one. This strategy allows a continuity for the block of modestly scaled structures and also visually reduces what is really a large project of over 80,000 square feet. Though it does not appear so, the 197 rooms are indeed in one large building, connected by a continuous looped, double-loaded corridor.

On the Second Avenue side, 202 Island Inn seems like three buildings, each segment having its own personality and color (fig. 66). The distinction is hardly noticeable in terms of the plan, but

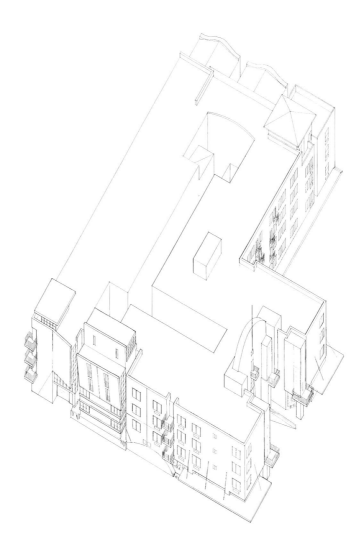

FIG. 65.   The L-shaped site for 202 Island
Inn creates several different contexts.

FIG. 66.   Along Second Avenue, 202
Island Inn looks like three distinctive
buildings.

the facades are quite diverse. On the side facing
the Chinese district the facade again looks like
three buildings, although these are quite similar
and sedate, in deference to the existing historic
building on the corner (fig. 67). On this side the
segments include live-work spaces that help the
ground floor fit in with the commercial activities
on that street.

The architect took two major risks in the design
of 202 Island Inn, and both have much to do with
the success and personality of the building. The
first is the grandness of the building's entry
(fig. 68). The large V-shaped opening rises above
the entry to the garage, but the actual pedestrian
access is up a small ramp to its side. This design
choice resulted from analyzing the various scales
of the building and finding ways of making utilitarian requirements serve higher purposes. A
building with so many tenants and visitors, and a
site that has three street frontages, needs a promi-

FIG. 67 (*above*).   The facade along the
Chinese district continues the form and
scale of an existing building.

FIG. 68 (*right*).   The entry performs many
functions: a grand front door, it also gives
access to parking and a view to the
courtyard beyond.

FIG. 69.   The narrow courtyard brings
light, landscaping, and liveliness into the
center of the building.

nent entry; it also needs a garage. The obvious response is to try to hide the garage, but given the
site constraints and the required size of the garage
opening, this would have been nearly impossible.
Quigley wisely combined both his desire for a
grand entry and the necessity of a large opening.[20]
The garage is actually below street level, and above

it is a very large gap revealing the public front
porch, which looks both to the street and back toward a narrow courtyard set in the middle of the
entire block of housing.

This courtyard is the second design risk, for it is
a strip of space only about ten feet wide in most
places (fig. 69). It is needed to bring light and air

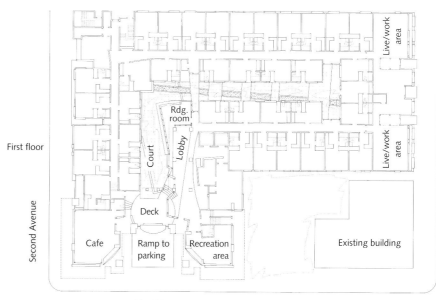

First floor

Second Avenue

Island Avenue

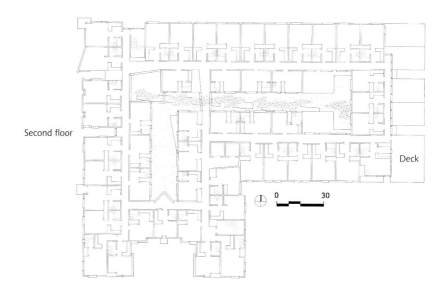

Second floor

FIG. 70. The floor plans for 202 Island Inn. A typical room measures 300 square feet and includes bathroom and kitchenette.

to the rooms that border it, but it is not in any sense a usable courtyard. In its size, form, and function, it is much more like the light shafts and ventilation wells of the early tenements. But what could have been a grim confined space is instead sunny and brightly colored, fulfilling its functional demands but also serving as a focal point and orienting device for the building. At various places along the hallways the court intrudes, bringing sunlight into the circulation while providing views along its length.

The slice of space between the blocks of buildings, with windows so close to each other, requires features that enhance privacy and reduce noise. For privacy, a landscaped screen of tall bamboo rises between the buildings, shielding the windows and filtering the sunlight that dabbles the walls. The bamboo brings color into the space, but so too do the brightly painted walls, some yellow and some green. The acoustic problem is handled by electronically producing a low-level "white noise" that masks other sounds. In a nearby SRO the same team used an even more rudimentary system, made from a common culvert pipe. The pipe, sliced in half, has one end suspended from the top floor, the other resting on the floor of the court. Water runs down it, creating a relaxing, and very inexpensive, waterfall that masks the noise emanating from the rooms.

The units are small, approximately 300 square feet each, and much like hotel rooms (fig. 70). Fully furnished, they have a minimal kitchen area and a private bathroom, but no frills other than a cable TV hook-up. In compensation, there are several community rooms, such as the corner cafe and a reading room off the lobby that projects into the narrow court. These provide the opportunity for this diverse group of tenants to interact, and they do. The spirit of the place is much like that of a European hostel: fun, energetic, and communal.

Ingenuity and careful risk-taking by the architect, combined with efficient planning and sensitivity to the neighborhood, are the ingredients that make 202 Island Inn successful. It fulfills its obligation to its tenants by making their modest dwellings seem much grander, and to the city by helping to repair its urban fabric. Like many of the other award-winning projects discussed in this chapter, 202 Island Inn is mixed-income housing. Many of the occupants—about an equal number of men and women, staying varying lengths of time—have jobs in downtown San Diego, only a few blocks away. This housing provides them with a well-located, affordable, dignified, and fun place to reside.

SCATTERED SITE INFILL HOUSING

Charleston, South Carolina
Designed by Bradfield Associates
Winner of National Honor Award (1986)
67 units

The benefits of a new building fitting comfortably into an existing context are many. The less disruptive a new building is to the fabric and sensibilities of the neighborhood, the more likely it will be accepted. Smaller, more discreet buildings also help the new tenants by making them feel less stigmatized and obvious. When a neighborhood's cultural and historical legacy is construed as part of the context for a new building, the opportunities for real integration of the new building and its residents are even more potent. That is the case in the scattered infill housing in Charleston.

A popular housing type in the eighteenth-century South was known as the Charleston Single. While it was indeed a single-family house, the name comes from its plan, which is typically a single room wide. These buildings, an interpretation of a West Indies type, are characterized both by the long, narrow plan and by extensive porches, called "piazzas," that run along the entire side of the building at each level.[21] The grander examples are often three floors high (fig. 71).

The building's form is a result of political and practical considerations. The lot configuration, specifically its narrowness, was a response to a city tax on street frontage: the less frontage, the lower the tax.[22] Because the house had little yard either in front or in back, the side became the important outdoor space, with the porch fronting it. The emphasis on the side yard is the antecedent for our current zoning type called "zero-lot line," a planning strategy that provides privacy, usable open space, and higher density. By recognizing that side yards for single houses have very little utility, this approach eliminates one side yard by placing the building directly on the property line, thereby making the other side yard larger and more usable.

In Charleston's humid climate, blessed with sea breezes, the narrow plan provides excellent cross-ventilation. The piazzas serve as outdoor rooms facing the breeze, their ample depth allowing the windows to remain open even during rain. They also shade the adjoining interior rooms from the sun. The piazza also serves as a formal architectural foil. It allows the main body of the house to be grand, symmetrical, and dignified—seeming larger than it is—while, by its eccentricity, it adds an informal, relaxed, and intimate quality to the dwelling.

Since the plan is only one room wide, one would have to traverse each room to access other parts of the dwelling if the entry were at the front. This inefficiency is avoided by placing the entry at the middle, a practical solution that isolates and minimizes interior circulation. To reach this entry, one first passes through a door at the end of the veranda. The porch thus becomes an exterior circulation path, in addition to its other duties. Its door is solid, much like an interior door, giving the porch some privacy from the street (fig. 72). There are in fact two entry doors: this first one at the end of the piazza, a ceremonial and often decorative entry, and a second in the middle of the long plan, which actually accesses the house.

This vernacular building is still a fixture in the older, now historic districts of the city. While they were originally rather large single-family homes, many for Southern aristocrats, the type has been well suited to people of all income levels. The reason so many still exist is twofold. First, Charleston was hard hit by the Civil War and took some time to recover economically. When it did, many of the buildings were intact, albeit dilapidated. There was little development during the Reconstruction, and no new types or styles supplanted the Charleston

FIG. 71 (*above*). A three-story Charleston Single, with the characteristic piazza.

FIG. 72 (*left*). The porch door is the formal entry to the house.

FIG. 73. Affordable housing in Charleston, South Carolina, emulates the historical type.

Single, which by the time the city recovered was valued for its intelligent response to the environment. Second, Charleston is serious about its architectural heritage. In 1931 it became the first city in the United States to pass legislation protecting historic districts, and the Historic Charleston Foundation was established fifteen years later.[23]

This resilience, the strong local sensibilities toward preserving the architectural past, and the po-litical wisdom of dispersing affordable housing on many sites eventually led the local housing authority and its architects to evoke the character of the Charleston Single in their new HUD-supported housing. Although Bradfield Architects did not intend to re-create the form, the more they grappled with the characteristics of the available sites, in part through careful analysis of many of the surrounding buildings, the more the results evolved into an adaptation of the vernacular type (fig. 73).

This wise and responsible approach was not without its problems. The HUD guidelines that envisioned a much different type of affordable housing—one with repetitive buildings and large-scale projects—had to be overridden. Even the material specifications, which called for brick facades, precluded a sensitive adaptation of the building type. Then the local authorities tiptoed into the endeavor. Sites that might otherwise be privately developed were eschewed, as were those not already zoned for multifamily use. The original intention of creating 139 units was reduced by 26 units, partly by NIMBY resistance and partly for technical reasons. The search of over 100 sites finally yielded 14 sites for the 113 units, of which the 67 designed by Bradfield Associates were subsequently selected for the Honor Award.[24]

The clearest example of deference to the vernacular type is the street facade, which has the cabled form, symmetrical windows, and a modest version of the piazza forming the entries to the dwellings. But in most cases this porch does not run the length of the building; it is instead interrupted by enclosed rooms or by stairs to the second-level apartment (fig. 74). The programmatic needs bumped up against the narrowness of the building type. Richard Bradfield indicates that although the continuous piazza was a feature of single houses for the wealthy, there were more modest traditional versions that had abridged porches like this new housing.[25] Unfortunately, however, the strengths of the type—cross-ventilation and a sizable, shaded outdoor space—are diminished in the new design.

Parking is generally located behind the dwellings, accessed through a narrow drive in the side yards. Not only is its placement cost-efficient, but it also avoids the problem of incorporating cars into a type of building that originated when there were none. When the architects were able to aggregate several such buildings on a site, never

FIG. 74. One-bedroom duplex floor plans. Unlike the traditional piazza, the porch does not extend the length of the building.

more than twenty-two in one place, the driveways are shared and parking is grouped in the rear.

Faithfulness to the overall form is critical to this design, but so too is the attention to detail. The wood siding, window moldings, balustrades, and shutters all give these dwellings a texture and style consistent with that of their historic neighbors. These embellishments are carefully considered; the architect measured several of the historic buildings before beginning their design. Neither slavish copies nor Disney-like replications, the buildings are respectful and modest adaptations. Local builders offered advice on how modern materials could emulate at least the intention of the original, for instance, by combining common wood sections for details that would have been molded for the original buildings. These new techniques help distinguish the new buildings from their predecessors.

That these new dwellings have their own personality is also a function of cultural changes. The front doors are much less elaborate than in the originals, for example. When the original Charleston Singles were built, visits to neighbors were important social events, and the elaborate streetside entrance to the piazza was a reflection not so much of the status of the owner but rather of the importance of the occasion.[26]

The strong stylistic and historical resonance of Charleston's scattered-site housing has made for satisfied neighbors. The projects have revitalized the neighborhoods and stimulated a benign gentrification. Other community residents are fixing their homes, not wanting to be outdone by affordable housing, and new homeowners have chosen to come into the community, building on the empty sites passed over by redevelopment.

ROOSEVELT SENIOR CITIZEN HOUSING

Roosevelt, New Jersey
Designed by Kelbaugh & Lee
Winner of National Honor Award (1985)
21 units for seniors [27]

In the late 1970s and early 1980s two design imperatives, one social and one technical, were overlaid on the traditional, formal design values in housing. The social issue was livability, and the technical issue was efficiency, motivated by the soaring cost of oil. Many energy-efficient efforts were misguided by the notion that the technological approaches to energy conservation required a new architecture. In a classic case of the tail wagging the dog, their designers eschewed sound planning, habitability, and even cultural preferences in deference to energy efficiency, sacrificing the social imperative to the technical one.

But several architects realized that it was not technical doodads that would make significant and efficient architecture, but rather more subtle and holistic approaches. They saw design as an integrative pursuit, one that balanced many concerns to produce a distinctive work. Kelbaugh & Lee were among them. They had already received recognition for some small energy-efficient buildings, including Doug Kelbaugh's own house, when they were asked to design this HUD-assisted senior project. For them the charge was both social and technical, and through meetings and questionnaires they set out to determine the needs and desires of the future occupants.

Roosevelt is an unusual American suburb, a town created in 1937 through the Works Progress Administration. It was a sort of social experiment, a cooperative venture, a bucolic alternative for urban workers, mostly Jewish immigrants who had been living in New York City and working in the garment district.[28] Along with these workers came many intellectuals and artisans who were attracted

FIG. 75. Roosevelt Senior Citizen
Housing in Roosevelt, New Jersey.

to the town's social purposes and brought a pioneering spirit to the community. By the 1980s this new senior housing was intended to keep them, or their parents, in the town. The first Roosevelt homes, many of which were modeled after Bauhaus ideas popular in Germany, were spartan, concrete-block forms with flat roofs. Some of these have now been embellished with roofs, shutters, and decorations. Kelbaugh & Lee vowed not to repeat this initial architecture, and their inclinations were corroborated by the results of their community surveys, which indicated a preference for "vernacular, rural."[29]

Their response was a softer design, one using a more archetypal house form (fig. 75). The National Honor Awards jury called it "warm, unpretentious, and playful."[30] The embellishments were various energy-efficient devices that looked like

FIG. 76.   Roosevelt's energy-saving features are incorporated into traditional architectural forms.

the chimneys or picture windows one might find in conventional houses (fig. 76). But these chimneys were rotary ventilators that exhausted warm air; and the large, south-facing glazing was part of a solarium that captured the sun's heat and used it to warm the dwelling (fig. 77). Pushing the envelope of energy efficiency, the designers also experimented with efficient water heater designs and recycled materials for insulation.

Orientation is the key to energy-efficient architecture, particularly for housing. Buildings should face south and north. The southern sun, which is most consistently focused on the building throughout the day, is the most easily controlled. Through various simple strategies the sun can be admitted or omitted from a south-facing building. In Roosevelt senior housing this is accomplished by operable shading screens and by the solarium,

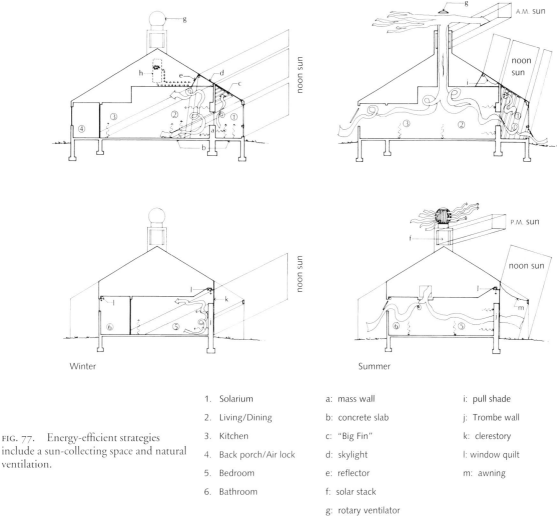

FIG. 77. Energy-efficient strategies include a sun-collecting space and natural ventilation.

A.M. sun

noon sun

P.M. sun

noon sun

noon sun

Winter

Summer

1. Solarium
2. Living/Dining
3. Kitchen
4. Back porch/Air lock
5. Bedroom
6. Bathroom

a: mass wall
b: concrete slab
c: "Big Fin"
d: skylight
e: reflector
f: solar stack
g: rotary ventilator
h: DHW heater/storage tank

i: pull shade
j: Trombe wall
k: clerestory
l: window quilt
m: awning

which can be physically isolated from the other parts of the dwelling. The north side receives little or no sunlight, so it too is easily controlled. It is cooler on the north of a building since it is in shade, and this differential between the north and south sides assists in natural cross-ventilation.

The most effective way to assure energy-efficient housing, then, is to make very long buildings oriented along the east-west axis, so that each building has extensive south- and north-facing facades. This is also a very efficient building plan, but the endless rows of south-facing buildings can be boring. One solution, used in the Pajaro project (discussed next), is a building block staggered and connected in a variety of ways that allow a southern orientation without the perception of continuous rows. The other solution, used in Roosevelt senior housing, accepts the connected

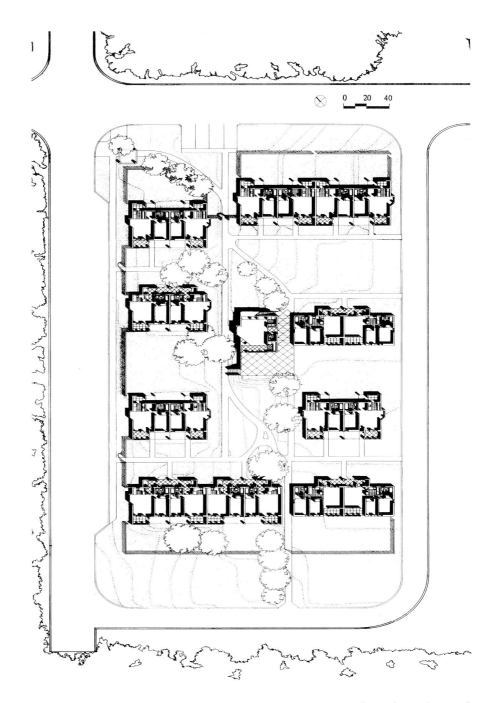

FIG. 78.   Roosevelt site plan, with rows of units staggered to make a series of court-yards along the walks. At its center is the community building.

house form but manipulates each row to diminish the repetitiveness. There are never more than four connected units, so the rows are not long, and each two share a cross-dormer on the north, which often spans the entry and makes them appear to be one house. These rows are then staggered on the site to create courts throughout the complex. The courts, often separated by the site's topography and by delicate, white fences, are quite intimate (fig. 78).

Late in the design, a query by a young student prompted the architects to rethink one point. They had placed all the entries to the units on the north, under the cross-gable, in order to make a recurring unit plan and to maximize the solar orientation. But the student wondered how this affected the social aspects of the design, since only half the units were entered through the courts. The entry sequence was thus unclear, with the front yards of half the dwellings serving as the backyards of the other half. The intent of this arrangement was to preserve the south-facing rooms for the living areas adjacent to private open space; the bedrooms were to be on the north. If energy orientation were not an issue, the pattern would be more like a conventional street. All residents would enter from the street, and the private yards would be on the opposite side of the dwelling, each abutting the adjoining private yard. The architects accepted the student's logic and redesigned the unit plans, at their own expense, within the same general form, allowing for south-facing entries in half of the units.[31]

The very low scale and low density of the housing component limited, in the architects' eyes, their ability to make a focal point in the project.[32] The community building would serve that function, but it too did not warrant enough space to make a large building. The architects pushed the funding agencies to allow for an additional dwelling, to be placed above the community facility, in order to make the facility grander, a perception that is enhanced by locating the building near the top of the hilly site. Thus, the project has twenty-one, not twenty, units. Since the funding did not allow for another subsidized dwelling, they argued for a market-rate dwelling, perhaps for a caretaker, in order to accomplish what they saw as a necessary architectural gesture.

The National Honor Awards jury praised the project as a "sensitive, innovative, and imaginative response to the special needs of the elderly."[33] It is somewhat ironic that the energetic, younger seniors whom the architects had anticipated as the residents had incomes too high to qualify for the project. Instead, infirm and very low-income seniors moved in. Had he known this, Kelbaugh would probably have chosen a different design.[34] Although the imagery and scale of Roosevelt senior housing continue to seem correct, the daily operation of the various energy devices to ensure optimal effectiveness was of little interest to the occupants, and many do not take advantage of the potential savings. The retractable awnings, for example, are left down and therefore become worn and soiled more quickly than expected. Kelbaugh's own analysis suggests that this strategy was a burden to the senior residents: "The shutters and curtains and greenhouses have to be operated by the tenants, and many are simply too old and forgetful. User interaction is a problem in projects involving the elderly."[35]

FIG. 79.   Pajaro, with its emphatic solar-collector roofs.

PAJARO

Davis, California
Designed by Sam Davis Architects
Winner of *Progressive Architecture* award (1981, as "Summertree")
36 units

Pajaro is the evolution of a larger, fully market-rate project called Summertree, which was the *Progressive Architecture* award winner. Reduced in size from 144 units to 36, then redesigned to make half the units affordable, as required by local inclusionary zoning, Pajaro was intended as an alternative to suburban single-family detached housing

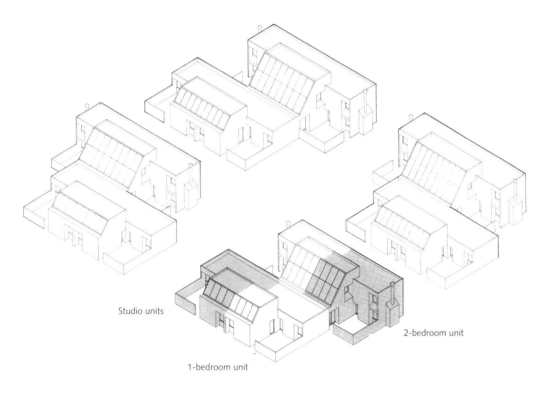

Studio units

1-bedroom unit

2-bedroom unit

FIG. 80.   Mirror images of Pajaro's
courtyard houses are connected, and these
combinations adjoin other, similar sets.

for either "empty nesters" or first-time buyers and as a demonstration of several energy-conserving features. The developers owned the active solar-energy system that provided domestic hot water, space heating, and some cooling for the units, and Pajaro was their first project that displayed how the system could be architecturally integrated into multifamily housing (fig. 79).

These two agendas, the energy imperative and the higher-density alternative to the house, had a dramatic impact on the design. The planning strategy entailed taking a single house form with a square plan and a corner patio, mirroring it, and attaching the two. The resulting two-unit building was then staggered with another, similar combination, making four connected dwellings (fig. 80).

Four such clusters were formed around a court-yard, which became a corral for cars close to each house (fig. 81). To make this an attractive alternative to the detached dwelling for the market-rate buyers, many house features were retained. For example, each dwelling is self-contained, with its own solar-energy system and its own private, enclosed patio that serves as both entry and yard. The private space, created by removing a corner from each square dwelling plan, is placed at either end of the building, so that no patio looks on or is adjacent to another.

This pattern of attached courtyard houses, all entered through their private open space, provides a clear entry sequence, but it does so by sacrificing the shared communal space created in the Roose-

FIG. 81.   The parking courtyard is formed by the groups of connected units.

velt Senior Citizen Housing plan. The spaces between the clusters are primarily for view and access, not for group activity. This compromise in Pajaro was based on the assumption that the likely occupants would want a self-contained dwelling with maximum privacy, even at increased density. It was also a result of the need for consistency in the plan and construction of the units, as a cost compensation for the extensive perimeter wall that the staggered form generated.

The difference between the market-rate and affordable units is size (fig. 82). The market-rate plans are based on a 36-foot square with an 18-foot court, the affordable units on a 32-foot square with a 16-foot court (fig. 83). The larger units also have attached garages, but all other features, including the energy systems, are identical. Each dwelling has a large closet that opens to its courtyard, where the solar water tanks and mechanical equipment are housed.

The most obvious visual features resulting from the energy agenda are the steeply sloped solar-collector roofs (fig. 84). The size and angle of these roofs are directly related to the amount of collector surface that was needed (20 percent of the floor area), but they further accommodated

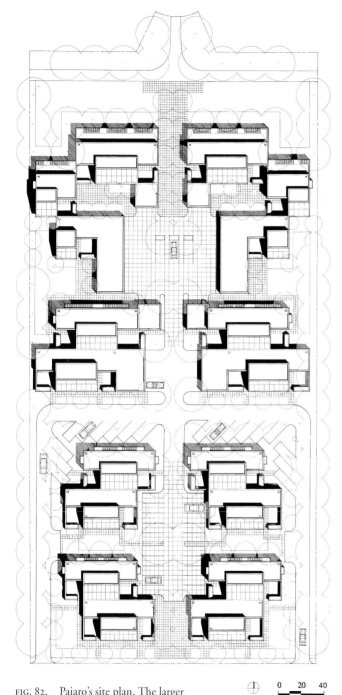

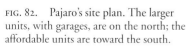

0   20   40

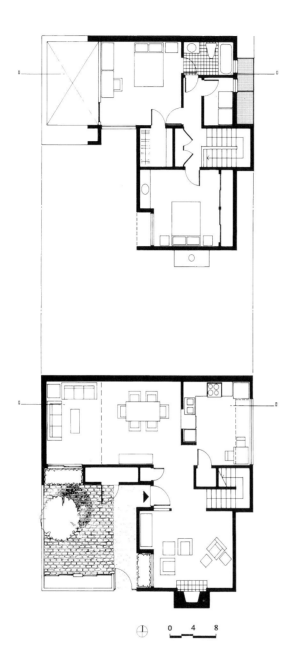

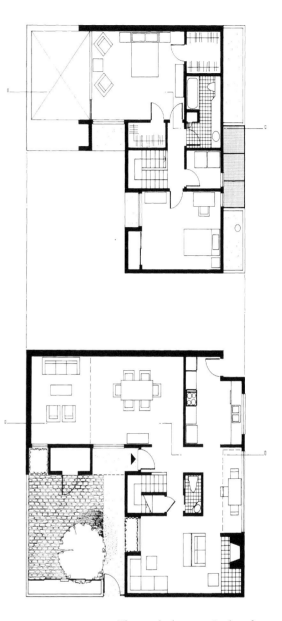

FIG. 83. The two-bedroom unit plans for Pajaro. The affordable dwellings (*left*) comprise four 16 × 16′ squares, whereas the market-rate units (*right*) are four 18 × 18′ squares.

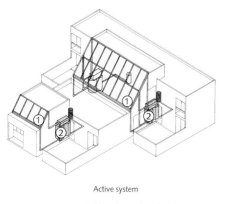

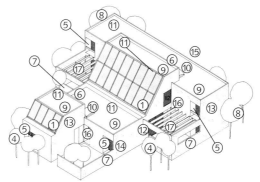

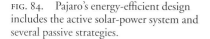

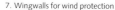

Active system		Passive system
1. Water-type solar collectors	7. Wingwalls for wind protection	13. Six-inch wall insulation
2. Solar storage tanks and controls	8. Landscaping for climate control	14. White stucco to reflect heat gain
3. Domestic hot-water tank	9. Gray roof gravel to equalize heat transfer	15. Minimal north windows
4. Deciduous trees for summer shade	10. Skylights for natural light	16. Protected south entrance
5. Recessed south-facing windows	11. Twelve-inch roof insulation	17. Trellis for east-west shading
6. Clerestory windows for natural light and ventilation	12. All double-glazed windows	

FIG. 84.   Pajaro's energy-efficient design includes the active solar-power system and several passive strategies.

the desire to create loft space and a high ceiling in the main living area of each dwelling (fig. 85). The dramatically sloping roofs also provide balanced lighting and assist in ventilation. Operable clerestory windows at the top of the north wall likewise bring soft daylight to the space and help stimulate natural ventilation. Because the units are aggregated tightly on the site, no such cross-ventilation would be possible for many units without these high windows. For the most part the energy-conserving features are truly passive, such as deep recesses for shading windows. The active solar-energy system is electronically monitored, requiring no manipulation by the residents.

The entire complex of connected square houses looks quite complicated, but apart from the dimensional difference between the affordable and market-rate components, the construction and detailing are nearly identical. The repetitive geometry creates a massing that seems irregular and varied, but in fact it is very simple and efficient. The smaller one-bedroom dwellings, which have only a loft on the second floor, are always placed in the front of a cluster to ensure that the solar collectors of the dwellings behind are not in shadow. The larger units, those with bedrooms on a second floor, are placed behind. The range of studios and one-, two-, and three-bedroom units from 500 to nearly 2,500 square feet is accommodated in this repeating, consistent, and closely packed geometry. Pajaro is a demonstration of variety within consistency. Its pueblo-like image tries to emphasize the individual character of the dwellings, but within a consistent whole. The locals

FIG. 85.   The living room of every dwelling has a high ceiling under the collector roof.

have nicknamed it "Little Egypt," not so much in reference to northern African design but more as a catchy moniker to give it a sort of landmark status. Since its construction, Pajaro has been surrounded by nondescript, multifamily development.

The distinctive image served to coalesce a small community of people who essentially value privacy and economy, but it also meant that only certain people were attracted to the project. Since the housing was always intended as for-sale, and thus included an element of choice, its distinctiveness was less of a problem than it would be for a rental project for people without housing options. The early occupants were mostly young professionals, first-time buyers who liked the low cost but also the uniqueness and independence. A young New York couple, recently arrived in California, appreciated the cosmopolitan aspect of the hard-edged geometry in a town where the housing was decidedly conventional. And while the project seemed quite immutable, many new owners created elaborate individualistic designs within their courtyards. Some covered theirs with trellises; others added wood decks and even fountains.

INFILL HOUSING

Santa Monica, California

Designed by Koning Eizenberg Architecture

Winner of *Progressive Architecture* award (1987)

19 units [36]

Santa Monica is one of the more affluent communities in an area west of central Los Angeles, and market-rate housing is extremely expensive. Like other large towns in the heavily populated region, Santa Monica has a diverse citizenry and its share of housing affordability problems. It is also a liberal, progressive town, and many residents were apprehensive when site after site succumbed to high-density, high-rise, high-cost housing. They reacted by creating the nonprofit CDC that sponsored these three projects.

The CDC astutely anticipated resistance to affordable housing and decided to combat it by having small infill projects. This strategy is often employed to limit the number of adversaries for any one development. If only a few units are to be built in a neighborhood, critics find it more difficult to argue about increased traffic and noise or the negative impact of a large number of low-income families. But while the adversaries for each site may be limited, there are more sites, each with its own naysayers, and each with its own set of hearings. After building these three projects the CDC tried the strategy again, proposing to place thirty units on four sites. Although this housing was eventually approved, it took three years of litigation, and the CDC had to agree to build no more affordable housing in that neighborhood for five years.[37] When it is possible to gain control of the individual sites and manage the approval processes concurrently, then at least the projects can be bid and built simultaneously. But this is a difficult proposition, and even if successful, the overall costs are likely to be higher than if the units were built on one site.

Given these exigencies of the scattered-site infill approach, architects hope to be able to develop a prototype that can be easily adapted to the conditions of the various sites. But in this case the circumstances demanded a somewhat different approach for each site. In Los Angeles the lots are generally narrow and deep, reaching from street to utility alley but still having access from both ends. Here, however, only one of the three sites, Berkeley Street, was of this type. The second, Fifth Street, was on a corner and did not reach to an alley; the third, Sixth Street, was landlocked in the middle of the block. Furthermore, the topographical conditions and parking requirements led the architects to different strategies.

FIFTH STREET—6 UNITS

Fifth Street is a tandem building, with one block of housing in front and one behind, both sharing the courtyard between. Since it is on the corner and the lot is relatively small, parking had to be placed at grade under the building. No other parking layout was feasible. This forced the courtyard up a level, above the parking, and pushed the building to three floors (fig. 86). The midblock court serves as both a front and back yard for the four units that adjoin it. It is their only defined common space and as such is asked to do many things: bring light and ventilation to the units, be a front porch and a usable patio, and provide emergency egress from the third level. Two sets of stairs go onto the court, and a catwalk that connects the front and rear buildings to the fire stair traverses it. As the architects see it, the courtyard is energized by these elements, which help organize the space and informally create separate zones within it (fig. 87).[38] The architects even provided a hole in the floor through which a tree, planted in the ground one story below, could penetrate to offer some shade and landscaping. (The tree was

FIG. 86.   Fifth Street places the courtyard above in order to accommodate the cars at street level.

gone after a few years.) But all these elements may also be seen as obstructions.

Julie Eizenberg, one of the architects, was pleased that in spite of the many demands on this space, at least the initial tenants for these two- and three-bedroom upper units seemed to be quite compatible and even shared child-care tasks, using the court as a play area. For her it was important to provide this open space, light, and cross-ventilation, regardless of the constraints of the site (fig. 88). Another objective was to ensure that the street was not ignored.[39] In this six-unit building, two of the units are entered not from the mid-block court but directly from Fifth Street. These two single-floor dwellings are the building's friendly front, with a pathway and a porch. Their private space is not shared, like the court; they each have a small, wall-enclosed patio at the side of the building.

FIG. 87.   The courtyard, at the second level, is both an entry and a shared play space.

Third floor

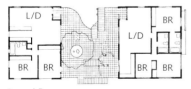

Second floor

FIG. 88.   Plan of Fifth Street infill housing. The upper-level deck above the parking separates front units from back and serves as both an entry and a semiprivate open space. The lower-level units face the street, much like neighboring buildings.

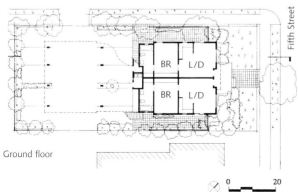

Hollister Avenue

Fifth Street

Ground floor

0   20

FIG. 89.   Sixth Street, with parking partly underground.

SIXTH STREET — 6 UNITS

At the Fifth Street buildings the court had to be raised one level to accommodate the surface parking, but at Sixth Street the topography and deep front-yard setback made a partly subterranean garage feasible (fig. 89). Here the tandem building is again employed, but its access is a narrow walkway from the street and along the north side of the building. This pathway is like a secret passage that leads to the mysteries of the midblock, a domain reserved only for these six units. It is the entry for all the dwellings, but each has at least a small private space as well (fig. 90). In this section of Los Angeles it is not uncommon to enter units in midblock. In the typical courtyard building, entry is through a narrow passage in the middle of the building and into a court surrounded by dwellings. In this way apartments guard the entryway and define the courtyard through which residents

Kit.

Study

L/D

LR

Kit./D

Ground floor

Sixth Street

0   10

BR

BR

BR

BR

L/D

Kit.

L/D

Kit.

BR

BR

BR

BR

BR

BR

BR

BR

Second floor (rear units)

Kit.

L/D

Kit.

L/D

BR

BR

BR

Second floor (front units)

FIG. 90.   Plan of Sixth Street infill housing. The front building, with four dwellings, is separated from the rear townhouses by a shared court accessed through a narrow side yard.

FIG. 91. The court separates rather than connects the buildings, and the building behind is stylistically different from the one in front.

pass to enter their units. But on these narrow lots, particularly when a driveway shares the frontage, the passage is forced to one side. For this six-unit building the combination of a site sloping down to the street and no access to either an alley or a side street meant no opportunity to have street-front entry to the dwellings.

The courtyard in the Sixth Street building is not so taxed as that for Fifth Street. While both are tandem buildings, the courtyard here separates rather than connects (fig. 91). This notion is reinforced by the separate architecture of the two structures, one with a vaulted roof and one with a flat roof, and each with a different palate of materials. Segmenting of structures, a recurring theme in the work of Koning Eizenberg, even entails changing exterior materials on the same structure.

BERKELEY STREET — 7 UNITS

The Fifth and Sixth Street buildings have several common features, not the least of which is the midblock court. But Berkeley Street has an entirely different strategy. This is partly a result of the long, narrow block that reaches through to an alley and allows for car access to a subterranean garage, but also because it was built later and with an additional sponsor.

Berkeley Street links four block forms—three nearly identical sets of stacked flats and one townhouse—into a building that looks like four dwellings but is actually seven (fig. 92). The blocks are slightly shifted and turned to further emphasize the notion that they are individual dwellings (fig. 93), and this perception is reinforced by the emphatic entries for each. Like Sixth Street, there

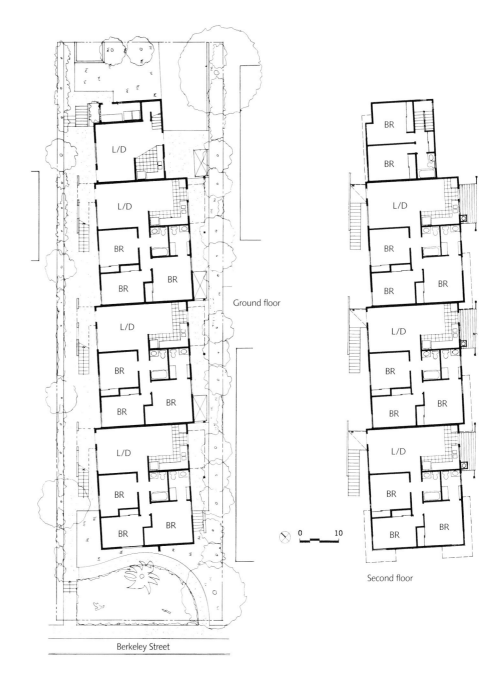

L/D

L/D

BR

BR BR

L/D

BR

BR BR

L/D

BR

BR BR

Ground floor

BR

BR

L/D

BR

BR BR

L/D

BR

BR BR

L/D

BR

BR BR

Second floor

0   10

Berkeley Street

FIG. 93.   Plan of Berkeley Street shows
four offset blocks, three of which have two
units.

FIG. 94.   Berkeley Street's side-yard entries.

is a side-yard access along the north side to the units, but here it reaches no hidden private oasis. It traverses the length of the site, ending in the alley. Along its way it serves as a very narrow front yard for all the units (fig. 94). Opposite, on the sunny south side of this long building, are the private outdoor spaces.

All three buildings are overtly modern, a choice, the architects explain, that was a function of the budget and the building norms in the area but also makes a historical reference.[40] Much as the Charleston houses were a nod to their past, these buildings allude to the European modernism brought to Los Angeles by Rudolph Schindler, Irving Gill, and Richard Neutra. The thin stucco walls with few embellishments and the seemingly random placement of windows, many oriented horizontally to further diminish the perception of the solidity of the walls, are characteristic of a modernism that was informed and tempered by

FIG. 95. A freestanding wall that marks the dwelling entries is an abstraction of a porch.

the moderate southern California climate. Perhaps the clearest example of the references to Los Angeles modernism is Berkeley Street's front facade: its solid, white stucco massing and flat roof are relieved at the top by horizontal corner windows reminiscent of Gill's Horatio West Court, built nearby in 1910 and still the epitome of the attached dwelling strategy in multifamily housing.

The architects freely acknowledge this legacy, which was recognized by the awards jury as praiseworthy, but Eizenberg also worries about the place of design choices and aesthetic experimentation in affordable housing. Are the designers imposing their ideas on those who have no housing choice? For her, the stylistic choices must yield amenity. The thin, projecting horizontal slabs do form in-

teresting compositions, but they also shade the bright California sun. Given her druthers, however, she would use trees rather than attachments to buildings for shading. But the advantage of this modernist architecture is that the desired embellishments can be abstracted, simplified, and inexpensive. Compare, for example, the entries of the similarly scaled houses of Charleston to those at Berkeley Street. The Charleston entries have painstaking details, carefully crafted, and wood molding and picket handrails. The Berkeley Street entries are simple, freestanding stucco walls placed in front of each downstairs unit. The walls, with their door and window cut-outs, are merely vestigial porches that identify the lower unit while hiding the stairs to the upper dwelling (fig. 95).

THE BEACH

Albuquerque, New Mexico

Designed by Antoine Predock

Winner of *Progressive Architecture* award (1985)

74 units

Some architects begin designs by developing impressions of a place and then interpreting these into a formal response. Antoine Predock, a New Mexico architect, began his career by making astounding sculptural houses that were visceral reactions to desert. His newer, public buildings, like the Las Vegas Library and Children's Museum, are visual poems about the essence of the site. The Beach is an example of this approach for affordable housing on a site caught between the sublime and the ridiculous. The building defers to neither, while recognizing both.

The 750-foot-long narrow stretch of land rests on an access road adjacent to Highway 66, a thoroughfare romanticized in a 1960s television series. But the highway is a dissonant mishmash of undistinguished strip commercial centers and uncoordinated signage. The site once held a motel called The Beach, which was something of a landmark because of its excessive neon lighting. The back of the site faces an exclusive country club and, in the distance, the Sandia Mountains (fig. 96). The architect describes the site as schizophrenic, "a cultural fault line, the habitat of the West Central Avenue, Route 66 custom cruiser meeting the white belts and white shoes of the Albuquerque Country Club."[41]

But what the site represents today is only part of the context that comes to bear on Predock's design. Although the neighborhood is now largely Hispanic, Albuquerque, like much of the Southwest, has a strong Native American history, encompassing a dramatic craft and cliff-dwelling tradition. The astonishing formal qualities of The Beach borrow from both cultures.

FIG. 96.   The Beach, caught between the commercial strip and the country club.

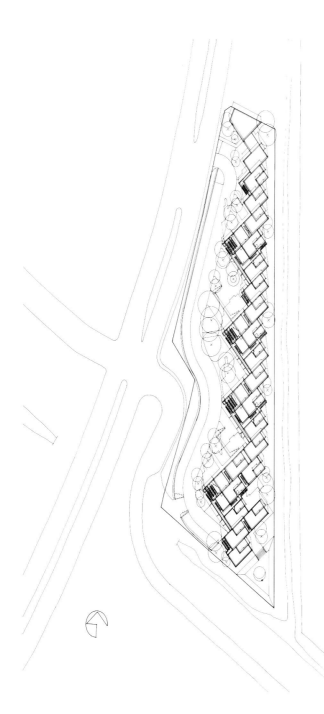

FIG. 97. Site plan for The Beach. What looks complex is actually rational and orthogonal.

The narrowness of the site, its forty-five-degree orientation to the mountains, and its dual character of gentility and crassness generate the dynamic site plan (fig. 97). A series of four major housing blocks, each nearly a square in plan, is turned forty-five degrees to the street. At each of the corners closest to the street, the building rises to a height of four floors, then cascades toward the golf course. The result is a metaphoric chain of mountains that refers to those in the distance. The rise to the top of these mountains is a series of steps, some large, made from the dwellings themselves, and some small, made from the stepping of parapets enclosing stairways and handrails. These smaller crenellations are references to Navajo rug and blanket designs.[42]

Most of the powerful variation is oriented toward, and focused on, the street side. Viewed from the street, the building has a clear visual and conceptual connection to the mountains, and the exuberance of the forms creates a continuity with the commercial strip. Moving up and down in elevation while moving in and out in plan, the building is outlined by thin neon strings. In daylight it is a mountain, a cliff dwelling, or a Navajo pattern; at night it is an integral, glowing part of the street (fig. 98). The opposite side, that which faces the mountains and the country club, is sedate by comparison. The mock-mountains descend to form an irregular hillside of rooftops, balconies, and patios.

One member of the *Progressive Architecture* jury suggested that this powerful imagery broke all the rules of affordable housing, and relative to cost it would certainly seem so.[43] First, the seventy-four units range from studios to four-bedrooms, and there is much variety even within the types. Second, there is an extensive amount of perimeter wall, one of the most costly components of a building. Third, there are many roof decks, patios, and stairways over enclosed area, features generally costly both to create and to maintain.

FIG. 98.   At night neon outlines the crenellated forms, emphasizing The Beach's proximity to and affinity for the strip.

The Beach is also an enigma relative to the amenities one would hope to find in affordable housing. It has no courtyard, no focus for the community. There is a park at one end of the site, but it is out of view and a substantial walk for residents living at the opposite end. The extensive stairways, while providing some privacy to the dwellings, have little overview for security, no "eyes on the street." And while the four "mountains" are apparent in the overall form, individual dwellings are not (fig. 99). This is clearly a highly visible, recognizable landmark, not subtle or discreet housing.

It does look costly, but like the other projects discussed here it was constructed on a very modest budget. How was this done? The "mountains," while visually complex, recur four times, gaining some efficiency in their repetition. And even though their plans seem angular, they are actually on an orthogonal system, with only ninety-degree corners, and with consistent cross-walls and regular structural spans (fig. 100). Another cost-saving strategy was the collaborative involvement of the contractor from the beginning. Had this project been competitively bid, the cost would have likely been much higher; from a builder's initial view it

FIG. 99. Two of The Beach's building "mountains."

FIG. 100. Ground floor of one of the four segments of The Beach.

looks frightening. But by working closely with the architect and seeing the subtle, hidden logic in the design, the builder found inexpensive ways to accommodate the architectural intentions.[44]

The project is not without its amenities. By turning this regular system forty-five degrees, Predock creates pockets of parking, each one closely associated to the adjacent units, and forecourts to each cluster. This scheme limits the number of cars in any one place. While staggering both in plan and in section produces extensive exterior walls, it also provides at least two orientations for most dwellings. The units get cross-ventilation, excellent natural light, and wonderful views, many to the mountains and golf course. But as two commentators of the design insightfully state, the real agenda for The Beach was "to find new, high-art housing with a viable price tag."[45] Its fulfillment of these conditions is its greatest amenity.

DAYBREAK GROVE AND SUNRISE PLACE

Escondido, California

Designed by Davids Killory Architects

Winner of *Progressive Architecture* awards (1991 and 1992)

21 units for homeless families [46]

René Davids and Christine Killory have the unique distinction of receiving back-to-back *Progressive Architecture* awards for two affordable housing projects for the same nonprofit client, both in the low-density southern California town of Escondido. One, originally called The Bridge but christened as Sunrise Place, is eight units of interim housing for homeless families; the other, Daybreak Grove, is thirteen units for single mothers and their children. Both rely heavily on the architects' interpretation of the California bungalow courtyard.

The architects believe strongly in the appropriateness of the bungalow court as a device to integrate housing into low-density neighborhoods and as a way of recognizing the sanctity of the individual dwelling, as well as its connection to the community.[47] For homeless families, who have neither community nor privacy, both are critical issues.

The unit planning on both sites underscores the architects' understanding of the residents' needs (fig. 101). The dwellings are linked two-story townhouses, each with clearly recognizable and independent entries. The units, particularly those for mothers and children, include layers of space, transitions from the most public to the most private areas. There is a porch in front and in back, making access to both the courtyard and the street very direct, and a private interior patio as well (no doubt inspired by the architects' own house, a traditional California bungalow that they have renovated to include these elements). These features provide a strong sense of retreat as one moves

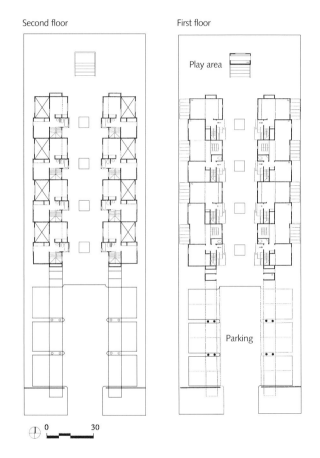

Second floor   First floor

Play area

Parking

0   30

FIG. 101.   Plans of Sunrise Place (*above*) and Daybreak Grove (*opposite*).

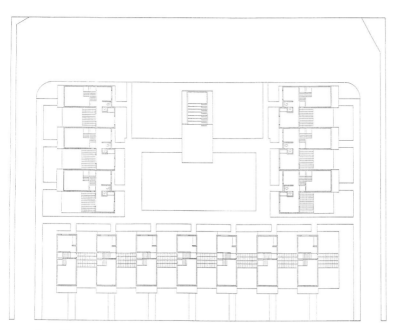

Second floor

Parking

Play area   Garden

Laundromat/Theater

Play area

First floor

0   20

FIG. 102a, b.   The courtyard at Sunrise Place, resembling a street with houses, leads to a small theater.

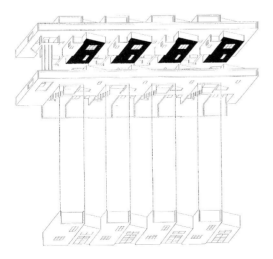

through the spatial layers, yet there is also the ever-present potential to connect to the outside world when one chooses. The kitchens are oriented to the courtyard for easy observation of children, but the living rooms are oriented to the city streets.

The architecture of both designs is a dramatic, somewhat abstract, very loose interpretation of the bungalow. It is a typological, not a stylistic, interpretation. The individual units are well identified, but they do not have the soft, rambling, humble feeling of their predecessors. In Sunrise Place, the individual houses are connected by interlocking L-shaped plans that allow each to have frontage on the courtyard. But more importantly and emphatically, they are connected by a continuous linear block that traverses all the dwellings on each side of the courtyard. The houses peek out from this strong axis, jutting both toward the neighbors on either side of the project and toward each other across their narrow courtyard. This architectural gesture serves several purposes. It is the consistent element, the group form, against which the individual houses are seen. Their length and rectilinear shape is urban, making the courtyard they define much more like a city street (fig. 102a, b). In fact the designers envisioned the court as an active street in a Latin American town, with canvas shading drawn across its width.[48] To capture this activity they have placed all the dwelling entries, the laundry facility, the children's play area, and a tiny outdoor theater along this inner street, which turns into a real street as it terminates in the parking court.

Daybreak Grove, for mothers and children, is somewhat more conventional both in its site plan and in its interpretation of the California bungalow court (fig. 103a, b). The dwellings are attached townhouses, each with a high volume that provides for a dramatic living space within, while emphasizing the unit's independence when seen from the exterior. They have a remarkable degree of

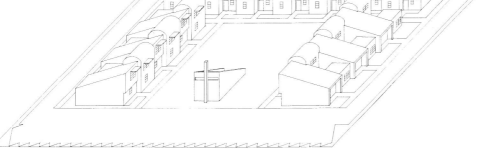

FIG. 103a, b. The courtyard at Daybreak
Grove is more conventional, with a play
yard surrounded by identifiable houses.

spatial variety within a mere 800 square feet: high spaces, interior patio, loft. These dwellings surround a playground on three sides. The fourth side, to the back of the lot, is parking. This is a sound urban gesture. It isolates the noise of the play within the project; protects the children from the street; moves the houses, with their entry paths, toward the street, as is the pattern in the neighborhood; and visually obscures the twenty cars from view.

The individual within the collective is a recurrent interest of the architects and is well represented in these designs. Their influences range from the Salk Institute, where individual laboratories are placed around a linear, symmetrical court-yard, to the Carthusian monasteries of Europe, where monks had private quarters placed around shared gardens. But in realizing these notions in affordable housing, the architects are quick to give credit to their client, Amy Roland, the director of the nonprofit North County Housing Foundation. A college acquaintance of theirs who at one time attended architecture school, she has what they feel is a critical understanding of the importance of design and a willingness to take some risks to make housing that does more than warehouse these previously homeless occupants.[49] Two separate architectural juries recognized the value in this approach.

What will save the ten award-winning projects from the fate of Acorn? Several are, after all, hard-edged, modern stucco structures. Thirty years from now will someone revisit these buildings, lamenting their condition and recounting both their promise and their problems? While there are no guarantees, these newer projects have several advantages over Acorn and other projects built in earlier decades. First, the award winners are relatively small in scale and therefore do not attempt to force dozens, much less hundreds, of very low-income families into one location; many, in fact, have residents of mixed incomes. Second, most of these buildings are owned and operated by community-based nonprofits that take pride in them and care deeply about their longevity and continued physical health. Finally, many of these projects carefully reflect the needs of the residents, not just for sound, commodious housing but also for other facilities and services.

These projects also represent a nascent movement to understand the various social dimensions of the nation's need for affordable housing. Why are so many people unable to afford market-rate housing? The most obvious reason, of course, is that their incomes are not high enough. But behind this general response lurk several more spe-cific deficiencies: inadequate education and job training, lack of accessible health care, and weak family, community, and social support.

Architects and developers of affordable housing are beginning to identify and then incorporate into projects the social services that can help residents surmount these deficiencies. In Los Angeles, the lawyer-turned–housing developer Kent Salve-son determined that the greatest need in the central city was better education for young children, many from single-parent households. He set out to develop an affordable housing project that included an educational component, complete with a classroom, computers, and tutors. The architecture of his EEXCEL Apartments reveals nothing unusual; the educational component occupies a unit identical to the other apartments. But his notion that an important service catering to the occupants be an integral part of both the creation and operation of housing is remarkable. It was not considered a mere amenity; the funding for the project included a line-item for tutors, a fact that met with resistance from most lenders.[1]

That housing should be combined with other uses is not a new idea. Mixed-use urban housing, dwellings coexisting with shops, is what makes cities vibrant and varied. In the suburbs many apartment developments include recreational facilities as an enticement for their young singles market. In affordable housing mixed-use planning can lead to senior housing with an on-site geriatrics clinic, housing for the homeless that includes job-training classrooms, shelters for abused women that have counseling facilities, and housing for single parents that has a child-care center. These strategies recognize that the needs of the occupants are not limited to shelter.

Such combinations do not necessarily change the architectural approaches. The community spaces may be larger to accommodate the new uses, or as at Colton Palms, there may be several special buildings for each use. More often there are subtle variations in the plan for the housing. For example, a bedroom suite may be placed between two apartments to allow its shared use, for instance, by visiting grandparents or by a child-care assistant. Or a room could be located near the dwelling's entry to serve as a home office for a parent or for a senior in poor health.

Many of these approaches also rely on the sharing of common spaces and activities. This is the premise behind "cohousing," a housing movement that originated in Scandinavia and is now finding its place in the United States.[2] Among its major physical characteristics are separate, often attached houses, each with a small kitchen, and a common house with a larger kitchen, used by the entire community. But cohousing is as much a social construct as a physical one. The proponents undertake the design collectively and, once the housing is built, may share responsibilities for collective meals, child care, and management of the project.

Although the presence of shared facilities allows for the design of smaller units, these approaches have not made housing less expensive to build, nor are they yet very prevalent. Part of the reason is that their financing is complicated. Once again, lenders view anything unconventional as suspect. And often the social component is funded by a

different source than the housing, bringing a second set of rules, regulations, and time frames. But the advantages of these approaches are increasingly becoming obvious; the housing is less institutional and gives the residents more control over their lives. Such experiments remind us that solving the housing problem requires creative attention to both physical and social factors.

The sober reality is that there will always be a demand for affordable housing. We are not witnessing a temporary condition that calls for quick emergency solutions. People with all types of lifestyles and needs—seniors, singles, families with children, homeless—share an affordable housing crisis. We need to provide them with sound buildings that require considerable architectural effort and reflect the values of the community, whether it be urban, suburban, or rural. And while technical advancements are welcome, they cannot substitute for sensitive design that incorporates the aspirations and visions of generations of residents who will live in the housing. Such a vast undertaking can only be accomplished by a consortium of architects, community development groups, local officials, and concerned citizens. Our collective will must also include a consistent assault on NIMBYism, to be waged as a war of attrition. Good architecture is the main weapon, with each good new project representing a small victory.

Recently I was telling a friend that my firm had again been retained to design affordable housing for a nonprofit developer. He asked what we were planning that was innovative. I think he was hoping I would cite some marvel of technology, some new high-tech system that could be constructed in hours, cost half what a normal dwelling would cost, have all the amenities that a family would need, and last for centuries without maintenance. What I said was that we were planning to build affordable housing that was better than market-rate, and to design housing that he would be proud to live in.

PREFACE

1. Bureau of the Census, *1990 Census of Population and Housing: Summary Social, Economic, and Housing Characteristics, United States* (Washington, D.C., 1992).
2. Interview with Tom Cook, deputy director of policy, California Department of Housing and Community Development (August 4, 1992).

INTRODUCTION

1. Cushing N. Dolbeare, "Federal Homeless Social Policies for the 1990s," *Housing Policy Debate* 2, no. 3 (1991): 1067.
2. James D. Wright and Beth A. Rubin, "Is Homelessness a Housing Problem?" *Housing Policy Debate* 2, no. 3 (1991): 949.
3. David S. Cordray and Georgine M. Pion, "What's Behind the Numbers? Definitional Issues in Counting the Homeless," *Housing Policy Debate* 2, no. 3 (1991): 606; Peter H. Rossi, *Down and Out in America: The Origins of Homelessness* (Chicago: University of Chicago Press, 1989), 81.
4. The various methods of counting the homeless and the different definitions of homelessness make accurate statistical representation of the problem complex. See "Counting the Homeless: The Methodologies, Policies, and Social Signifi-
cance Behind the Number" (papers presented at the Fannie Mae Annual Housing Conference, May 14, 1991), in *Housing Policy Debate* 2, no. 3, (1991); and Courtenay M. Slater and George E. Hall, eds., *1992 County and City Extra: Annual Metro, City, and County Data Book* (Lanham, Md.: Bernan Press, 1992), 20.
5. Bureau of the Census, *1990 Housing Highlights, United States* (Washington, D.C., 1991); and idem, "Money Income of Households, Families, and Persons in the United States: 1990," *Current Population Reports: Consumer Income*, ser. P-60, no. 174 (Washington, D.C., 1991), table B-12.
6. Bureau of the Census and Department of Housing and Urban Development, "American Housing Survey for the United States in 1989," *Current Housing Reports*, ser. H-150 (Washington, D.C., 1991), table C; Eric N. Lindblom, "Toward a Comprehensive Homelessness-Prevention Strategy," *Housing Policy Debate* 2, no. 3 (1991): 994.
7. Cushing N. Dolbeare, *The Widening Gap: Housing Needs of Low-Income Families* (Washington, D.C.: Low-Income Housing Information Service [LIHIS], 1992), 20.
8. Bureau of the Census, *1990 Census of Population and Housing: Summary Tape File STF3a* (Washington, D.C., 1990).

9. By most estimates the soft cost of construction—that not directly related to labor and materials (bonds, fees, permits, etc.)—is between 25 and 30 percent of the total cost. All other costs relate directly to decisions about design and structure. (The total cost considered here excludes aspects unrelated to construction, such as land and financing.)

10. Bureau of the Census, *Statistical Abstract of the United States: 1992* (Washington, D.C., 1992), tables 12 and 49.

11. Martin Mayer, *The Builders: Houses, People, Neighborhood, Government, Money* (New York: Norton, 1978), 120.

12. Sam Davis, ed., *The Form of Housing* (New York: Van Nostrand Reinhold, 1977), vii.

CHAPTER 1

1. Richard Plunz, *A History of Housing in New York City: Dwelling Type and Social Change in the American Metropolis* (New York: Columbia University Press, 1990), 22, 47.

2. In his *History of Housing*, Plunz provides a thorough study of the evolution of housing types and the social and regulatory forces that influenced them. Since his focus is New York, he covers all manner of urban housing, from early tenements through late twentieth-century projects.

3. Gwendolyn Wright, *Building the Dream: A Social History of Housing in America* (New York: Pantheon Books, 1981), 122.

4. Paul Groth, "Nonpeople: A Case Study of Public Architects and Impaired Social Vision," in Russell Ellis and Dana Cuff, eds., *Architects' People* (New York: Oxford University Press, 1989), 222.

5. Robert C. Spencer Jr., "The Work of Frank Lloyd Wright," *Architectural Review* 7 (June 1900): 71.

6. Spiro Kostof, *America by Design* (New York: Oxford University Press, 1987), 101–2.

7. Wright, *Building the Dream,* 221.

8. Ursula Cliff, "Oskar Stonorov: Public Housing Pioneer," *Design and Environment* 2, no. 3 (Fall 1971): 52.

9. Warren Shaw, "First Houses," *Metropolis* 12, no. 6 (January/February, 1993): 27–31.

10. Catherine Bauer, *Modern Housing* (Boston: Houghton Mifflin Company, 1934), 129.

11. Roger Montgomery, "High Density, Low-Rise Housing and the Changes in the American Housing Economy," in Davis, ed., *The Form of Housing,* 83–111.

12. Federal Housing Administration, *Minimum Property Standards for Multifamily Housing,* FHA no. 2600 (Washington, D.C.: Government Printing Office, 1963).

13. The sociologist Lee Rainwater, the planner and architect Roger Montgomery, and the architect Mary Comerio have all written about Pruitt-Igoe. Each shows how the problems were as much social, political, and administrative as they were architectural.

14. Mary C. Comerio, "Pruitt-Igoe and Other Stories," *Journal of Architectural Education* 34, no. 4 (1981): 26–31.

15. Jane Jacobs, *The Death and Life of Great American Cities* (New York: Random House, 1961), 35.

16. For a fuller discussion of how advocacy movements altered the course of projects, see Chester Hartman, "Housing Struggles and Housing Form," in Davis, ed., *The Form of Housing,* 113–37.

17. Murray L. Weidenbaum remarks that project approval under the law today takes as much as two years—the same amount of time it took to construct the Empire State Building in the 1930s (*Business, Government, and the Public,* 4th ed. [New York: Prentice Hall, 1990], 100–102).

18. Victor B. Scheffer, *The Shaping of Environmentalism in America* (Seattle: University of Washington Press, 1991), 145.

19. Urban Institute, *Housing America: Learning from the Past, Planning for the Future* (Washington, D.C.: Urban Institute Press, 1990), 11.

20. Montgomery, "High Density, Low-Rise Housing," 100.

21. Jacqueline Cutler and Jacqueline Frost, "Scant Shelter," *Oakland Tribune,* Sunday, November 29, 1992, A-1.

22. Joel Warren Barna, "CDCs, a New Force in Public Housing," *Progressive Architecture* 72, no. 6 (June 1991): 116, and Robert Miller, "Will HOPE Starve out HOME?" *Architectural Record* 180, no. 9 (September 1992): 36–37; Bradley Inman, "Building a Future for Nonprofit Housing," *San Francisco Examiner*, Sunday, October 11, 1992, F-8–F-9.

23. Inman, ibid.

24. *California Credit Counter* 3, no. 4 (December 1992): 3.

25. Karin Kirsch, *The Weissenhofsiedlung: Experimental Housing Built for the Deutscher Werkbund, Stuttgart, 1927* (New York: Rizzoli, 1989), 17. The quote is from the policy statement of the Württemberg Werkbund in 1926.

26. Michael Pyatok, "Housing as a Social Enterprise: The Ambivalent Role of Design Competitions," *Journal of Architectural Education* 46, no. 3 (February 1993): 148.

27. For a discussion of the features of these designs, see Sam Davis, "The House versus Housing," in Davis, ed., *The Form of Housing*, 1–39.

28. From the report by Phillip Johnson, chair of the jury, in City of New York Housing and Development Administration et al., *Record of Submissions and Awards Competition for Middle-Income Housing at Brighton Beach, Brooklyn 1968* (New York: City of New York, 1968; not paginated).

29. Marta Gutman, "Housers and Other Architects: Pragmatism and Aesthetics in Recent Competitions," *Journal of Architectural Education* 46, no. 3 (February 1993): 131–46. Gutman discusses the series of modest competitions held each year between 1984 and 1991. Only one yielded a building.

30. Harvey Sherman, Preface to Harvey Sherman and Elizabeth Spring, eds., *The New American House Competition* (Minneapolis: Minneapolis College of Art and Design, 1984).

31. Jacqueline Leavitt, "Two Prototypical Designs for Single Parents," in Karen A. Franck and Sherry Ahrentzen, eds., *New Households, New Housing* (New York: Van Nostrand Reinhold, 1989), 182–83.

32. Interview with Rob Wellington Quigley (August 7, 1992).

33. Bryan Irwin, David Pollak, and Anne Tate, "The *PA* House," *Progressive Architecture* 73, no. 8 (August 1992): 44–51.

34. Ashok Chaluvadi, "Market Share of Top Builders," *Housing Economics* (August 1991): 13–14.

35. See Richard Bender and John Parman, "A Framework for Industrialization," in Davis, ed., *The Form of Housing*, 172–89. The authors describe other analogies for systems, such as that of Karl Popper, who evokes the difference between a clock movement, which is predictable and exact, and a cloud movement, which is predictable but not exact.

36. Nabeel Hamdi, *Housing without Houses: Participation, Flexibility, Enablement* (New York: Van Nostrand Reinhold, 1991), 51–74.

37. John F. C. Turner, *Housing by People: Toward Autonomy in Building Environments* (New York: Pantheon Books, 1977).

38. John N. Habraken, *Supports: An Alternative to Mass Housing* (London: Architectural Press, 1972).

39. See Peter G. Rowe, *Modernity and Housing* (Cambridge, Mass.: MIT Press, 1993), 230–44.

40. "Habitat," *Architectural Review* 142, no. 846 (August 1967): 143.

41. Interview with Moshe Safdie (June 21, 1992).

42. Moshe Safdie, "Habitat at 25," *Architectural Record* 180, no. 7 (July 1992): 40–42.

CHAPTER 2

1. Department of Housing and Community Development, State of California, *The Effects of Subsidized and Affordable Housing on Property Values: A Survey of Research* (Sacramento: Department of Housing and Community Development, 1990). This research reviews fifteen published papers, fourteen of which conclude there are no significant negative effects from affordable housing, and indeed some positive impact, on property values of surrounding neighborhoods. See also Paul M. Cummings with John D. Landis, *Relationships*

between Affordable Housing Developments and Neighboring Property Values (Berkeley: University of California at Berkeley, Institute of Urban and Regional Development, 1993), a study of three thousand home sales in California within a quarter mile of new affordable housing that shows that single-family home prices are not lowered because of such projects (17).

2. Interview with Steve Kodama (June 2, 1992).

3. Interview with Robert Marquis (July 7, 1992).

4. This estimate, by Philip Bettencourt of The Preview Company in Orange County, California, is cited in U.S. Advisory Commission on Regulatory Barriers to Affordable Housing, *"Not in My Back Yard": Removing Barriers to Affordable Housing* (Washington, D.C.: U.S. Department of Housing and Urban Development, 1991), 2–12.

5. Timothy Noah, "The Money Trail: Why Federal Dollars Meant for the Poor Seem to Disappear," *Wall Street Journal*, July 24, 1992, 1.

6. Interview with Michael Pyatok (July 2, 1992).

7. Interview with Robert Marquis (July 7, 1992).

8. Debra Stein, *Winning Community Support for Land Use Projects* (Washington, D.C.: Urban Land Institute, 1992), 25–26.

9. Carol T. Robbins, *Removing Regulatory Barriers to Affordable Housing: How States and Localities Are Moving Ahead* (Washington, D.C.: Department of Housing and Urban Development, Office of Policy Development and Research, 1992), 17.

10. Donald A. Schön, *Educating the Reflective Practitioner* (San Francisco: Jossey-Bass, Inc., 1987).

CHAPTER 3

1. Allyson Watts and Frank J. Rockwood, *The Cost of Affordable Housing: An Analysis of Development Cost* (Sacramento: Department of Housing and Community Development, State of California, 1992).

2. Bay Area Economics and ARCH.Research, *The California Affordable Housing Cost Study: Initial Comparison of Market Rate and Affordable Rental Projects* (n.p.: Local Initiatives Support Corpora-

tion and California Tax Credit Allocation Committee, 1993), i.

3. Watts and Rockwood, *Cost of Affordable Housing*, 3; and Bay Area Economics and ARCH.Research, *California Affordable Housing*, ii.

4. Interview with Robert Marquis (July 7, 1992). This insight is part of his comment that "a rich man's amenity may be a poor man's necessity."

5. Watts and Rockwood, *Cost of Affordable Housing*, 5.

6. Ibid., 4.

7. Anne Gelbspan, *The Affordable Housing Challenge: Case Studies of Selected Developments* (Boston: Boston Society of Architects Housing Committee, 1988), 6. This document also has a good overview of the issues of modular building.

8. Interview with David Baker (June 2, 1992).

9. Interview with Howard Backen (July 7, 1992).

10. U.S. Advisory Commission on Regulatory Barriers to Affordable Housing, *"Not in My Back Yard,"* 3–6.

11. Anthony Downs, "The Advisory Commission on Regulatory Barriers to Affordable Housing: Its Behavior and Accomplishments," *Housing Policy Debate* 2, no. 4 (1991): 1104.

12. This figure is approximate. Because many construction costs are fixed regardless of the size of the project, there is a diminishing cost on a square-foot basis for larger buildings. The last square foot does not cost as much as the first.

13. Christine Benglia Bevington, "One Size Doesn't Fit All," *Interior Design* 63, no. 11 (August 1992): 81.

14. Interview with Rob Wellington Quigley (August 7, 1992).

15. U.S. Advisory Commission on Regulatory Barriers to Affordable Housing, *"Not in My Back Yard,"* 3–7.

16. Downs, "Advisory Commission," 1109, 1112.

17. Donald MacDonald, "Home Sweet Home: The Fading American Dream," *Sooner Magazine* (University of Oklahoma) (Spring 1988): 13.

18. The lack of comparative construction data is a recurrent dilemma recounted in the literature on

affordable housing. There are data on single-family house construction and costs, but the product is more definable and less variable than multifamily projects. Part of the problem is related to record-keeping. Even bid documents from contractors do not follow a consistent form, so that some aspects of construction are categorized differently. Both of the California studies revealed that the basis for comparing projects (e.g., people per unit or bedrooms per unit) yielded a different, and more favorable, picture of affordable housing than either square-foot or total unit costs.

19. Downs, "Advisory Commission," 1106.
20. Chester Hartman, "Comment on Anthony Downs's 'The Advisory Commission on Regulatory Barriers to Affordable Housing: Its Behavior and Accomplishments,' " *Housing Policy Debate* 2, no. 4 (1991): 1161–68. Much of Hartman's writings and those of his Poverty and Race Research Action Council are on this theme.

CHAPTER 4

1. Moshe Safdie, *Beyond Habitat* (Cambridge: MIT Press, 1970), 160.
2. Sam Davis, "The House versus Housing," in Davis, ed., *The Form of Housing*, 1–39.
3. Elizabeth Cromley, "Apartments and Collective Life in Nineteenth Century New York," in Franck and Ahrentzen, eds., *New Households, New Housing*, 20–46.
4. John Nolon and Duo Dickinson, "Intricately Financed Nonprofit Development: Yorkshire Terrace," in *Common Walls/Private Homes: Multiresidential Design* (New York: McGraw-Hill, 1990), 128–34; and John Pastier, "Caring Design of Assisted Housing," *Architecture* 77, no. 7 (July 1988): 73–75.
5. Interview with Cynthia Weese (July 16, 1992).
6. Werner Hegemann and Elbert Peets, *An Architects' Handbook of Civic Art* (New York: Architectural Book Publishing Co., 1922), 268–69.
7. Stefanos Polyzoides, Roger Sherwood, and James

Tice, *Courtyard Housing in Los Angeles* (Berkeley: University of California Press, 1982), 12–18.

8. Clare Cooper Marcus has long been a proponent of cluster housing, which in most of her writings is embodied in a courtyard form. See, for example, Clare Cooper Marcus and Wendy Sarkissian, *Housing As If People Mattered* (Berkeley: University of California Press, 1986).
9. Interview with René Davids and Christine Killory (August 7, 1992).
10. Allan B. Jacobs, *Great Streets* (Cambridge: MIT Press, 1993), 262.
11. Interview with William Rawn (June 21, 1992).
12. See, for example, John Macsai, *Housing* (New York: John Wiley & Sons, 1976).
13. Federal Public Housing Authority, *Public Housing Design: A Review of Experience in Low-Rent Housing* (Washington, D.C.: Government Printing Office, 1946), 108.
14. Franck and Ahrentzen, eds., *New Households, New Housing*, xi–xv.
15. Interview with Donald MacDonald (June 26, 1992).
16. Hamdi, *Housing without Houses*; and Sam Davis and Cathy Simon, "Interiors: Accommodating Diversity," in Davis, ed., *The Form of Housing*, 191–215.
17. Brent C. Brolin, *The Failure of Modern Architecture* (New York: Van Nostrand Reinhold, 1976).
18. Bradley Inman, "Acorn Housing Project: Tenant, Owner Pride Rises after Years of Neglect," *San Francisco Examiner*, February 23, 1992, F-1.
19. Interview with Edmund Burger (June 29, 1992). Burger recalls the comment made after the jury deliberations.
20. Tim Findley, "Integration of an Oakland Ghetto," *San Francisco Chronicle*, October 9, 1968, 6.
21. Interview with Burger (June 29, 1992).

CHAPTER 5

1. Dana Cuff, *Architecture: The Story of Practice* (Cambridge: MIT Press, 1991), 195–245.

2. Interview with Michael Pyatok (July 2, 1992).

3. Federal Public Housing Authority, *Public Housing Design*, 112.

4. The *Progressive Architecture* awards usually include both "awards" and "citations," the former being the higher honor. The profession and the general readership usually do not distinguish between the two, simply identifying them as the "*PA* Awards."

5. *AIA Honor Awards Program, 1949–1992* (Washington, D.C.: American Institute of Architects, 1992).

6. *The 1959 National Honor Awards Report of the Jury* (Washington, D.C.: American Institute of Architects, 1959).

7. "AIA Awards Top 1993 Honors to 18 Projects," press release by the American Institute of Architects, Washington, D.C., January 26, 1993.

8. I have selected from among projects built before 1993, when this book went to press, that won a national award between 1980 and 1993 and were financed with some type of assistance. In most cases the financing was mixed, with some government subsidy, tax credits, or grants. In one case the market-rate portion financed the affordable portion through required inclusionary zoning. Several award-winning affordable housing designs between 1980 and 1992 are single-family detached houses, and these are not discussed. A few multifamily projects that were built in the 1970s and won Honor Awards after 1980 are also not included.

Three projects received the American Institute of Architects National Honor Award in 1993: the Charleston Navy Yard rowhouses by William Rawn, discussed in Chapter 4; Daybreak Grove by Davids Killory, included in this chapter as a recipient of the *Progressive Architecture* award in 1991; and the Simone Hotel in Los Angeles, a single-room-occupancy facility designed by Koning Eizenberg. The San Antonio Family and Senior Housing, a mixed-use affordable project in Oakland designed by Michael Pyatok and The Ratcliff Architects, won a 1994 *Progressive Architecture* award; construction began that same year.

9. See Jim Murphy, "Vaguely Familiar," *Progressive Architecture* 73, no. 2 (February 1992): 84–91, for further information.

10. *Progressive Architecture* 72, no. 1 (January 1991): 102–3; interview with Joseph Valerio (March 8, 1993); interview with Colton Palms resident (October 1, 1992).

11. See Donald Canty, "Bright and Serene," *Architectural Record* 180, no. 8 (August 1991): 90–99, for further information.

12. Chester Hartman has written about Yerba Buena several times, most extensively in *Yerba Buena: Land Grab and Community Resistance in San Francisco* (San Francisco: Glide Publications, 1974). See also his "Housing Struggles and Housing Form," in Davis, ed., *The Form of Housing*, 113–37.

13. Interview with Robert Herman (June 6, 1992).

14. Hartman, "Housing Struggles," 119–20.

15. Nancy Levinson, "Mixed Incomes," *Architectural Record* 180, no. 7 (July 1992): 94–97.

16. Interview with Joan Goody (June 19, 1992).

17. See Aaron Betsky, "Island of Domesticity," *Architectural Record* 180, no. 7 (July 1992): 79–82, for further information.

18. Paul Groth, "Nonpeople: A Case Study of Public Architects and Impaired Social Vision," in Russell Ellis and Dana Cuff, eds., *Architects' People* (New York: Oxford University Press, 1989), 213–37.

19. Robert Campbell, "Shattering Old Housing Myths," *Architectural Record* 180, no. 7 (July 1992): 70–71.

20. Interview with Rob Wellington Quigley (August 7, 1992).

21. Deirdre Stanforth, *Restored America* (New York: Praeger, 1975), 17.

22. Michael J. Crosbie, "Gentle Infill in a Genteel City," *Architecture* 74, no. 7 (July 1985): 45.

23. Stanforth, *Restored America*, 18.

24. Crosbie, "Gentle Infill," 44–48. Middleton McMillan Architects of Charleston designed forty-six of the infill units.

25. Interview with Richard Bradfield (January 22, 1993).

26. Jim Kemp, *American Vernacular: Regional Influ-*

ences in Architecture and Interior Design (New York: Viking Penguin, 1987), 212.

27. See Thomas Fisher, "Living with the Sun," *Progressive Architecture* 67, no. 7 (July 1984): 66–68, for further information.

28. James A. Moore and Donald Prowler, *The Solar Village: The Roosevelt (NJ) Senior Citizens Housing Project* (Washington, D.C.: ACSA Press, 1990), 9.

29. Moore and Prowler, *Solar Village,* 26.

30. Carleton Knight III, "Elderly Housing as a Solar Village," *Architecture* 74, no. 5 (May 1985): 291.

31. Moore and Prowler, *Solar Village,* 10.

32. Interview with Doug Kelbaugh (January 20, 1993).

33. Knight, "Elderly Housing," 291.

34. Interview with Kelbaugh (January 20, 1993)

35. Moore and Prowler, *Solar Village,* 26.

36. See "Low-Cost Housing," *Progressive Architecture* 69, no. 10 (October 1988): 70–75, for further information.

37. Morris Newman, "The Struggle to Provide Affordable Homes: In Santa Monica, Neighborhood Politics Prevail," *New York Times*, March 8, 1992, real estate section, 29.

38. "Affordable Housing," *Progressive Architecture* 68, no. 1 (January 1987): 84.

39. Interview with Julie Eizenberg (January 15, 1993).

40. Ibid.

41. Donald Canty, "Colorful Regional 'Landscape' Celebrates Route 66," *Architecture* 75, no. 10 (October 1986): 78.

42. Nolon and Dickinson, "Neon Navajo Motifs and Tax-Exempt Financing," in *Common Walls/Private Homes*, 118.

43. "The Beach," *Progressive Architecture* 66, no. 1 (January 1985): 108–9.

44. Nolon and Dickinson, "Neon Navajo Motifs," 121.

45. Ibid.

46. See Dirk Sutro, "Escondido Innovations for Housing Are Winners," *Los Angeles Times* (San Diego County), January 30, 1992, E-1 and E-5; and "Housing for Homeless Mothers and Children," *Progressive Architecture* 72, no. 1 (January 1991): 96–97, for further information.

47. Interview with René Davids and Christine Killory (August 7, 1992).

48. "Housing for Homeless Families," *Progressive Architecture* 73, no. 1 (January 1992): 54–56.

49. Interview with Davids and Killory (August 7, 1992).

AFTERWORD

1. Morris Newman, "Apartment House with a Live-in Tutorial," *New York Times*, March 14, 1993, real estate section, 30.

2. Kathryn M. McCamant and Charles R. Durrett, "Cohousing in Denmark," in Franck and Ahrentzen, eds., *New Housing/New Households*, 95–126.

Fig. 1. Photo from the Jacob A. Riis Collection, reproduced by permission of the Museum of the City of New York. Architect: William Field.

Fig. 2. Photo courtesy of The Art Institute of Chicago. Architect: Frank Lloyd Wright.

Fig. 3. Photo courtesy of American Heritage Center, University of Wyoming; copyright restricted. Architects: Oskar Stonorov and Alfred Kastner.

Fig. 4. Reproduced by permission of LaGuardia and Wagner Archives, LaGuardia Community College, City University of New York.

Fig. 5. Photo by A. J. Josephs, Media Image + Design. Architect: Aaron Green.

Fig. 6. Drawings by Michael Pyatok.

Fig. 7. Architect: Troy West; urban planner: Jacqueline Leavitt; competition director: Harvey Sherman.

Fig. 8. Photo by Abacus Architects & Planners.

Fig. 9. From Joseph Carreiro et al., *The New Building Block: A Report on the Factory-Produced Dwelling Module,* Cornell University Center for Housing and Environmental Studies Research Report, no. 8 (Ithaca, 1968); reproduced by permission of Cornell University.

Figs. 10, 11. General exterior view: photo by Jerry Spearman. Balcony view: photo by Taal Safdie. Architect: Moshe Safdie.

Fig. 12. Photo by Sam Davis. Architect: Davis & Joyce Architects.

Fig. 13. Sam Davis Architects.

Figs. 14, 15. Photo © Jane Lidz. Architect: Sam Davis Architects.

Fig. 16. Photo by Janet Delaney. Architect: Pyatok Associates.

Fig. 17. Photo by Michael Pyatok.

Fig. 18. Photo by John Sutton Photography. Architect: David Baker & Associates, Architects.

Fig. 19. Davis & Joyce Architects.

Fig. 20, 21. Photo © Jane Lidz. Architect: Davis & Joyce Architects.

Fig. 22. Photo by Sam Davis. Architect: Backen, Arrigoni, and Ross

Fig. 23. Davis & Joyce Architects.

Fig. 24. Drawing courtesy Ben Weese.

Fig. 25. Photo by Norman F. Carver Jr., from his *Italian Hilltowns* (Kalamazoo, Mich.: Documan Press, 1980); reproduced by permission.

Fig. 26. Davis & Joyce Architects.

Fig. 28. Photo by Magnus Stark. Architect: MacDonald Architects.

Fig. 29. Photo by Steve Proehl. Architect: MacDonald Architects.

Fig. 30. Photo by Mark Citret. Architect: Sam Davis Architects and Shen/Glass Architects.

Fig. 31. Davis & Joyce Architects.

Fig. 32. Sam Davis Architects and Shen/Glass Architects.

Fig. 33. John V. Mutlow Architects.

Figs. 34, 37. Photo by John Sutton Photography. Architect: Davis & Joyce Architects.

Fig. 35. Photo by Sam Davis. Architect: Weese, Langley, Weese Architects.

Fig. 38a. Photo by Sam Davis. Architect: William Merchant.

Fig. 38b. Photo © Christopher Irion. Architect: Solomon Architecture and Planning.

Figs. 39, 40. Photo © Steve Rosenthal. Architect: William Rawn Associates.

Fig. 41. MacDonald Architects.

Fig. 42. Photo credit: © Henry Bowles. Architect: MacDonald Architects.

Fig. 43. Sam Davis Architects and Shen/Glass Architects.

Fig. 44. Photo by Sam Davis. Architect: Ricardo Bofill.

Fig. 45. Photo © Jane Lidz. Architect: Davis & Joyce Architects.

Fig. 46. Margaret Bach, from the Historic American Buildings Survey (1968).

Fig. 47. Photo © Christopher Irion. Architect: Solomon Architecture and Planning.

Figs. 48, 50. Photo by Kaz Tsuruta. Architect: Burger & Coplans, Inc., Architects.

Figs. 49, 51. Burger & Coplans, Inc., Architects.

Fig. 52. Photo by Sam Davis. Architect: Burger & Coplans, Inc., Architects.

Figs. 53, 55. Photo by Karant + Associates, Inc. Architect: Valerio Associates.

Figs. 54, 56. Valerio Associates.

Figs. 57, 58, 60. Photo by Richard Barnes. Architect: Herman Stoller Coliver Architects (formerly Robert Herman Associates).

Fig. 59. Herman Stoller Coliver Architects (formerly Robert Herman Associates).

Figs. 61, 62, 63. Photo © Steve Rosenthal. Architect: Goody, Clancy & Associates, Inc., Architects.

Fig. 64. Goody, Clancy & Associates, Inc., Architects.

Figs. 66, 67, 68, 69. Photo by David Hewitt and Anne Garrison Photographs. Architect: Rob Wellington Quigley.

Figs. 65, 70. Rob Wellington Quigley.

Fig. 72. Photo by Paul Beswick, courtesy of The Housing Authority of the City of Charleston. Architect: Bradfield Associates, Architects, Inc.

Fig. 73. Photos by D. J. Johnson, courtesy of The Housing Authority of the City of Charleston. Architect: Bradfield Associates, Architects, Inc.

Fig. 74. Bradfield Associates, Architects, Inc.

Figs. 75, 76. Photo by Otto Baitz. Architect: Kelbaugh & Lee.

Figs. 77, 78. Kelbaugh & Lee.

Figs. 79, 81, 85. Photo by Rob Super. Architect: Sam Davis Architects.

Figs. 80, 82, 83, 84. Sam Davis Architects.

Figs. 86, 87, 89, 91, 92, 94, 95. Photo by Grant Mudford. Architect: Koning Eizenberg Architecture.

Figs. 88, 90, 93. Koning Eizenberg Architecture.

Figs. 96, 98, 99. Photo by Timothy Hursley. Architect: Antoine Predock.

Figs. 97, 100. Antoine Predock.

Figs. 101, 102b, 103b. Davids Killory Architects.

Figs. 102a, 103a. Photo by Loisos/Ubbelohde Architecture and Energy. Architect: Davids Killory Architects.